Czech

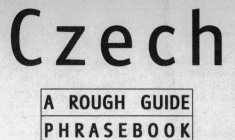

A ROUGH GUIDE
PHRASEBOOK

Compiled
by Lexus

Credits

Compiled by Lexus with Václav Řeřicha

Lexus Series Editor:	Sally Davies
Rough Guides Phrase Book Editor:	Jonathan Buckley
Rough Guides Series Editor:	Mark Ellingham

This first edition published in 1995 by Rough Guides Ltd, 1 Mercer Street, London WC2H 9QJ.

Distributed by the Penguin Group.

Penguin Books Ltd, 27 Wrights Lane, London W8 5TZ
Penguin Books USA Inc., 375 Hudson Street, New York 10014, USA
Penguin Books Australia Ltd, 487 Maroondah Highway, PO Box 257, Ringwood, Victoria 3134, Australia
Penguin Books Canada Ltd, Alcorn Avenue, Toronto, Ontario, Canada M4V 1E4
Penguin Books (NZ) Ltd, 182–190 Wairau Road, Auckland 10, New Zealand

Typeset in Rough Serif and Rough Sans to an original design by Henry Iles.
Printed by Cox & Wyman Ltd, Reading.

© Lexus Ltd 1995
240pp.

British Library Cataloguing in Publication Data
A catalogue for this book is available from the British Library.

ISBN 1-85828-148-2

CONTENTS

INTRODUCTION

The Rough Guide Czech phrasebook is a highly practical introduction to the contemporary language. Laid out in clear A-Z style, it uses key-word referencing to lead you straight to the words and phrases you want – so if you need to book a room, just look up 'room'. The Rough Guide gets straight to the point in every situation, in bars and shops, on trains and buses, and in hotels and banks.

The main part of the Rough Guide is a double dictionary: English-Czech then Czech-English. Before that, there's a page explaining the pronunciation system we've used, then a section called **The Basics**, which sets out the fundamental rules of the language, with plenty of practical examples. You'll also find here other essentials like numbers, dates and telling the time.

Forming the heart of the guide, the **English-Czech** section gives easy-to-use transliterations of the Czech words wherever pronunciation might be a problem, and to get you involved quickly in two-way communication, the Rough Guide includes dialogues featuring typical responses on key topics – such as renting a car and asking directions. Feature boxes fill you in on cultural pitfalls as well as the simple mechanics of how to make a phone call, what to do in an emergency, where to change money, and more. Throughout this section, cross-references enable you to pinpoint key facts and phrases, while asterisked words indicate where further information can be found in the Basics.

In the **Czech-English** dictionary, we've given not just the phrases you're likely to hear, but also all the signs, labels, instructions and other basic words you might come across in print or in public places.

Finally the Rough Guide rounds off with an extensive **Menu Reader**, giving a run-down of food and drink terms that you'll find indispensable whether you're eating out, stopping for a quick drink, or browsing through a local food market.

šťastnou cestu!
have a good trip!

PRONUNCIATION

In this phrasebook, the Czech has been written in a system of
imitated pronunciation so that it can be read as though it were
English, bearing in mind the notes on pronunciation given
below:

ah	long 'a' as in 'father'
ay	as in may
e	as in get
d^yeh	a very slight 'dy' sound as in dew
g	always hard as in goat
H	a harsh 'ch' as in the Scottish way of pronouncing loch
i	as in pit
ī	as the 'i' sound in might
J	as the 's' sound in measure
n^yeh	a very slight 'ny' sound as in nuance
o	as in not
oo	as in book
oo	'oo' as in fool
ow	as in now
rJ	a rolled 'r' followed by an 's' sound as in measure
ts	as in hats
t^yeh	a very slight 'ty' sound as in stupid
u, uh	'u' as in but
y	as in yes

Czech Pronunciation

a	'u' as in but
á	'a' as in father
aj	'i' as in might
au	'ow' as in now
c	'ts' as in hats
č	'ch' as in chocolate
ď	a very slight 'dy' sound as in dew
dž	'j' as in `jam'
é	'e' as in get but longer
ě	'ye' as in yes
ej	'ay' as in may

h	as in **h**at, but sometimes pronounced like Czech **ch**
ch	a harsh 'ch' as in the Scottish way of pronouncing lo**ch**
í	'ee' as in s**ee**d
j	'y' in **y**es
ň	a very slight 'ny' sound as in **nu**ance
o	as in n**o**t
ó	'aw' as in **aw**ful
oj	'oy' as in b**oy**
ou	'oh' as in the exclamation **oh**
q	'qu' as in **qu**ite
ř	a rolled 'r' followed by an 's' sound as in mea**s**ure
š	'sh' as in **sh**op
ť	a very slight 'ty' sound as in **st**upid
u	'oo' as in b**oo**k
ú, ů	'oo' as in f**oo**l
w	'v' as in 'vote'
y	'i' as in p**i**t
ý	'ee' as in s**ee**d
ž	's' as in mea**s**ure

In Czech, the stress is always on the first syllable of the word.

When e (or é) occurs at the end of a Czech word, it is always pronounced, for example **stanice** (station, stop) is pronounced 'stunyitseh'.

The combination **mě** is always pronounced 'mnyeh'.

ABBREVIATIONS

acc	accusative	loc	locative
adj	adjective	m	masculine
anim	animate	n	neuter
dat	dative	nom	nominative
f	feminine	pl	plural
fam	familiar	pol	polite
gen	genitive	sing	singular
inan	inanimate	voc	vocative
instr	instrumental		

THE CZECH ALPHABET

The Czech-English section and Menu Reader are in Czech alphabetical order which is as follows:

a, b, c, č, d, e, f, g, h, ch, i, j, k, l, m, n, o, p, q, r, ř, s, š, t, u, v, w, x, y, z, ž

NOTE

An asterisk (*) next to a word in the English-Czech or Czech-English means that you should refer to the Basics section or conversion tables for further information.

The Basics

NOUNS, ARTICLES AND CASES

There are no articles (a, an, the) in Czech:

okno
okno
window/a window/
the window

ručník
rootch-nyeek
towel/a towel/the towel

Context clarifies the equivalent English article:

bude vám vadit, když otevřu okno?
boodeh vahm vudyit gudiJ
otevrJoo okno
do you mind if I open the window?

mohu dostat ručník?
mohoo dostut rootch-nyeek
can I have a towel?

Czech nouns have one of three genders – masculine, feminine or neuter. Most masculine nouns end in a consonant:

vagón   otec   přítel
vugawn   otets   prJeetel
carriage father friend (male)

Most feminine nouns end in -a:

cukrárna   matka
tsookrarna   mutka
cake shop   mother

překladatelka
prJekludutelka
translator (woman)

Most neuter nouns end in -o or -í:

jídlo   oddělení
yeedlo   od-dyelenyee
food   department

jméno   poschodí
yumeno   posHodyee
(first) name   floor, storey

Exceptions to the above rules are shown in the English-Czech section of this book.

Words for human adults are either masculine or feminine:

učitel   učitelka
ootchitel   ootchitelka
teacher (man)   teacher (woman)

Words for children and young animals are usually neuter:

děťátko   dítě   kotě
dyet-yahtko   dyee-tyeh   kotyeh
baby   child   kitten

Cases

Czech has seven cases: nominative, accusative, genitive, dative, locative, instrumental and vocative. In the English-Czech section we have indicated which case needs to be used with certain words and phrases. Usually, words following prepositions change their form according to which case they are in.

Nominative Case

The nominative is the case of the subject of a sentence. In the following examples, **obchod** and **Petr** are in the nominative:

> **obchod je nyní otevřený**
> opHot yeh ninyee otevrJenee
> the shop is open now

> **Petr přijel dnes**
> petr prJi-yel dnes
> Peter arrived today

Accusative Case

The object of most verbs takes the accusative. In the following examples the object is in the accusative:

> **chceme vidět starou Prahu**
> Hutsemeh vidyet sturoh pruhoo
> we want to see the old part of Prague

> **prodáváte známky?**
> prodahvahteh znahmki
> do you sell stamps?

> **mohu použít váš telefon?**
> mohoo pohJeet vahsh telefon
> may I use your phone?

Some prepositions indicating motion or direction towards something are followed by the accusative:

> **na**
> na
> onto, to

> **skrz**
> skurs
> through

> **přes**
> prJes
> across, through

> **jedeme na hory zítra**
> yedemeh na hori zeetra
> we are going to the mountains tomorrow

> **přes cestu**
> prJes tsestoo
> across the road

> **půjdu přes park**
> pOO-iudoo prJes purk
> I'll walk through the park

Genitive Case

The genitive is used to indicate possession:

> **dopis Petra**
> Peter's letter

There is no word for 'of' in Czech. The genitive is used to translate 'of':

> **šálek čaje**
> shahlek chī-eh
> a cup of tea

> **tabulka čokolády**
> tuboolka chokolahdi
> a bar of chocolate

The genitive is also used after some prepositions, for example:

do
do
until; to

u	**vedle**
oo	vedleh
by; at	beside

jak se dostanu do centra?
yuk seh dostunoo do tsentra
how do I get to the centre?

seděli jsme u stolu
sedyeli smeh oo stoloo
we were sitting at the table

Dative Case

The dative is used for indirect objects with verbs like 'to give' and 'to send'. It often corresponds to 'to' (as in 'to me') in English:

koupil jsem sestře broušené sklo
kohpil sem sestrJeh brohsheneh sklo
I've bought my sister some cut glass

dal jsem mu to
dul sem moo to
I gave it to him

See the forms of Personal Pronouns on page 18.

The dative is also used after some prepositions, for example:

k	**proti**
k	protyi
to, towards	opposite

poslali dceru k Heleně
posluli dutseroo k helenyeh
they've sent their daughter to Helena's

je to proti kostelu
yeh to protyi kosteloo
it's opposite the church

Locative Case

The locative is used with most prepositions:

na	**o**	**v, ve***	**po**
na	o	v, veh	po
on	about	in, on	after

v letadle	**ve městě**
vletudleh	veh mnyestyeh
on the plane	in the town, downtown

na ulici	**po obědě**
na oolitsi	po obyedyeh
on the street	after lunch

hovořili o dětech
hovorJili o dyeteH
they were talking about the children

* ve is used before words beginning with v or f or to ease the running together of two consonants as in ve městě above

Instrumental Case

The instrumental is used to show by whom or by what means an action is carried out. It is used to translate 'by' when referring to means of transport:

> **přijeli jsme vlakem/autem**
> prJi-yeli smeh vlukem/owtem
> we came by train/by car

> **dopis poslaný leteckou poštou**
> dopis poslunee letetskoh poshtoh
> a letter sent by airmail

The instrumental is also used with some prepositions:

pod	**před**	**s**
pot	prJet	s
under	before	with

> **piju čaj s mlékem**
> pi-yoo chī smlekem
> I take tea with milk

> **pod kobercem**
> pot kobertsem
> under the carpet

> **před obědem**
> prJet obyedem
> before lunch

Vocative Case

The vocative is used when addressing people directly:

> **dámy a pánové**
> dahmi a pahnoveh
> ladies and gentlemen

> **Václave!**
> vahtsluveh
> Václav!

Numbers and Cases

Numbers in Czech also determine the case of the noun. 1 and all numbers ending in 1 (eg 21, 31 and so on) are followed by a noun in the nominative singular; 2, 3, and 4 (and all numbers ending in 2, 3 or 4) take the nominative plural; all other numbers take the genitive plural:

jedno pivo	**dvě piva**
yedno pivo	dvyeh piva
one beer	two beers

tři dny	**dvacet jeden den**
trJi dni	dvutset yeden den
three days	21 days

> **třicet sedm korun**
> trJitset sedum koroon
> 37 crowns

> **sto korun**
> sto koroon
> 100 crowns

Noun Cases

As illustrated above, noun endings change depending on the case. The case endings used depend on the following factors:

whether the noun is masculine, feminine or neuter

whether the noun is singular or plural

whether the nominative singular ending contains a hard or soft consonant

There are three types of consonants in Czech:

hard consonants
d, h, ch, k, r, t, n

soft consonants
c, č, ď, j, ň, ř, š, ť, ž

either hard or soft consonants*
b, f, l, m, p, s, v, z

* g, w, x and q in Czech are used mainly in foreign words and do not fall into the above categories.

Masculine Nouns

The case endings of masculine nouns ending in a consonant are also dependent on whether the noun is animate (people or animals) or inanimate (objects):

Masculine Inanimate Nouns

	hard ending		soft ending	
	singular	plural	singular	plural
	dopis letter		**kartáč** brush	
nom	**dopis**	**dopisy**	**kartáč**	**kartáče**
	dopis	dopisi	kurtahtch	kurtahtcheh
acc	**dopis**	**dopisy**	**kartáč**	**kartáče**
	dopis	dopisi	kurtahtch	kurtahtcheh
gen	**dopisu**	**dopisů**	**kartáče**	**kartáčů**
	dopisoo	dopisoo	kurtahtcheh	kurtahtchoo
dat	**dopisu**	**dopisům**	**kartáči**	**kartáčům**
	dopisoo	dopisoom	kurtahtchi	kurtahtchoom
loc	**dopise/dopisu**	**dopisech**	**kartáči**	**kartáčích**
	dopiseh/dopisoo	dopiseH	kurtahtchi	kurtahtcheeH
instr	**dopisem**	**dopisy**	**kartáčem**	**kartáči**
	dopisem	dopisi	kurtahtchem	kurtahtchi

GRAMMAR

Masculine Animate Nouns

	hard ending singular	plural	soft ending singular	plural
	doktor doctor		**nosič** porter	
nom	**doktor**	**doktoři**/	**nosič**	**nosiči**/
	doktor	**doktorové**	nositch	**nosičové**
		doktorЈi/		nositchi/
		doktoroveh		nositchoveh
acc	**doktora**	**doktory**	**nosiče**	**nosiče**
	doktora	doktori	nositcheh	nositcheh
gen	**doktora**	**doktorů**	**nosiče**	**nosiču**
	doktora	doktorОО	nositcheh	nositchoo
dat	**dotorovi**/	**doktorům**	**nosičovi**/	**nosičům**
	doktoru	doktorООm	**nosiči**	nositchООm
	doktorovi/		nositchovi/	
	doktoroo		nositchi	
loc	**dotorovi**/	**doktorech**	**nosičovi**/	**nosičích**
	doktoru	doktoreН	**nosiči**	nositcheeН
	doktorovi/		nositchovi/	
	doktoroo		nositchi	
instr	**doktorem**	**doktory**	**nosičem**	**nosiči**
	doktorem	doktori	nositchem	nositchi
voc	**doktore!**		**nosiči!**	
	doktoreh		nositchi	

The case endings of masculine nouns ending in **-a** or **-e** are dependent on whether the consonant preceding the final vowel is hard or soft, but there is no distinction for animate and inanimate nouns:

Masculine Animate or Inanimate Nouns

	hard ending singular	plural	soft ending singular	plural
	cyklista cyclist		**průvodce** guide; guidebook	
nom	**cyklista**	**cyklistové**	**průvodce**	**průvodci/**
	tsiklista	tsiklistoveh	proovot-tseh	**průvodcové**
				proovot-tsi/
				proovot-tsoveh
acc	**cyklistu**	**cyklisty**	**průvodce**	**průvodce**
	tsiklistoo	tsiklisti	proovot-tseh	proovot-tseh
gen	**cyklisty**	**cyklistů**	**průvodce**	**průvodců**
	tsiklisti	tsiklistoo	proovot-tseh	proovot-tsoo
dat	**cyklistovi**	**cyklistům**	**průvodci/**	**průvodcům**
	tsiklistovi	tsiklistoom	**průvodcovi**	proovot-tsoom
			proovot-tsi/	
			proovot-tsovi	
loc	**cyklistovi**	**cyklistech**	**průvodci/**	**průvodcích**
	tsiklistovi	tsikliteн	**průvodcovi**	proovot-tseeн
			proovot-tsi/	
			proovot-tsovi	
instr	**cyklistou**	**cyklisty**	**průvodcem**	**průvodci**
	tsiklistoh	tsiklisti	proovot-tsem	proovot-tsi
voc	**cyklisto!**			
	tsiklisto			

Feminine Nouns

There are two types of feminine noun endings: those preceded by a hard consonant and those preceded by a soft consonant. Feminine noun endings change as follows:

	hard ending		soft ending	
	singular	plural	singular	plural
	žena woman		**růže** rose	
nom	**žena**	**ženy**	**růže**	**růže**
	Jena	Jeni	rooJeh	rooJeh
acc	**ženu**	**ženy**	**růži**	**růže**
	Jenoo	Jeni	rooJi	rooJeh
gen	**ženy**	**žen**	**růže**	**růží**
	Jeni	Jeni	rooJeh	rooJee
dat	**ženě**	**ženám**	**růži**	**růžím**
	Jenyeh	Jenahm	rooJi	rooJeem
loc	**ženě**	**ženách**	**růži**	**růžích**
	Jenyeh	JenahH	rooJi	rooJeeH
instr	**ženou**	**ženami**	**růží**	**růžemi**
	Jenoh	Jenumi	rooJee	rooJemi
voc	**ženo!**	**ženy!**		
	Jeno	Jeni		

Feminine nouns that don't have either of the above endings (e.g. **báseň** or **radost**) are declined according to the ending of the genitive singular (which will have to be learnt) and change as follows:

nom	**báseň**	poem	**radost**	happiness
gen	**básně**		**radosti**	

	genitive ending in -ě		genitive ending in -i	
	singular	plural	singular	plural
nom	**báseň**	**básně**	**radost**	**radosti**
	bahsen^{yeh}	bahsnyeh	rudost	rudostyi
acc	**báseň**	**básně**	**radost**	**radosti**
	bahsen^{yeh}	bahsnyeh	rudost	rudostyi
gen	**básně**	**básní**	**radosti**	**radostí**
	bahsnyeh	bahsnyee	rudostyi	rudostyee
dat	**básni**	**básním**	**radosti**	**radostem**
	bahsnyi	bahsnyeem	rudostyi	rudostem
loc	**básni**	**básních**	**radosti**	**radostech**
	bahsnyi	bahsnyeeH	rudostyi	rudosteH
instr	**básní**	**básněmi**	**radostí**	**radostmi**
	bahsnyee	bahsnyemi	rudostyee	rudostmi

Neuter Nouns

Neuter nouns have one of three endings:

the hard ending -o   (slovo word)
the soft ending -e   (pole field)
the ending -í   (nádraží railway station)

	hard ending		soft ending	
	singular	plural	singular	plural
nom	**slovo**	**slova**	**pole**	**pole**
	slovo	slova	poleh	poleh
acc	**slovo**	**slova**	**pole**	**pole**
	slovo	slova	poleh	poleh
gen	**slova**	**slov**	**pole**	**polí**
	slova	slof	poleh	polee
dat	**slovu**	**slovům**	**poli**	**polím**
	slovoo	slovoOm	poli	poleem
loc	**slově/slovu**	**slovech**	**poli**	**polích**
	slovyeh/slovoo	sloveH	poli	poleeH
instr	**slovem**	**slovy**	**polem**	**poli**
	slovem	slovi	polem	poli

	the ending -í	
	singular	plural
nom	**nádraží**	**nádraží**
	nahdruJee	nahdruJee
acc	**nádraží**	**nádraží**
	nahdruJee	nahdruJee
gen	**nádraží**	**nádraží**
	nahdruJee	nahdruJee
dat	**nádraží**	**nádražím**
	nahdruJee	nahdruJeem
loc	**nádraží**	**nádražích**
	nahdruJee	nahdruJeeн
instr	**nádražím**	**nádražími**
	nahdruJeem	nahdruJeemi

ADJECTIVES AND ADVERBS

Adjectives

There are two types of Czech adjectives: the first type express basic qualities (qualities which aren't derived from nouns, adverbs or verbs):

nový [novee]   **zdravý** [zdravee]
new   healthy

The second type are derived from nouns, adverbs or verbs:

dřevo   **dřevěný**
drJyevo   drJyevyenee
wood   wooden

pít [peet]   **pitný** [pitnee]
to drink   drinkable

Most adjectives have one of the following endings in the nominative case:

-ní, -ný, -ský, -cký or -ový

Czech adjectives agree in case, gender and number with the nouns to which they refer. There are two types of adjective endings: hard and soft.

	Hard Ending: singular	**šťastný** happy	
	m animate	f	n
nom	**šťastný**	**šťastná**	**šťastné**
	shtyastnee	shtyastnah	shtyastneh
acc	**šťastného***	**šťastnou**	**šťastné**
	shtyastneho	shtyastnoh	shtyastneh
gen	**šťastného**	**šťastné**	**šťastného**
	shtyastneho	shtyastneh	shtyastneho
dat	**šťastnému**	**šťastné**	**šťastnému**
	shtyastnemoo	shtyastneh	shtyastnemoo
loc	**šťastném**	**šťastné**	**šťastném**
	shtyastnem	shtyastneh	shtyastnem
instr	**šťastným**	**šťastnou**	**šťastným**
	shtyastneem	shtyastnoh	shtyastneem

* use the nominative when describing a masculine inanimate noun

Hard Ending: plural

	m animate	f/m inanimate	n
nom	šťastní	šťastné	šťastná
	shtyast-nyee	shtyastneh	shtyastnah
acc	šťastné	šťastné	šťastná
	shtyastneh	shtyastneh	shtyastnah
gen	šťastných	šťastných	šťastných
	shtyastneeH	shtyastneeH	shtyastneeH
dat	šťastným	šťastným	šťastným
	shtyastneem	shtyastneem	shtyastneem
loc	šťastných	šťastných	šťastných
	shtyastneeH	shtyastneeH	shtyastneeH
instr	šťastnými	šťastnými	šťastnými
	shtyastneemi	shtyastneemi	shtyastneemi

Soft Ending:

	singular		plural
	m/n	f	
	cizí foreign		
nom	cizí	cizí	cizí
	tsizee	tsizee	tsizee
acc	cizího*	cizí	cizí
	tsizeeho	tsizee	tsizee
gen	cizího	cizí	cizích
	tsizeeho	tsizee	tsizeeH
dat	cizímu	cizí	cizím
	tsizeemoo	tsizee	tsizeem
loc	cizím	cizí	cizích
	tsizeem	tsizee	tsizeeH
instr	cizím	cizí	cizími
	tsizeem	tsizee	tsizeemi

* use the nominative form instead of the accusative when the adjective is describing a masculine inanimate or neuter noun

GRAMMAR

Comparatives

The comparative of adjectives is generally formed by removing the final -ý from the adjective and adding either -ejší or -ší:

rychlý	rychlejší
riHlee	riHlayshee
fast	faster
tvrdý	tvrdší
tvurdee	tvurtshee
hard	harder

Some common irregular comparative forms:

dlouhý	delší
dloh-hee	delshee
long	longer
malý	menší
mulee	menshee
small	smaller
velký	větší
velkee	vyetshee
big	bigger
dobrý	lepší
dobree	lepshee
good	better
zlý	horší
zlee	horshee
bad	worse

Superlatives

To form the superlative add the prefix nej- to the comparative:

rychlejší	nejrychlejší
riHlayshee	nayriHlayshee
faster	fastest
tvrdší	nejtvrdší
tvurtshee	naytvurtshee
harder	hardest

Adverbs

To form the adverb, remove the final ý of the adjective and replace it with -e or -ě:

pěkný	pěkně
pyeknee	pyeknyeh
nice	nicely
špatný	špatně
shputnee	shput-nyeh
bad	badly
rychlý	rychle
riHlee	riHleh
quick	quickly
dobrý	dobře
dobree	dobrJeh
good	well

DEMONSTRATIVES

The Czech demonstrative adjectives and pronouns are:

ten/ta/to

These mean both 'this (one)' and 'that (one)' and the forms change according to gender and case:

	m/n	f
nom	**ten/to**	**ta**
	ten/to	ta
acc	**toho*/to**	**tu**
	toho/to	too
gen	**toho**	**té**
	toho	teh
dat	**tomu**	**té**
	tomoo	teh
loc	**tom**	**té**
	tom	teh
instr	**tím**	**tou**
	tyeem	toh

* use the nominative form instead of the accusative when the adjective is describing a masculine inanimate noun

The plurals 'these (ones)', 'those (ones)' are:

ti/ty/ta

The forms change according to gender, number and case:

	m	f	n
nom	**ty/ti***	**ty**	**ta**
	ti/tyi	ti	ta
acc	**ty**	**ty**	**ta**
	ti	ti	ta
gen	**těch**	**těch**	**těch**
	tyeH	tyeH	tyeH
dat	**těm**	**těm**	**těm**
	tyem	tyem	tyem
loc	**těch**	**těch**	**těch**
	tyeH	tyeH	tyeH
instr	**těmi**	**těmi**	**těmi**
	tyemi	tyemi	tyemi

* the inanimate form is **ty** and the animate form is **ti**

POSSESSIVES

Nearly all the forms of possessive pronouns/adjectives change according to gender, case and number. The exceptions are 'his', 'her(s)' and 'their(s)' which always have the same form:

můj/má/mé/mí my, mine

singular

	m	f	n
nom	**můj**	**má**	**mé**
	moo-i	mah	meh
acc	**mého**	**mou**	**mé**
	meho	moh	meh
gen	**mého**	**mé**	**mého**
	meho	meh	meho
dat	**mému**	**mé**	**mému**
	memoo	meh	memoo
loc	**mém**	**mé**	**mém**
	mem	meh	mem
instr	**mým**	**mou**	**mým**
	meem	moh	meem

GRAMMAR

	plural		
	m anim	m inan/f	n
nom	mí	mé	má
	mee	meh	mah
acc	mé	mé	má
	meh	meh	mah
gen	mých	mých	mých
	meeH	meeH	meeH
dat	mým	mým	mým
	meem	meem	meem
loc	mých	mých	mých
	meeH	meeH	meeH
instr	mými	mými	mými
	meemi	meemi	meemi

tvůj/tvá/tvé/tví your(s) (follows the same pattern as **můj**)

jeho [yeho] his (does not change)
její [yeh-yi] her(s) (does not change)

náš/naše/naši/naše our(s)

	singular	
	m/n	f
nom	náš/naše	naše
	nahsh/nusheh	nusheh
acc	našeho*	naši
	nusheho	nuhshi
gen	našeho	naši
	nusheho	nuhshi
dat	našemu	naši
	nushemoo	nuhshi
loc	našem	naši
	nushem	nuhshi
instr	naším	naší
	nusheem	nushee

* the forms **náš/naše** are used when the possessive refers to

a masculine inanimate or neuter noun

	plural
nom	naši*/naše
	nushi/nusheh
acc	naše
	nusheh
gen	našich
	nushiH
dat	našim
	nushim
loc	našich
	nushiH
instr	našimi
	nushimi

* the form **naši** is used when the possessive refers to a masculine animate noun; otherwise the forms for masculine, feminine and neuter plurals are the same

váš/vaše/vaši/vaše our(s) (follows the pattern of **náš**)
jejich [yeh-yiH] their(s) (does not change)

jeho pokoj	jeho peníze
yeho pokoy	yeho penyeezeh
his room	his money

náš pokoj	naše peníze
nahsh pokoy	nusheh penyeezeh
our room	our money

s mou sestrou
smoh sestroh
with my sister

s mými sestrami
smeemi sestrumi
with my sisters

There is a possessive pronoun
and adjective **svůj** which
follows the pattern of **můj** and
tvůj. It is used as a possessive
pronoun or adjective when it
refers to something
possessed by the subject of
the sentence and when the
identity of the possessor is
clear:

já si beru svoje auto
yah si beroo svo-yeh owto
I'm taking my car

ty si bereš svoje auto?
ti si beresh svo-yeh owto
are you taking your car?

Anna si bere svoje auto
Anna si bereh svo-yeh owto
Anna is taking her car

PRONOUNS

Personal Pronouns

já [yah]	I
ty [ti]	you (sing, fam)
on/ona/ono	he/she/it
[on/ona/ono]	
my [mi]	we
vy [vi]	you (pl or pol)
oni m/**ony** f/**ona** n	they
[onyi/oni/ona]	

There are two ways of saying
'you' in Czech: **ty** is the
singular, familiar form used
when speaking to friends,
family and children – it's also
used among young people
and students; **vy** is the
singular, polite form and is
used to speak to strangers or
older people; **vy** is also the
form to use when addressing
more than one person.

Personal pronouns are
usually omitted when they are
the subject of a sentence but
may be retained for special
emphasis.

co kupuje?
tso koopoo-yeh
what's she buying?

nevím
neveem
I don't know

In the following example, the
pronouns **ona** and **on** are used
to avoid confusion:

ona řídí, ale on spí
ona rJeedyee uleh on spee
she is driving, but he is
asleep

The forms of personal pronouns change according to case:

nom	já	ty	on	ona	ono
	yah	ti	on	ona	ono
acc	mne/mě	tebe/tě	jeho/něho*	ji/ni*	je/ně*
	mneh/mnyeh	tebeh/tyeh	yeho/nyeho	yi/nyi	yeh/nyeh
gen	mne/mě	tebe/tě	jeho/něho*	jí/ní*	jeho/něho*
	mneh/mnyeh	tebeh/tyeh	yeho/nyeho	yee/nyee	yeho/nyeho
dat	mně/mi	tobě/ti	jemu/němu*	jí/ní*	jemu/němu*
	mnyeh/mi	tobyeh/ti	yemoo/ nyemoo	jee/nyee	yemoo/ nyemoo
loc	mně	tobě	něm	ní	něm
	mnyeh	tobyeh	nyem	nyee	nyem
instr	mnou	tebou	jím/ním*	jí/ní*	jím/ním*
	mnoh	teboh	yeem/nyeem	yee/nyee	yeem/nyeem

nom	my	vy	oni/ony/ona
	mi	vi	onyi/oni/ona
acc	nás	vás	je/ně*
	nahs	vahs	yeh/nyeh
gen	nás	vás	jim/nim*
	nahs	vahs	yim/nyim
dat	nám	vám	jich/nich*
	nahm	vahm	yiH/niH
loc	nás	vás	nich
	nahs	vahs	niH
instr	námi	vámi	jimi/nimi*
	nahmi	vahmi	yimi/nyimi

* forms beginning ně-, ni- or ní- must be used when the pronoun is preceded by a preposition

dal jsem to jemu	neviděl jsem ji
dul sem to yemoo	nevidyel sem yi
I gave it to him	I haven't seen her

s námi	pro nás
snahmi	pro nahs
with us	for us

Note how the following is expressed in Czech:

> **to je on/ona**
> yeh on/ona
> that's him/her

Some examples of pronouns used with prepositions:

> **uděláte to pro ně?**
> oo-dyelahteh to pro nyeh
> will you do it for them?

> **přijela s ním**
> prJi-yela snyeem
> she arrived with him

VERBS

Verb Aspects

The basic form of the verb given in the dictionaries in this book is the infinitive (e.g. to drive, to go etc). Most Czech verbs have two forms known as the imperfective and perfective aspects. In the English-Czech section of this book, where useful, the two aspects of common verbs are given in this order:

imperfective/perfective

For example the verb 'to do' is:

> **dělat** [dyelut]/**udělat** [oodyelut]

In general the imperfective aspect is used to form what in English would be the present and imperfect (continuous) tenses and the future (with the future tense of být).

The perfective aspect is used to form what in English would be expressed by the perfect tense.

Czech regular verbs usually have one of three endings:

-at   **hledat** to look for
-it   **řídit** to drive
consonant plus -t   **vézt** to take/carry

To form the various tenses, the ending of the verb is removed and appropriate endings are added to the basic stem.

Present Tense

The present tense corresponds to 'I leave' and 'I am leaving' in English. Using the imperfective aspect of the verb, the conjugation patterns for the present tense are as follows:

hledat	[hledut]	to look for
hledám	[hledahm]	I look for
hledáš	[hledahsh]	you look for (sing, fam)
hledá	[hledah]	he/she/it looks for
hledáme	[hledahmeh]	we look for
hledáte	[hledahteh]	you look for (pl or pol)
hledají	[hledī-ee]	they look for
řídit	[rJeedyit]	to drive
řídím	[rJee-dyeem]	I drive
řídíš	[rJee-deesh]	you drive (sing, fam)
řídí	[rJee-dyee]	he/she drives
řídíme	[rJee-dyeemeh]	we drive
řídíte	[rJee-dyeeteh]	you drive (pl or pol)
řídí	[rJee-dyee]	they drive
vézt	[vest]	to take, to carry
vezu	[vezoo]	I take
vezeš	[vezesh]	you take (sing, fam)
veze	[vezeh]	he/she/it takes
vezeme	[vezemeh]	we take
vezete	[vezeteh]	you take (pl or pol)
vezou	[vezoh]	they take

The following verbs are irregular in the present tense:

být	[beet]	to be
jsem	[sem]	I am
jsi	[si]	you are (sing, fam)
je	[yeh]	he/she/it is
jsme	[smeh]	we are
jste	[steh]	you are (pl or pol)
jsou	[soh]	they are

chtít	[Hutyeet]	to want
chci	[Hutsi]	I want
chceš	[Hutsesh]	you want (sing, fam)
chce	[Hutseh]	he/she/it wants
chceme	[Hutsemeh]	we want
chcete	[Hutseteh]	you want (pl or pol)
chtějí	[Hutyay-ee]	they want
jíst	[yeest]	to eat
jím	[yeem]	I eat
jíš	[yeesh]	you eat (sing, fam)
jí	[yee]	he/she/it eats
jíme	[yeemeh]	we eat
jíte	[yeeteh]	you eat (pl or pol)
jedí	[yedyee]	they eat
vědět	[vyedyet]	to know
vím	[veem]	I know
víš	[veesh]	you know (sing, fam)
ví	[vee]	he/she/it knows
víme	[veemeh]	we know
víte	[veeteh]	you know (pl or pol)
vědí	[vyedyee]	they know

The Past Tense: Imperfective and Perfective Forms

The imperfective form describes an action which is seen as continuing:

kupovali dům
koopovuli doom
they were buying a house

The perfective form describes an action which is seen as completed:

koupili dům
kohpili doom
they bought a house

The perfective verbs can be simple, for example, **vysvětlit** 'to explain', or with a prefix **napsat** 'to write' (to finish writing).

Perfective verbs can sometimes be identified because they look like a simpler form of the imperfective, for example:

vysvětlovat/vysvětlit (imperfective/
   perfective)
vis-vyetlovut/vis-vyetlit
to explain

In many cases the dropping
of the prefix (napsat – psát)
will change the perfective
verb into the imperfective:

psát/napsat (imperfective/
   perfective)
pusaht/napsut
to write

psal svému příteli
pusul svemoo prJeeteli
he was writing to his friend

napsal svému příteli
nupsul svemoo prJeeteli
he wrote to his friend, he
   has written to his friend

To form the past tense of
both the imperfective and
perfective forms, use the past
participle of the appropriate
verb followed by the
appropriate person of the
present tense of 'to be' **být**.
The exceptions to this are the
third persons singular and
plural, when **být** is omitted.

To form the past participle
for the imperfective or
perfective aspect, replace the
final -t of the infinitive with
one of the following endings.
There are different past tense
endings for masculine,
feminine and neuter subjects,
in the singular and plural:

m	f	n	mpl	fpl	npl
-l	-la	-lo	-li	-ly	-la

hledat	[hledut]	to look for
hledal jsem m/	[hledul sem]	I looked for
hledala jsem f		
hledal jsi m/**hledala jsi** f	[hledul si]	you looked for (sing, fam)
hledal/hledala/hledalo	[hledul]	he looked for/she looked for/it looked for
hledali jsme m/	[hleduli smeh]	we looked for
hledaly jsme f		
hledali jste m/	[hleduli steh}	you looked for (pl or pol)
hledaly jste f		
hledali m anim/	[hleduli]	they looked for
hledaly f/m inan/	[hleduli]	
hledala n	[hledula]	

řídit	[rJeedyit]	to drive
řídil jsem m/**řídila jsem** f	[rJeedyil sem]	I drove
řídil jsi m/**řídila jsi** f	[rJeedyil si]	you drove (sing, fam)
řídil/**řídila**/**řídilo**	[rJeedyil]	he/she/it drove
řídili jsme m/**řídily jsme** f	[rJeedili smeh]	we drove
řídili jste m/**řídily jste** f	[rJeedili steh]	you drove (pl or pol)
řídili m/**řídily** f/	[rJeedili]	they drove
řídila n	[rJeedila]	

vézt	[vest]	to take, to carry
vezl jsem m/**vezla jsem** f	[vezul sem/vezla]	I took
vezl jsi m/**vezla jsi** f	[vezul si/vezla]	you took (sing, fam)
vezl/**vezla**/**vezlo**	[vezul/vezla/vezlo]	he/she/it took
vezli jsme m/**vezly jsme** f	[vezli smeh]	we took
vezli jste m/**vezly jste** f	[vezli steh]	you took (pl or pol)
vezli m anim/	[vezli]	they took
vezly f/m inan/	[vezli]	
vezla n	[vezla]	

The verb 'to be' has an irregular past tense:

byl jsem m/**byla jsem** f	[bil sem/bila sem]	I was
byl jsi m/**byla jsi** f	[bil si/bila si]	you were (sing, fam)
byl/**byla**/**bylo**	[bil/bila/bilo]	he/she/it was
byli jsme m/**byly jsme** f	[bili smeh/bili smeh]	we were
byli jste m/**byly jste** f	[bili steh/bili steh]	you were (pl or pol)
byli m anim/**byly** f/m inan/	[bili/bili]	they were
byla n	[bila]	

The following are common exceptions to the above rules and the stem given should be used to form the past participle:

infinitive			past participle stem	
číst	[cheest]	to read	četl	[chetul]
chtít	[Hutyeet]	to want	chtěl	[Hutyel]
jíst	[yeest]	to eat	jedl	[yedul]
jít	[yeet]	to go	šel m/šla f/šlo n	[shel/shla/shlo]
mít	[meet]	to have	měl	[mnyel]
moci	[motsi]	to be able	mohl	[mohul]
péct	[petst]	to bake	pekl	[pekul]
plést	[plest]	to knit	pletl	[pletul]
říct	[rJeetst]	to say	řekl	[rJekul]
vést	[vest]	to lead	vedl	[vedul]
vzít	[vzeet]	to take	vzal	[vuzul]
začít	[zatcheet]	to start	začal	[zutchul]

Future Tense

The future tense is formed with the infinitive of the main verb (imperfective aspect) and the future tense of 'to be' být:

budu	[boodoo]	I will be
budeš	[boodesh]	you will be (sing, fam)
bude	[boodeh]	he/she/it will be
budeme	[boodemeh]	we will be
budete	[boodeteh]	you will be (pl or pol)
budou	[boodoh]	they will be

chodit [Hodyit]	to go, to walk
budu chodit	I will go
budeš chodit	you will go (sing, fam)
bude chodit	he/she/it will go
budeme chodit	we will go
budete chodit	you will go (pl or pol)
budou chodit	they will go

The future can also be expressed using the 'present' tense of perfective verbs. The conjugation patterns are the same as those for the **Present Tense** on page 20.

dělat/udělat to do	uděláte to pro mě? [oo-dyelahteh to pro mnyeh]
	will you do it for me?

Negatives

To form a negative sentence, add the prefix **ne-** to the verb or to the appropriate form of **být**:

jsem	I am	**nejsem**	I am not
sem		naysem	
jím	I eat	**nejím**	I don't eat
yeem		nay-yeem	
byl jsem	I was	**nebyl jsem**	I was not
bil sem		nebil sem	
bude	he/she it will be	**nebude**	he/she it will not be
boodeh		neboodeh	

Double negatives are common:

nic nothing
nyits

nikdy never
nigdi

nechtěl jsem nic
neHutyel sem nyits
I didn't want anything

nikdy jsem tam nebyl/nebyla
(said by man/woman)
nigdi sem tum nebil/nebila
I've never been there

není it is not; there is not
nenyee

nikdo tam není
nigdo tum nenyee
there's nobody there

Imperative

The imperative form of the verb is used to express a command (such as 'come here!', 'let's go' etc). Generally, to form the familiar imperative, take the infinitive and make the following changes, depending on whether the verb ends in -at, -it or -t:

spěchat to hurry	**risknout** to risk	**nést** to carry
spyeHut	risknoht	nest
spěchej!	**riskni to!**	**nes to!**
spyeHay	risknyi to	nes to
hurry up!	risk it!	carry it!

The forms of the plural or polite imperatives are as follows:

> **spěchejte!**
> spyeHayteh
> hurry up!

> **riskněte to!**
> risknyeteh to
> risk it!

> **neste to!**
> nesteh to
> carry it!

QUESTIONS

The word order in questions is often the same as in English:

> **co je to?**
> tso yeh to
> what is it?

> **mohu mluvit s Václavem?**
> mohoo mloovit svahtsluvem
> may I speak to Václav?

DATES

Use the ordinal numbers on page 28 to express the date; the ordinal number is always in the genitive case and follows the declension patterns of adjectives (see page 12).

prvního dubna [purvnyeeho doobna] the first of April

třetího března [trJetyeeho brJezna] the third of March

dvacátého prvního června [dvutsahteho purvnyeeho chervna] the twenty first of June

TIME

what time is it? kolik je hodin? [kolik yeh ho-dyin]

one o'clock jedna hodina [yedna ho-dyina]

two/three/four o'clock dvě/tři/čtyri hodiny [dvyeh/trJi/chutirJi ho-dyini]

five o'clock[1] pět hodin [pyet ho-dyin]

it's one o'clock je jedna hodina [yeh yedna ho-dyina]

it's two/three/four o'clock jsou dvě/tři/čtyři hodiny [soh dvyeh/trJi/chutirJi ho-dyini]

it's five o'clock[1] je pět hodin [yeh pyet ho-dyin]

five past one jedna hodina a pět minut [yedna ho-dyina a pyet minoot]

ten past two dvě hodiny a deset minut [dvyeh ho-dyini a deset minoot]

quarter past one[2] čtvrt na dvě [chutvurt na dv-yeh]

quarter past two čtvrt na tři [chutvurt na trJi]

half past one[3] půl druhé [pool drooheh]

half past ten půl jedenácté [pool yedenahtsteh]

twenty to ten za dvacet minut deset [za dvutset minoot deset]

quarter to two tři čtvrtě na dvě

[trɟi chutvurtyeh na dvyeh]

quarter to ten tři čtvrtě na
deset [trɟi chutvurtyeh na deset]

at one o'clock v jednu hodinu
[vyednoo ho-dyinoo]

at two/three/four o'clock ve dvě/
tři/čtyři hodiny [veh dvyeh/
trɟi/chutirɟi ho-dyini]

at five o'clock[1] v pět hodin
[fpyet ho-dyin]

at half past four v půl páté
[fpool pahteh]

14.00 čtrnáct hodin
[chuturnahtst ho-dyin]

17.30 sedmnáct třicet
[sedumnahtst trɟitset]

noon poledne [poledneh]

midnight půlnoc [poolnots]

a.m. (12 p.m. to 5 a.m.) v noci
[vnotsi]

a.m. (5 to 9 a.m.) ráno [rahno]

a.m. (9 to 12 a.m.) dopoledne
[dopoledneh]

p.m. (12 to 5 p.m.) odpoledne
[otpoledneh]

p.m. (5 to 10 p.m.) večer [vetcher]

p.m. (10 to 12 p.m.) v noci [vnotsi]

hour hodina [ho-dyina]

minute minuta [minoota]

second sekunda [sekoonda]

quarter of an hour čtvrt hodiny
[chutvurt ho-dyini]

half an hour půl hodiny [pool
ho-dyini]

three quarters of an hour tři
čtvrtě hodiny [trɟi chutvurtyeh
ho-dyini]

[1] for numbers from five to
twelve use hodin

[2] when expressing time past
the hour, always refer to the
next hour

[3] when expressing 'half past',
the neuter form of the ordinal
adjective is used, see pages
12 and 28

NUMBERS

See also page 6.

0	nula	[noola]
1	jeden/jedna/jedno[1] [yeden/yedna/yedno]	
2	dva/dvě[2]	[dva/dvyeh]
3	tři	[trɟi]
4	čtyři	[chutirɟi]
5	pět	[pyet]
6	šest	[shest]
7	sedm	[sedum]
8	osm	[osum]
9	devět	[devyet]
10	deset	[deset]
11	jedenáct	[yedenahtst]
12	dvanáct	[dvunahtst]
13	třináct	[trɟinahtst]
14	čtrnáct	[chuturnahtst]
15	patnáct	[putnahtst]
16	šestnáct	[shestnahtst]
17	sedmnáct	[sedumnahtst]
18	osmnáct	[osumnahtst]
19	devatenáct [devutenahtst]	
20	dvacet	[dvutset]
21	dvacet jeden/jedna/jedno[1] [dvutset yeden/yedna/yedno]	

22	dvacet dva/dvě[2] [dvutset dva/dvyeh]
23	dvacet tři [dvutset trɹi]
30	třicet [trɹitset]
31	třicet jeden/jedna/ jedno[1] [trɹitset yeden/ yedna/yedno]
32	třicet dva/dvě[2] [trɹitset dva/dvyeh]
33	třicet tři [trɹitset trɹi]
40	čtyřicet [chutirɹitset]
50	padesát [pudesaht]
60	šedesát [shedesaht]
70	sedmdesát [sedumdesaht]
80	osmdesát [osumdesaht]
90	devadesát [devudesaht]
100	sto [sto]
101	sto jeden/jedna/jedno[1] [sto yeden/yedna/yedno]
102	sto dva/dvě[2] [sto dva/ dvyeh]
200	dvě stě [dvyeh styeh]
300	tři sta [trɹi sta]
400	čtyři sta [chutirɹi stah]
500	pět set [pyet set]
600	šest set [shest set]
700	sedm set [sedum set]
800	osm set [osum set]
900	devět set [devyet set]
1,000	tisíc [tyiseets]
2,000	dva tisíce [dva tyiseetseh]
3,000	tři tisíce [trɹi tyiseetseh]
4,000	čtyři tisíce [chutirɹi tyiseetseh]
5,000[3]	pět tisíc [pyet tyiseets]

1,000,000	milión [mili-yawn]

[1] masculine, feminine and neuter forms
[2] masculine and feminine/ neuter forms
[3] for 5,000 or more use tisíc

Ordinals

1st	první [purvnyee]
2nd	druhý [droohee]
3rd	třetí [trɹetyee]
4th	čtvrtý [chutvurtee]
5th	pátý [pahtee]
6th	šestý [shestee]
7th	sedmý [sedmee]
8th	osmý [osmee]
9th	devátý [devahtee]
10th	desátý [desahtee]
11th	jedenáctý [yedenahtsutee]
12th	dvanáctý [dvunahtsutee]
13th	třináctý [trɹinahtsutee]
14th	čtrnáctý [chuturnahtsutee]
15th	patnáctý [putnahtsutee]
16th	šestnáctý [shestnahtsutee]
17th	sedmnáctý [sedumnahtsutee]
18th	osmnáctý [osumnahtsutee]
19th	devatenáctý [devutenahtsutee]
20th	dvacátý [dvutsahtee]
21st	dvacátý první [dvutsahtee purvnyee]
22nd	dvacátý druhý [dvutsahtee droohee]
23rd	dvacátý třetí [dvutsahtee trɹetyee]
24th	dvacátý čtvrtý [dvutsahtee chutvurtee]

25th dvacátý pátý [dvutsahtee pahtee]

26th dvacátý šestý [dvutsahtee shestee]

27th dvacátý sedmý [dvutsahtee sedmee]

28th dvacátý osmý [dvutsahtee osmee]

29th dvacátý devátý [dvutsahtee devahtee]

30th třicátý [trɈitsahtee]

31st třicátý první [trɈitsahtee purvnyee]

CONVERSION TABLES

1 centimetre = 0.39 inches	1 inch = 2.54 cm

1 metre = 39.37 inches = 1.09 yards

1 foot = 30.48 cm

1 yard = 0.91 m

1 kilometre = 0.62 miles = 5/8 mile

1 mile = 1.61 km

km	1	2	3	4	5	10	20	30	40	50	100
miles	0.6	1.2	1.9	2.5	3.1	6.2	12.4	18.6	24.8	31.0	62.1

miles	1	2	3	4	5	10	20	30	40	50	100
km	1.6	3.2	4.8	6.4	8.0	16.1	32.2	48.3	64.4	80.5	161

1 gram = 0.035 ounces

1 kilo = 1000 g = 2.2 pounds

g	100	250	500
oz	3.5	8.75	17.5

1 oz = 28.35 g

1 lb = 0.45 kg

kg	0.5	1	2	3	4	5	6	7	8	9	10
lb	1.1	2.2	4.4	6.6	8.8	11.0	13.2	15.4	17.6	19.8	22.0

kg	20	30	40	50	60	70	80	90	100
lb	44	66	88	110	132	154	176	198	220

lb	0.5	1	2	3	4	5	6	7	8	9	10	20
kg	0.2	0.5	0.9	1.4	1.8	2.3	2.7	3.2	3.6	4.1	4.5	9.0

1 litre = 1.75 UK pints / 2.13 US pints

1 UK pint = 0.57 l	1 UK gallon = 4.55 l
1 US pint = 0.47 l	1 US gallon = 3.79 l

centigrade / Celsius

$C = (F - 32) \times 5/9$

C	-5	0	5	10	15	18	20	25	30	36.8	38
F	23	32	41	50	59	64	68	77	86	98.4	100.4

Fahrenheit

$F = (C \times 9/5) + 32$

F	23	32	40	50	60	65	70	80	85	98.4	101
C	-5	0	4	10	16	18	21	27	29	36.8	38.3

English-Czech

A

a, an*

about (concerning) o (+ loc)

  about 20 asi dvacet [usi]

  it's about 5 o'clock je asi pět
  hodin [yeh]

  a film about Moravia film o
  Moravě

above nad (+ instr) [nut]

abroad v zahraničí
  [zuhrunyitchee]

absolutely (I agree) určitě
  [oorchityeh]

accelerator plyn [plin]

accept přijmout [prJeemoht]

accident nehoda

  there's been an accident stala
  se nehoda [stula seh]

accommodation ubytování
  [oobitovah-nyee]

accurate přesný [prJesnee]

ache bolest f

  my back aches bolí mě záda
  [bolee mnyeh zahda]

across: across the road přes
  cestu [prJes tsestoo]

adapter (for voltage) adaptér
  [udupter]

  (plug) rozdvojka [rozdvoyka]

address adresa [udresa]

  what's your address? jaká je
  vaše adresa? [yukah yeh
  vusheh]

Addresses are written with the
title (either **Vážený pan** or
Pan for 'Mr', **Paní** 'Mrs' or
Slečna 'Ms') on a separate line, →

followed by the name, then the
street and number, the postcode
and town (in this case **Praha**)
and then, if appropriate, the
suburb:

Vážený pan   or   Pan
Pavel Novák   Pavel Novák
Ztracená 36
160 00 Praha 6 – Dejvice

address book adresář [udresarJ]

admission charge vstupné n
  [fstoopneh]

adult (man/woman) dospělý
  [dos-pyelee]/dospělá

advance: in advance předem
  [prJedem]

aeroplane letadlo [letudlo]

after po (+ loc)

  after you až po vás [ush]

  after lunch po obědě

afternoon odpoledne n
  [otpoledneh]

  in the afternoon odpoledne

  this afternoon dnes odpoledne

aftershave voda po holení
  [holenyee]

aftersun cream krém po
  opalování [opalovah-nyee]

afterwards potom

again znovu [znovoo]

against proti [protyi]

age věk [vyek]

ago: a week ago před týdnem
  [prJet]

  three days ago před třemi dny

  an hour ago před hodinou

agree: I agree souhlasím [soh-
  hluseem]

air vzduch [vzdooH]
  by air letadlem [letudlem]
air-conditioning klimatizace f [klimutizatseh]
airmail: by airmail letecky [letetski]
airmail envelope letecká obálka [letetskah obahlka]
airport letiště n [letyish-tyeh]
  to the airport, please na letiště, prosím
airport bus autobus na letiště [owtoboos]
aisle seat sedadlo v chodbičce [sedudlo fHodbitch-tseh]
alarm clock budík [boo-dyeek]
alcohol alkohol [ulkohol]
alcoholic (adj) alkoholický [ulkoholitskee]
all: all the boys všichni chlapci [fshiHnyi]
  all the girls všechny dívky [fsheHni]
  all of it to všechno
  all of them ti všichni
  that's all, thanks to je všechno, děkuji [yeh – dyekoo-yi]
allergic: I'm allergic to ... jsem alergický na ... [sem alergitskee]
allowed: is it allowed? je to dovoleno? [yeh]
all right dobře [dobrJeh]
  I'm all right jsem v pořádku [sem fporJahtkoo]
  are you all right? jste v pořádku? [steh]
almond mandle f [mundleh]

almost skoro
alone sám m [sahm], sama f [suma]
alphabet abeceda [abetseda]

a ah	ch Hah	q kveh	x iks
b beh	i ee	r er	y ipsilon
c tseh	j yeh	ř erJ	z zet
č cheh	k kah	s es	ž Jet
d deh	l el	š esh	
ď dʸᵉʰ	m em	t teh	
e eh	n en	ť tʸᵉʰ	
f ef	ň enʸᵉʰ	u oo	
g geh	o aw	v veh	
h hah	p peh	w dvo-yiteh veh	

already už [oosh]
also také [tukeh]
although ačkoliv [utchkolif]
altogether celkem [tselkem]
always vždy [vuJdi]
am*: I am já jsem [yah sem]
a.m.: at seven a.m. v sedm hodin ráno [rahno]
amazing (surprising) zvláštní [zvlahsht-nyee]
  (very good) fantastické [fantastitskeh]
ambulance sanitka [sunitka]
  call an ambulance! volejte sanitku! [volayteh sunitkoo]

> Dial 155 for an ambulance.

America Amerika [umerika]
American americký [umeritskee]
  I'm American (man/woman) jsem Američan/Američanka [sem umerichun]
among mezi (+ instr)

amount množství [mnoJustvee]

amp: a 13-amp fuse pojistka na třináct ampérů [po-yistka – umperoo]

and a

angry rozzlobený [rozlobenee]

animal zvíře n [zveerJeh]

ankle kotník [kotnyeek]

anniversary (wedding) výročí [veerotchee]

annoy: this man's annoying me ten člověk mě zlobí [chlo-vyek mnyeh zlobee]

annoying nepříjemný [neprJee-yemnee]

another (different) jiný [yinee] (one more) ještě jeden [yeshtyeh yeden]

can we have another room? můžeme dostat jiný pokoj? [mooJemeh dostut]

another beer, please ještě jedno pivo [yedno]

antibiotics antibiotikum n [unti–]

antifreeze nemrznoucí směs f [nemurz-nohtsee smnyes]

antihistamine antihistamin [untihistumin]

antique starožitnost f [staroJitnost]

antiseptic antiseptikum n [unti–]

any: have you got any bread/ tomatoes? máte nějaký chleba/nějaká rajčata? [mahteh nyeh-yukee – nyeh-yukah]

do you have any change? máte drobné?

sorry, I don't have any bohužel, nemám [bo-hooJel nemahm]

anybody někdo [nyegdo] (in negative sentence) nikdo [nyigdo]

does anybody speak English? mluví někdo anglicky? [mloovee – unglitski]

there wasn't anybody there nikdo tam nebyl [tum nebil]

anything něco [nyetso] (in negative sentence) nic [nyits]

•••••• DIALOGUES ••••••

anything else? ještě něco? [yeshtyeh]

nothing else, thanks už ne, děkuji [oosh neh dyekoo-yi]

would you like anything to drink? dáte si něco k pití? [dahteh – kupityee]

I don't want anything, thanks ne, nechci nic, děkuji [neh neHutsi]

apart from kromě [kromnyeh]

apartment byt [bit]

appendicitis zánět slepého střeva [zahnyet – strJeva]

appetizer předkrm [prJetkurm]

aperitif aperitiv [uperitif]

apology omluva [omloova]

apple jablko [yabluko]

appointment schůzka [sHooska]

•••••• DIALOGUE ••••••

good afternoon, sir, how can I help you? dobrý den, pane, mohu vám pomoci? [dobree den puneh mohoo vahm pomotsi]

I'd like to make an appointment chci si domluvit schůzku [Hutsi si domloovit suHOOskoo]

what time would you like? v kolik hodin? [fkolik ho-dyin]

three o'clock ve tři hodiny [veh – ho-dyini]

I'm afraid that's not possible, is four o'clock all right? obávám se, že to nebude možné, hodí se vám to ve čtyři hodiny? [obahvahm seh Jeto neboodeh moJneh ho-dyee seh vahm]

yes, that will be fine ano, to bude výborné [uno to boodeh veeborneh]

what was the name? jak se, prosím, jmenujete? [yuk seh proseem yumenoo-yeteh]

apricot meruňka [meroon^{yeh}ka]
April duben [dooben]
are*: we are my jsme [mismeh]
  you are vy jste [visteh]
  they are oni jsou [onyi soh]
area oblast f
area code směrové číslo [smnyeroveh cheeslo]
arm paže f [puJeh]
arrange: will you arrange it for us? zařídíte to pro nás? [zarJee-dyeeteh pro nahs]
arrival příjezd [prJee-yest]
arrive přijet [prJi-yet]
  when do we arrive? kdy tam přijedeme? [gudi tum prJi-yedemeh]
  has my fax arrived yet? už přišel můj fax? [oosh prJishel mOO-i]

we arrived today přijeli jsme dnes [prJi-yeli smeh]
art umění [oo-mnyenyee]
art gallery galerie f [guleri-eh]
artist (man/woman) umělec [oo-mnyelets]/umělkyně [oo-mnyelki-nyeh]
as: as big as velký jako [velkee yuko]
  as soon as possible co nejdříve [tso naydrJeeveh]
ashtray popelník [popel-nyeek]
ask žádat [Jahdut]/požádat
  I didn't ask for this (said by man/woman) to jsem nechtěl/nechtěla [sem neHutyel]
  could you ask him to …? (to man/woman) mohl/mohla byste ho požádat, aby …? [mohul/mo-hla bisteh – ubi]
asleep: she's asleep ona spí [spee]
aspirin aspirin [uspirin]
asthma astma n [ustma]
astonishing udivující [oo-dyivoo-yeetsee]
at: at the hotel v hotelu
  at the station na nádraží
  at six o'clock v šest hodin
  at Jan's u Jana [oo yuna]
athletics atletika
attractive atraktivní [utruktiv-nyee]
August srpen [surpen]
aunt teta
Austerlitz Slavkov [sluvkof]
Australia Austrálie f [owstrahli-eh]
Australian australský

[owstrulskee]
I'm Australian (man/woman)
jsem Australan/Australanka
[sem owstrulun]
Austria Rakousko [rukohsko]
Austrian (adj) rakouský
[rukohskee]
automatic automatický
[owtomutitskee]
automatic teller bankovní
automat [bunkov-nyee
owtomat]
autumn podzim
in the autumn na podzim
average (not good) obyčejný
[obitchaynee]
(ordinary) průměrný
[proomnyernee]
on average v průměru
[proomnyeroo]
awake: is he awake? je vzhůru?
[yeh vuzh0oroo]
away: go away! jděte pryč!
[yudyeteh pritch]
is it far away? je to daleko?
[yeh to duleko]
awful hrozný [hroznee]
axle náprava [nahpruva]

B

baby děťátko [dyetyahtko]
baby food kojenecká výživa
[ko-yenetskah veeJiva]
baby's bottle kojenecká láhev f
[lah-hef]
baby-sitter paní na hlídání f
[punyee na hleedah-nyee]
back (of body) záda npl [zahda]

(back part) **zadní část** f
[zudnyee chahst]
at the back vzadu [vzudoo]
can I have my money back?
mohu dostat zpátky peníze?
[mohoo dostut spahtki
penyeezeh]
to come/go back vrátit se
[vrahtyit seh]
backache bolest zad f [zud]
bacon anglická slanina
[unglitskah slunyina]
bad špatný [shputnee]
a bad headache silné bolesti
hlavy [silneh bolestyi hluvi]
badly špatně [shput-nyeh]
bag taška [tushka]
(handbag) **kabelka** [kubelka]
(suitcase) **kufr** [koofr]
baggage zavazadla npl
[zuvuzudla]
baggage check (US) úschovna
zavazadel [0osHovna zuvuzudel]
baggage claim výdej zavazadel
[veeday]
bagpipes dudy fpl [doodi]
bakery pekárna
balcony balkón [bulkawn]
a room with a balcony pokoj s
balkónem [pokoy]
bald plešatý [pleshutee]
ball (large) balón [balawn]
(small) **míček** [meetchek]
ballet balet [bulet]
ballpoint pen kuličková tužka
[koolitch-kovah tooshka]
banana banán [banahn]
band (musical) skupina
[skoopina]

bandage obvaz [obvus]
Bandaids® náplasti fpl [nahplustyi]
bank (money) banka [bunka]

Banks are open from Monday to Friday and on Saturday morning. Hours of opening vary, but all open about 7.30-8 a.m. and close at the earliest at 3.30 p.m. Some stay open at lunchtime, but most are closed between noon and 1 p.m. Money can be changed in banks, at large travel agencies and bureaux de change – the latter will be clearly marked in four different languages. Rates are broadly similar, but it may be worth comparing a few places.

---

bank account bankovní konto [bunkov-nyee]
bar bar

The Czech Republic is basically a beer-drinking country with many breweries and excellent beers. This is only challenged by wine in South Moravia. The word for 'pub' is **pivnice** and the more local ones are called **hospoda** or **hostinec**. The more basic types of pubs are sometimes open as early as six in the morning. In the countryside, they usually close at 9 p.m. and in towns 10 or

---

11 p.m. is more usual. In Prague, some pubs are open until midnight. There is not such a wide choice of beers as in Western Europe, but each pub sells a lager-type beer and often a dark beer too. To be served you take a seat and when the waiter comes, you order. The waiter will mark down what you have on a chit of paper which is left on the table and you settle the bill before you leave. If you want to ask for the bill say '**zaplatím, prosím**', literally 'I'll pay, please'. Since pubs are traditionally male preserves, women tend instead to head for a **vinárna** (wine bar). A **vinárna** generally has slightly later opening hours, often doubling as an upmarket restaurant or nightclub.
see **beer**

---

a bar of chocolate tabulka čokolády [tuboolka chokolahdi]
barber's holičství [holitchstvee]
basket koš [kosh]
(in shop) košík [kosheek]
bath koupel f [kohpel]
can I have a bath? mohu se vykoupat? [mohoo seh vikohpat]
bathroom koupelna [kohpelna]
with a private bathroom s vlastní koupelnou [svlast-nyee kohpelnoh]

bath towel ručník [rootch-nyeek]
battery baterie f [bateri-eh]
be* být [beet]
beans fazole fpl [fuzoleh]
  broad beans boby mpl [bobi]
beard bradka [brutka]
beautiful krásný [krahsnee]
because protože [protoJeh]
  because of ... kvůli (+ dat) ...
  [kvOOli]
bed postel f
  I'm going to bed now jdu spát
  [doo spaht]
bed and breakfast nocleh se
  snídaní [notsleH seh snyeedun-
  yee]
  see **hotel**
bedroom ložnice f [loJ-nyitseh]
beef hovězí [hovyezee]
beer pivo
  two beers, please dvě piva,
  prosím

There are two basic types of
beer – **světlé pivo** [svyetleh],
which is light, pale beer, and
černé pivo [cherneh], which is
dark beer, usually sweet by
British and American standards,
though you can have a mixture
of light and dark, called **řezané**
[rJezuneh]. The beers are
usually called 10° (**desítka**),
11° (**jedenáctka**) or 12° (**dván-
áctka**); alcohol by volume
normally varies from about 4.2%
for a '10' to about 5% for a '12'.
In pubs, '10' or '11' on draught
is the most common.

before před (+ instr) [prJet]
begin: when does it begin? kdy
  to začíná? [gudi to zutcheenah]
beginner (man/woman)
  začátečník [zutchahtetch-
  nyeek]/začátečnice [–nyitseh]
beginning: at the beginning na
  začátku [zutchahtkoo]
behind za (+ instr)
  behind me za mnou [mnoh]
beige béžový [beJovee]
believe věřit [vyerJit]
below pod (+ instr) [pot]
belt pásek [pahsek]
bend (in road) zatáčka
  [zutahtchka]
beside: beside the ... vedle
  (+ gen) ... [vedleh]
best nejlepší [naylepshee]
better lepší
  are you feeling better? cítíš se
  lépe? [tsee-tyeesh seh lepeh]
between mezi (+ instr)
beyond za (+ instr)
bicycle kolo
big velký [velkee]
  too big příliš velký
  [prJeelish]
  it's not big enough není to
  dost velké [nenyee – velkeh]
bike kolo
  (motorbike) motorka
bikini bikiny fpl [bikini]
bill účet [OOtchet]
  (US) bankovka [bunkovka]
  could I have the bill, please?
  mohu dostat účet, prosím?
  [mohoo dostut]

In a restaurant or a pub it is unusual to get your change back, then hand the waiter a tip. What you should do is to round up the amount, so if the bill comes to 26 crowns, you should round it up to 30 crowns, if you can afford it. If you give 50 crowns for a 30-crown bill, you should say the amount you intend to pay as you hand over the money, otherwise you might not get any change. Generally, you are not expected to give a large amount as a tip. Czech restaurants do not usually include a service charge in the bill.

bin popelnice f [popel-nyitseh]

binding (ski) lyžařské vázání [liJarJskeh vahzah-nyee]

bird pták [ptahk]

birthday narozeniny fpl [narozenyini]

happy birthday! všechno nejlepší k narozeninám! [fsheHno naylepshee]

biscuit sušenka [sooshenka]

bit: a little bit trochu [troHoo]

a big bit velký kus [velkeh koos]

a bit of ... kousek (+ gen) ... [kohsek]

a bit expensive trochu drahé [draheh]

bite (noun: by insect) štípnutí [shtyeepnoo-tyee]

(by dog) **kousnutí** [kohsnoo-tyee]

bitter (taste etc) hořký [horJkee]

black černý [chernee]

blanket deka

bleach (for toilet) odbarvovač [odbarvovutch]

bless you! požehnej Pánbůh! [poJehunay pahnbOOH]

blind slepý [slepee]

blinds okenice fpl [okenitseh]

blister puchýř [puHeerJ]

blocked ucpaný [ootspunee]

block of flats činžovní dům [chinJov-nyee dOOm]

blond (adj) světlovlasý [svyetlovlusee]

blood krev f [kref]

high blood pressure vysoký krevní tlak [visokee krev-nyee tluk]

blouse halenka [hulenka]

blow-dry foukaná [fohkunah]

I'd like a cut and blow-dry prosím ostříhat a vyfoukat [ostrJeehut a vifohkat]

blue modrý [modree]

blusher růž f [rOOsh]

boarding house penzión [penzyawn]

boarding pass palubní vstupenka [paloob-nyee fstoopenka]

boat (small) člun [chloon]

(for passengers) **loď** f [lod^yeh]

body tělo [tyelo]

Bohemia Čechy fpl [cheHi]

Bohemian (adj) český [cheskee]

boil (verb) **vařit** [varJit]/**uvařit** [oovarJit]

boiled egg vařené vejce n [varJeneh vaytseh]

boiler bojler [boyler]

bone kost f

bonnet (car) kapota [kupota]

book (noun) kniha [kunyiha]
(verb) rezervovat [reservovut]
can I book a seat? mohu si rezervovat místo? [mohoo – meesto]

• • • • • DIALOGUE • • • • •

I'd like to book a table for two (said by man/woman) chtěl/chtěla bych si zamluvit stůl pro dva [Hutyel – biHsi zamloovit stool]

what time would you like it booked for? na kolik hodin si ho chcete zamluvit? [ho-dyin – Hutseteh zamloovit]

half past seven na půl osmé [pool osmeh]

that's fine dobře [dobrJeh]

and your name? na jaké jméno? [yukeh yumeno]

bookshop knihkupectví [kuniH-koopets-tvee]

bookstore knihkupectví

boot (footwear) bota
(of car) zavazadlový prostor [zuvuzudlovee], kufr [koofr]

border (of country) hranice f [hrunyitseh]

bored: I'm bored nudím se [noodyeem seh]

boring nudný [noodnee]

born: I was born in Manchester (said by man/woman) narodil/narodila jsem se v Manchesteru [narodyil – sem seh]

I was born in 1963 (said by man/woman) narodil/narodila jsem se v roce tisíc devět set šedesát tři [rotseh]

borrow půjčit si [poo-ichit]
may I borrow ...? mohu si půjčit ...? [mohoo]

both oba

bother: sorry to bother you promiňte, že vás obtěžuji [promin^{yeh}teh Jeh vahs op-tyeJoo-yi]

bottle láhev f [lah-hef]
a bottle of red wine láhev červeného vína [cherveneho veena]

bottle-opener otvírák [otveerahk]

bottom (of person) zadek [zudek]
at the bottom of ... (road etc) na konci ... [kontsi]
(hill) na úpatí ... [oopatyee]

box krabice f [krubitseh]

box office pokladna [pokludna]

boy chlapec [Hlupets]

boyfriend přítel [prJeetel]

bra podprsenka [potprsenka]

bracelet náramek [narumek]

brake brzda [burzda]

brandy koňak [konyuk]

bread chléb [Hlep]
white bread bílý chléb [beelee]
brown bread černý chléb [chernee]
wholemeal bread celozrnný chléb [tselozurnnee]

break (verb: something) rozbít
[rozbeet]
(arm etc) zlomit
I've broken the ... (said by man/
woman) rozbil/rozbila jsem ....
[sem]
I think I've broken my wrist
(said by man/woman) zlomil/
zlomila jsem si zápěstí
[zahpyes-tyee]
break down: I've broken down
mám poruchu [mahm
porooHoo]
breakdown (car) porucha
[porooHa]

If you break down dial 123 or
0123 at the nearest phone for
Yellow Angels (Žlutí andělé
[Jloo-tyee undyeleh]) – the 24-
hour emergency road service. Or
you could try to get a tow from a
passing motorist to the nearest
autoservis or autoopravna (car
repairs). If you just have a flat
tyre, however, you can go to the
nearest pneuservis. For peace
of mind, it might be worth taking
out an insurance policy like the
AA Five-Star scheme or AA
Europe cover, which will pay for
any on-the-spot repairs, and in
the case of emergencies, ship
you and all your passengers
back home free of charge.

breakdown service havarijní
služba [huvureenyee slooJba]
breakfast snídaně f

[snyeedunyeh]
break-in: I've had a break-in
vloupali se ke mně [vlohpali
seh keh mnyeh]
breast prs [purs]
breathe dýchat [deeHut]
breeze vánek [vahnek]
bridge (over river) most [mosst]
brief stručný [strootchnee]
briefcase aktovka [uktofka]
bright (light etc) jasný [yusnee]
bright red jasně červený
[jusnyeh]
brilliant (idea, person) skvělý
[skvyelee]
bring přinést [prJinest]
I'll bring it back later přinesu
to zpět později [prJinesoo to
spyet pozdyay-yi]
Britain Velká Británie f [velkah
britahni-eh]
British britský [britskee]
I'm British jsem z Británie
[sem zbritahni-eh]
brochure brožura [broJoora]
broken rozbitý [rozbitee]
(bone) zlomený [zlomenee]
it's broken je to rozbité [yeh to
rozbiteh]
bronchitis bronchitida
[bronHitida]
brooch brož f [brosh]
broom koště n [kosh-tyeh]
brother bratr [brutr]
brother-in-law švagr [shvagr]
brown hnědý [hnyedee]
bruise modřina [modrJina]
brush (for hair, cleaning) kartáč
[kurtahtch]

(artist's) **štětec** [shutyetets]

Budweis (place) **České Budějovice** [cheskeh boodyeh-yovitseh]

bucket kýbl [keebl]

buffet car jídelní vůz [yeedel-nyee voos]

buggy (for child) **kočárek** [kotcharek]

building budova [boodova]

bulb (light bulb) **žárovka** [Jarofka]

bumper nárazník [naruz-nyeek]

bunk lůžko [lOOshko]

bureau de change směnárna [smnyenarna]
see **bank**

burglary vloupání [vlohpah-nyee]

burn (noun) **spálenina** [spahlenyina]
(verb: of fire) **hořet** [horJet]
(sensation) **pálit** [pahlit]/**spálit**

burnt: this is burnt to je spálené [yeh spahleneh]

burst: a burst pipe prasklá trubka [prusklah troopka]

bus autobus [owtoboos]
what number bus is it to ...?
který autobus jede do ...?
[kuteree – yedeh]
when is the next bus to ...?
kdy jede příští autobus do ...? [gudi yedeh prJeesh-tyee]
what time is the last bus? kdy jede poslední autobus?
[posled-nyee]
could you let me know when we get there? dáte mi vědět, až tam budeme? [dahteh mi

vyedyet ush tum boodemeh]

•••••• D I A L O G U E ••••••

does this bus go to ...? jede tento autobus do ...?
no, you need a number ... ne, musíte jet autobusem číslo ...
[neh mooseeteh yet – cheeslo]

You should buy your tickets for town buses in advance from newspaper kiosks, tobacconists or automatic machines. In Prague, this will entitle you to an hour on the underground, or one ride on a bus or tram. You validate the ticket as you get on the bus/tram or as you enter a metro station. If you are caught without a valid ticket you will be fined (usually 200 crowns). On country buses, the tickets are sold by the driver and for long-distance bus journeys they are either sold by the driver or can be bought at the coach station. Travel agencies sell tickets for international coach journeys. For many popular long-distance routes you'll need to book in advance.

business obchod [opHot]

bus station autobusové nádraží [owtoboosoveh nahdraJee]

bus stop autobusová zastávka [–ovah zustahfka]

bust hruď f [hrootʸᵉʰ]

busy (restaurant etc) **rušný**

[rooshnee]
**I am busy tomorrow zítra
mám napilno** [zeetra mahm
nupilno]
but ale [aleh]
butcher's řeznictví [rJez-nyits-
tvee]
butter máslo [mahslo]
button knoflík [kunofleek]
buy kupovat [koopovut]/**koupit**
[kohpit]
   **where can I buy ...? kde mohu
   koupit ...?** [gudeh mohoo]
**by: by bus/car autobusem/
autem**
   written by ... napsáno
   (+ instr) ... [nupsahno]
   by the window u okna [oo]
   by the sea u moře
   by Thursday do čtvrtka
bye nashle [nusHleh]

C

cabbage zelí [zelee]
cable car lanovka [lunofka]
café kavárna [kuvarna]

You can sometimes get coffee
and cakes in a **cukrárna**
[tsookrarna] (cake shop). In a
kavárna (café) you can buy
coffee, soft and alcoholic drinks,
cakes and sandwiches. If you
want something quick and
savoury try a **bufet** [boofet]
(snack bar) or **občerstvení**
[optcher-stvenyee] (literally 'refreshments').

---

cagoule pláštěnka [plahsh-
tyenka]
cake dort
cake shop cukrárna [tsookrarna]
call říkat [rJeekut]/**říct** [rJeetst]
(+ dat)
(to phone) **telefonovat**
[telefonovut] (+ dat)
   **what's it called? jak se tomu
   říká?** [yuk seh tomoo rJeekah]
   **he/she is called ... jmenuje
   se ...** [yumenoo-yeh seh]
   **please call the doctor
   zavolejte doktora, prosím**
   [zuvolayteh]
   **please give me a call at 7.30
   a.m. tomorrow zatelefonujte
   mi, prosím, zítra v půl osmé
   ráno** [zutelefonoo-iteh]
   **please ask him to call me
   řekněte mu, prosím, aby mi
   zatelefonoval** [rJeknyeteh moo
   – abi mi zutelefonovul]
**call back: I'll call back later
přijdu později** [prJeedoo
pozdyay-yi]
   (phone back) **zatelefonuji
   později** [zutelefonoo-yi]
**call round: I'll call round
tomorrow přijdu zítra**
[prJee-doo]
camcorder videokamera [videh-
o-kumera]
camera fotoaparát [foto-
upuraht]
**camera shop fotografické
potřeby fpl** [fotogrufitskeh
potrJebi]
camp kempovat [kempovut]

can we camp here? můžeme tady stanovat? [mooJemeh tudi stanovut]

camping gas butan [bootun]

Camping gas canisters can be bought either from a **železářství** [Jelezarjstvee] (hardware store) or from some sports shops, where you can find out about the nearest filling point (usually attached to the local gasworks).

campsite tábořiště n [tahborJish-tyeh]
(more luxurious) **autokempink** [owto–]

There is no shortage of campsites. You can buy a map showing the sites marked in a bookshop or travel agency. Services are variable, ranging from basic to very good. Standards are likely to be higher in an **autokempink** which is a type of motel where you can also camp and which allows cars. Officially you can't camp anywhere you like.

can konzerva
a can of beer plechovka piva [pleHofka]

can: can you ...? můžeš ...? [mooZhesh]
can I have ...? mohu dostat ...? [mohoo dostut]
I can't ... nemohu ...

Canada Kanada [kunuda]
Canadian kanadský [kunutskee]
I'm Canadian (man/woman) jsem Kanaďan/Kanaďanka [sem kunudyun]

canal kanál [kunahl]
cancel rušit [rooshit]/zrušit
candies bonbóny [bonbawni]
candle svíčka [sveetchka]
canoe kanoe f [kano-eh]
canoeing jízda na kanoi [yeezda na kano-i]
can-opener otvírák konzerv [otveerahk konzerf]
cap (hat) čepice f [chepitseh]
(of bottle) zátka [zahtka]
car auto [owto]
by car autem
caravan karavan [kuruvun]
caravan site kemp pro přívěsy [prJee-vyesi]
carburettor karburátor [kurboorahtor]
card (birthday etc) blahopřání [bluhoprJah-nyee]
(business) navštívenka [nufsh-tyeevenka]
here's my (business) card zde je má navštívenka [zdeh yeh mah]
cardigan pletená zapínací vesta [pletenah zapeenatsee]
cardphone telefon na kartu [kurtoo]
careful opatrný [oputurnee]
be careful! buď te opatrný! [bood^{yeh}teh]
caretaker (man/woman) správce m [sprahftseh]/správcová

car hire pronájem automobilů [pronī-em owtomobil00]
see **rent**

car park parkoviště n [purkovish-tyeh]

carpet koberec [koberets]

carriage (of train) vagón [vagawn]

carrier bag nákupní taška [nahkoop-nyee tushka]

carrot mrkev f [murkef]

carry nést

carry-cot taška na přenášení dítěte [tushka na prJenahshenyee dyee-tyeteh]

carton krabice f [krubitseh]

carwash umývárna automobilů [oomeevarna owtomobil00]

case (suitcase) kufr [koofr]

cash hotové peníze mpl [hotoveh penyeezeh]
(verb) proměnit [pro-mnyenyit]
will you cash this for me? proměníte mi to? [pro-mnyenyeeteh]

cash desk pokladna [pokludna]

cash dispenser bankovní automat [bunkov-nyee owtomut]

cashier pokladní m/f [poklud-nyee]

cassette kazeta [kuzeta]

cassette recorder kazetový magnetofon [kuzetovee mug–]

castle zámek [zahmek]

casualty department úrazová ambulance f [ooruzovah umbooluntseh]

cat kočka [kotchka]

catch chytnout [Hitnoht]

where do we catch the bus to ...? kde chytneme autobus do ...? [gudeh Hitnemeh]

cathedral katedrála [kutedrahla]

Catholic (adj) katolický [kutolitskee]

cauliflower květák [kvyetahk]

cave jeskyně f [yeski-nyeh]

ceiling strop

celery celer [tseler]

cellar (for wine) vinný sklep [vinee]

cemetery hřbitov [hurJbitof]

centigrade* stostupňový [stostoop-nyovee]

centimetre* centimetr [tsentimetr]

central centrální [tsentrahl-nyee]

central heating ústřední topení [00strJed-nyee topenyee]

centre střed [strJet]
how do we get to the city centre? jak se dostaneme do středu města? [yuk seh dostanemeh do strJedoo mnyesta]

cereal müsli [misli], vločky fpl [vlotchki]

certainly určitě [oortchi-tyeh]
certainly not určitě ne [neh]

chair židle f [Jidleh]

champagne šampaňské n [shumpan^(yeh)skeh]

change (noun: money) drobné [drobneh]
(verb: money) proměnit [pro-mnyenyit]
(trains) přesedat [prJesedat]
(clothes) převlékat se

[prJevlekut seh]/**převléknout
se** [prJevleknoht]
can I change this for ...? mohu
si toto proměnit za ...?
[mohoo]
I don't have any change
nemám drobné [nemahm]
**can you give me change for a
hundred crown note?** můžete
mi dát drobné za sto korun?
[mooJeteh mi daht – koroon]

•••••• DIALOGUE ••••••

do we have to change (trains)?
musíme přesedat? [mooseemeh
prJesedut]
**yes, change at Brno/no, it's a direct
train** ano, přesedáte v Brně/ne, je
to přímý spoj [uno prJesedahteh v
brunyeh/neh yeh to prJeemee spoy]

changed: to get changed
převléci se [prJevletsi seh]
chapel kaple f [kupleh]
charge poplatek [poplutek]
(verb) účtovat [OOtchtovut]
charge card
see **credit card**
cheap levný [levnee]
do you have anything cheaper?
máte něco levnějšího?
[mahteh nyetso lev-nyaysheeho]
check (US: noun) šek [shek]
see **cheque**
(US: bill) účet [OOtchet]
see **bill**
(verb) kontrolovat
[kontrolovut]/zkontrolovat
**could you check the ...,
please?** (to man/woman) mohl/

**mohla byste zkontrolovat ...,
prosím?** [mohul/mo-hla bisteh]
checkbook šeková knížka
[shekovah kunyeeJka]
check in (verb) dostavit se k
odbavení [dostuvit seh k
odbuvenyee]
where do we have to check in?
kam se máme dostavit k
odbavení? [kumseh mahmeh]
check-in odbavení [odbuvenyee]
cheek tvář f [tvahrJ]
cheerio! ahoj! [uhoy]
cheers! (toast) na zdraví!
[zdruvee]
cheese sýr [seer]
chemist's lékárna

If you need items such as toothpaste, toothbrushes, soap and
sunglasses, go to a **drogerie**. If
you need medical items go to
a **lékárna** (pharmacy). Each
lékárna will have the address of
the nearest late-night or all-
night pharmacy on the door. In
most pharmacies, you'll find a
separate prescription counter
(**výdej na recepty**) and cash
desk (**prodej za hotové**).

cheque šek [shek]
do you take cheques? berete
šeky? [bereteh sheki]

The Czech Republic is still
predominantly a cash society.
Major credit cards and cheques →

can be used in the centre of Prague and other major cities and are accepted in hotels, more up-market restaurants and shops specialising in glass and luxury goods. Cash dispensing machines are beginning to appear in Prague and other major towns.

cheque book šeková knížka [shekovah kunyeeshkah]

cheque card bankovní průkaz majitele konta n [bunkov-nyee prookas muh-yiteleh]

cherry třešeň f [trJeshen^yeh]

chess šachy mpl [shaHi]

chest (body) hruď f [hroot^yeh]

chewing gum žvýkačka [Jveekutchka]

chicken (bird) kuře n [koorJeh] (meat) kuřecí maso [koorJetsee muso]

chickenpox plané neštovice fpl [planeh neshtovitseh]

child dítě n [dyeetyeh]

child minder paní k dětem f [punyee gudyetem]

children děti [dyetyi]

Children are welcome in the more upmarket restaurants in the morning and at lunchtime. They are rarely seen in pubs or cafés, apart from open-air places.

children's pool dětský bazén [dyetskee buzen]

children's portion dětská porce f [dyetskah portseh]

chin brada [bruda]

china porcelán [portselahn]

Chinese (adj) čínský [cheenskee]

chips hranolky mpl [hrunolki] (US) lupínky mpl [loopeenki]

chocolate čokoláda [chokolahda]
  milk chocolate mléčná čokoláda [mletchnah]
  plain chocolate hořká čokoláda [horJkah]
  a hot chocolate (horká) čokoláda

choose vybírat [vibeerut]/vybrat [vibrut]

Christian name křestní jméno [krJest-nyee yumeno]

Christmas Vánoce mpl [vahnotseh]
  Christmas Eve Štědrý večer [shtyedree vetcher]
  merry Christmas! Veselé Vánoce! [veseleh]

church kostel

cider kvašený jablečný mošt [kvushenee yubletchnee mosht]

cigar doutník [doht-nyeek]

cigarette cigareta [tsigureta]

Cigarettes can be bought in supermarkets and grocery stores (**potraviny**) and from tobacconists (**tabák, trafika**) or newspaper kiosks. International brands of cigarettes, tobacco and cigars are available, as are many, rougher, local brands.

cigarette lighter zapalovač
[zupulovutch]

cinema kino

Most bigger cinemas show films
at 5.30 p.m. and again at 8 p.m.
Comedies and very successful
films are usually dubbed, other
films are subtitled.

---

circle kruh [krooH]

city město [mnyesto]

city centre střed města [strJet
mnyesta]

clean (adj) čistý [chistee]
can you clean these for me?
můžete mi to vyčistit?
[mOOJeteh – vitchis-tyit]

cleaning solution (for contact
lenses) čisticí roztok na
kontaktní čočky [chis-tyitsee –
kontaktnyee chotchki]

cleansing lotion pleťový
čisticí krém [pletyovee chis-
tyitsee]

clear jasný [yusnee]
(obvious) jasné [yusneh]

clever chytrý [Hitree]

cliff útes [OOtes]

climbing horolezectví
[horolezets-tvee]

cling film fólie f [fawli-eh]

clinic klinika

cloakroom šatna [shutna]

clock hodiny fpl [ho-dyini]

close zavírat [zuveerut]/zavřít
[zuvurJeet]

what time do you close? kdy
zavíráte? [gudi zaveerahteh]

**we close at 8 p.m. on weekdays
and 6 p.m. on Saturdays** ve všední
dny v osm hodin a v sobotu v
šest hodin [veh fshed-nyee dni –
fsobotoo]

do you close for lunch? zavíráte v
poledne?
[zuveerahteh fpoledneh]

yes, between 1 and 2 p.m. ano,
mezi jednou a druhou [uno]

closed zavřeno [zavurJeno]

cloth (fabric) látka [lahtka]
(for cleaning etc) hadr [hudr]

clothes šaty mpl [shuti]

clothes line šňůra na prádlo
[shnyOOra na prahdlo]

clothes peg kolík na prádlo
[koleek]

cloud mrak [mruk]

cloudy zamračeno
[zamrutcheno]

clutch (noun: car) spojka [spoyka]

coach (bus) autobus [owtoboos]
(on train) vagón [vagawn]

coach station autobusové
nádraží [owtoboosoveh
nahdruJee]

coach trip výlet autobusem
[veelet]

coat (long coat) kabát [kubaht]
(jacket) bunda [boonda]

coathanger ramínko na šaty
[rumeenko na shuti]

cockroach šváb [shvahp]

cocoa kakao [kuka-o]

code (when dialling) **směrové číslo** [smnyeroveh cheeslo]
　what's the (dialling) code for Brno? jaké je směrové číslo pro Brno? [yakeh yeh – burno]
coffee káva [kahva]
　two coffees, please dvě kávy, prosím [kahvi]

Coffee is generally served black and known as **turecká káva**. The most common types of coffee are:

turecká káva [tooretskah] Turkish coffee – small, dark, strong with grounds at the bottom
vídeňská káva [viden^yeh^skah] Viennese coffee – coffee with whipped cream on top
espresso (or **presso**) – strong, black coffee
capuccino (or **kapucín**) – espresso with hot milk
ledová káva – cold, black coffee, often served with ice cream and whipped cream

---

coin mince f [mintseh]
Coke® kokakola
cold (adj: weather, food etc) **studený** [stoodenee]
　I'm cold je mi zima [yeh]
　I have a cold jsem nachlazený [sem nuh-Hluzenee]
collapse: he's collapsed je zničený [yeh znyichenee]
collar límec [leemets]
collect sbírat [zbeerut]/**sebrat**

[sebrut]
　I've come to collect ... sbírám ... [zbeerahm]
collect call hovor na účet volaného [ootchet]
college fakulta [fukoolta]
colour barva [burva]
　do you have this in other colours? máte to v jiné barvě? [mahteh – yineh burvyeh]
colour film barevný film [burevnee]
comb (noun) **hřeben** [hrJeben]
come přijít [prJi-yeet]

•••••• D I A L O G U E ••••••

where do you come from? odkud jste? [otkoot steh]
I come from Edinburgh jsem z Edinburgu [sem]

come back vrátit se [vrahtyit seh]
　I'll come back tomorrow vrátím se zítra [vrah-tyeem]
come in vstoupit [fstohpit]
comfortable pohodlný [pohodlnee]
compact disc kompaktní disk [kompakt-nyee]
company (business) **společnost** f [spoletchnost]
compartment (on train) **oddělení** [od-dyelenyee]
compass kompas [kompus]
complain stěžovat si [styeJovut si]
complaint stížnost f [styeeJnost]
　I have a complaint mám stížnost [mahm]

completely úplně [OOpul-nyeh]

computer počítač [potcheetutch]

concert koncert [kontsert]

concussion otřes mozku [otrJes moskoo]

conditioner (for hair) vlasový regenerátor [vlusovee regenerahtor]

condom prezervativ [–vutif], kondom

conference konference f [konferentseh]

confirm potvrdit [potvurdyit]

congratulations! blahopřeji! [bluhoprJay-i]

connecting flight letové spojení [letoveh spo-yenyee]

connection spoj [spoy]

conscious při vědomí [prJi vyedomee]

constipation zácpa [zahtspa]

consulate konzulát [konzoolaht]

contact kontaktovat [kontuktovut]

contact lenses kontaktní čočky fpl [kontaktnyee chotchki]

contraceptive antikoncepční prostředek [untikontseptch-nyee prostrJedek]

convenient (time, location) vhodný [vhodnee]

that's not convenient to se nehodí [seh nehodyee]

cook (verb) vařit/uvařit [oovarJit]

not cooked nedovařený [nedovurJenee]

cooker vařič [vurJitch]

cookie sušenka [sooshenka]

cooking utensils kuchařské

náčiní n sing [kooHarJskeh nahtchi-nyee]

cool chladný [Hludnee]

cork korková zátka [–ovah zahtka], špunt [shpunt]

corkscrew vývrtka [veevurtka]

corner: on the corner na rohu [rohoo]

in the corner v rohu

cornflakes pražené kukuřičné vločky fpl [praJeneh kookoorJitchneh vlotchki]

correct (right) správný [sprahvnee]

corridor chodba [Hodba]

cosmetics kosmetika

cost stát [staht]

how much does it cost? kolik to stojí? [sto-yee]

cot dětská postýlka [dyetskah posteelka]

cotton bavlna [buvulna]

cotton wool vata [vuta]

couch (sofa) pohovka [pohofka]

couchette lehátkový vůz [lehahtkovee vOOs]

cough (noun) kašel [kushel]

cough medicine lék na kašel

could: could you ...? (to man/ woman) mohl/mohla byste ...? [mohul/mo-hla bisteh]

could I have ...? (said by man/ woman) mohl/mohla bych dostat ...? [biH dostut]

I couldn't ... (said by man/woman) nemohl/nemohla bych ...

country (nation) země f [zemnyeh]

(countryside) venkov [venkof]

countryside krajina [krī-ina]
couple (two people) pár, dvojice f
[dvo-yitseh]
  a couple of ... několik
  (+ gen) ... [nyekolik]
courier kurýr [kooreer]
course (main course etc) chod
[Hot]
  of course samozřejmě
[sumozrJay-mnyeh]
  of course not samozřejmě ne
[neh]
cousin (male/female) bratranec
[brutrunets]/sestřenice f
[sestrJenyitseh]
cow kráva [krahva]
crab krab [krub]
crackers (biscuits) krekery fpl
crash (noun) srážka [srahshka]
  I've had a crash srazil jsem se
[sem seh]
crazy bláznivý [blahz-nyivee]
cream (on milk, in cake) smetana
[smetuna]
  (lotion) krém
  (colour) smetanový
[smetunovee]
creche jesle fpl [yesleh]
credit card platební karta
[plutebnyee]
  see **cheque**

•••••• D I A L O G U E ••••••

can I pay by credit card? mohu
platit platební kartou? [mohoo
plutyit plutebnyee kartoh]
which card do you want to use?
kterou kartou chcete platit?
[kuteroh kartoh Hutseteh]

yes, sir ano, pane [uno puneh]
what's the number? jaké máte
číslo? [yakeh mahteh cheeslo]
and the expiry date? do kdy platí?
[dog-di plutyee]

crisps lupínky mpl [loopeenki]
crockery nádobí [nahdobee]
crossroads křižovatka
[krJiJovutka]
crowd dav [daf]
crowded plný lidí [pulnee
lidyee]
crown (on tooth) korunka
[koroonka]
  (currency) koruna [koroona]
crutches berle fpl [berleh]
cry plakat [plukut]
crystal křišťálové sklo [krJish-
tyahloveh]
cucumber okurka [okoorka]
cup šálek [shahlek]
  a cup of ..., please šálek ...,
prosím
cupboard skříň s policemi f
[skrJeen^yeh s politsemi]
cure léčení [letchenyee]
curly kudrnatý [koodurnutee]
current proud [proht]
curtains (at window) záclona
[zahtslona]
  (in theatre) opona
cushion polštář [polshtarJ]
custom zvyk [zvik]
Customs clo [tslo]
cut (verb) říznout [rJeeznoht]
  I've cut myself (said by man/
woman) říznul/říznula jsem se
[rJeeznool – sem seh]

cut glass broušené sklo
[brohsheneh]

cutlery příbor [prJeebor]

cycling cyklistika [tsiklistika]

cyclist (man/woman) cyklista m/
cyklistka

Czech (adj) český [cheskee]
(language) čeština [chesh-tyina]
(man) Čech [cheH]
(woman) Češka [cheshka]
the Czechs Češi [cheshi]

Czech Republic Česká
republika [cheskah]

D

dad tatínek [tutyeenek]

daily (adj) denní [denyee]

damage (verb) poškodit
[poshkodyit]
I'm sorry, I've damaged this
(said by man/woman) je mi to
líto, že jsem to poškodil/
poškodila [yeh – leeto Jeh sem]

damaged poškozený
[poshkozenee]

damn! hrome! [hromeh]

damp (adj) vlhký [vulH-kee]

dance (noun) tanec [tunets]
(verb) tancovat [tuntsovat]
would you like to dance?
smím prosit? [smeem]

dangerous nebezpečný
[nebespetchnee]

Danish dánský [dahnskee]

Danube Dunaj [doonĭ]

dark (adj: colour) tmavý [tmuvee]
(hair) tmavovlasý
[tmuvovlasee]

it's getting dark stmívá se
[stmeevah seh]

date*: what's the date today?
kolikátého je dnes?
[kolikahteho yeh]
**let's make a date for next
Monday** domluvme si
schůzku na pondělí
[domloovmeh si suHOOskoo na
pondyelee]

dates (fruit) datle fpl [dutleh]

daughter dcera [dutsera]

daughter-in-law snacha [snaHa]

dawn (noun) úsvit [OOsvit]
at dawn za úsvitu [OOsvitoo]

day den
the day after den poté [poteh]
the day after tomorrow pozítří
[pozeetrJee]
the day before den předtím
[prJet-tyeem]
the day before yesterday
předevčírem [prJedef-
cheerem]
every day každý den [kuJdee]
all day celý den [tselee]
in two days' time za dva dny
[duni]
have a nice day! přeji vám
příjemný den! [prJayvi vahm
prJee-yemnee]

day trip celodenní výlet
[tselodenyee veelet]

dead mrtvý [murtvee]

deaf hluchý [hlooHee]

deal (business) obchod [opHot]
it's a deal! ujednáno! [oo-
yednahno]

death smrt f [smurt]

decaffeinated coffee bez kofeinu [bes kofaynoo]

December prosinec [prosinets]

decide rozhodnout se [rozhodnoht seh]

we haven't decided yet ještě jsme se nerozhodli [yeshtyeh smeh seh]

decision rozhodnutí [rozhodnoo-tyee]

deckchair lodní lehátko [lod-nyee lehahtko]

deduct odečíst [odecheest]

deep hluboký [hloobokee]

definitely určitě [oorchityeh]

definitely not určitě ne [neh]

degree (qualification) akademická hodnost f [ukudemitskah]

delay (noun) zpoždění [spoJ-dyenyee]

deliberately záměrně [zahmnyer-nyeh]

delicatessen lahůdky fpl [lah-hOOtki]

delicious lahodný [lahodnee]

deliver dodávat [dodahvut]

delivery (of mail) donáška pošty [donahshka poshti]

Denmark Dánsko [dahnsko]

dental floss zubní nit' f [zoob-nyee nit^yeh]

dentist (man/woman) zubní lékař [zoob-nyee lekurJ]/zubní lékařka

•••••• DIALOGUE ••••••

it's this one here je to tady ten [yeh to tudi]

this one? tenhle? [ten-hleh]

no that one ne, tady ten [neh]

here? tady?

yes ano [uno]

dentures zubní protéza [zoobnyee]

deodorant deodorant [deh-odorunt]

department oddělení [od-dyelenyee]

department store obchodní dům [opHod-nyee dOOm]

departure odjezd [od-yest]

departure lounge čekárna [chekarna]

depend: it depends to záleží [zahleJee]

it depends on ... to záleží na ...

deposit (as security) zástava [zahstuva]

(as part payment) záloha

> You usually have to leave a deposit when hiring something; the amount will vary, but if you are asked to leave your passport, do not.

description popis

dessert dezert

destination cíl [tseel]

develop rozvinout [rozvinoht]

•••••• DIALOGUE ••••••

could you develop these films? mohli byste vyvolat tyto filmy? [mohuli bisteh vivolut tito filmi]

when will they be ready? kdy to

bude hotové? [gudi-to boodeh
hotoveh]
tomorrow afternoon zítra
odpoledne
how much is the same day service?
kolik by stálo vyvolání dnes? [bi
– vivolah-nyee]

diabetic (man/woman) diabetik/
diabetička [diabetitchka]
   diabetic foods potraviny pro
   diabetiky
dial volit číslo [cheeslo]
dialling code směrové číslo
[smnyeroveh cheeslo]

For direct international calls
from the Czech Republic, dial
the country code (given below),
the area code (minus the first
0), and finally the subscriber
number:
UK: 0044
Australia: 0061
Ireland: 00353
New Zealand: 0064
US & Canada: 001

---

diamond diamant [di-amunt]
diaper plenka
diarrhoea průjem [proo-yem]
diary (business etc) diář [di-arJ]
   (for personal experiences) deník
   [denyeek]
dictionary slovník [slov-nyeek]
didn't
   see **not**
die umírat/zemřít [zemrJeet]
diesel (fuel) motorová nafta

[–ovah nufta]
diet dieta [di-eta]
   I'm on a diet držím dietu
   [drJeem di-yetoo]
   I have to follow a special diet
   musím držet speciální dietu
   [mooseem drJet spetsi-ahlnyee]
difference rozdíl [rozdyeel]
   what's the difference? jaký je v
   tom rozdíl? [yakee yeh]
different jiný [yinee]
   this one is different tento je
   jiný [yeh]
   a different table jiný stůl
   [stool]
difficult obtížný
   [op-tyeeJnee]
difficulty potíž f [po-tyeesh]
dinghy malý člun
   [mulee chlun]
dining room jídelna [yeedelna]
dinner (evening meal) večeře f
   [vetcherJeh]
   to have dinner večeřet
   [vetcherJet]
direct (adj) přímý [prJeemee]
   is there a direct train? je tam
   přímý spoj? [yeh tum]
direction směr [smnyer]
   which direction is it? jakým je
   to směrem? [yukeem yeh to
   smnyerem]
   is it in this direction? je to
   tímto směrem? [yeh to
   tyeemto]
directory enquiries telefonní
   informace [telefon-nyee
   informatseh]

In larger towns, the number for local directory enquiries is 120. In smaller towns you have to ring the nearest large town using the town code first. International directory enquiries is 0149.

dirt špína [shpeena]
dirty špinavý [shpinavee]
disabled invalidní [invulid-nyee]
 is there access for the disabled? dostanou se tam invalidé? [dostunoh seh tum invulideh]
disappear zmizet
 it's disappeared zmizelo to
disappointed zklamaný [sklumunee]
disappointing zklamání [sklumah-nyee]
disaster katastrofa [kutustrofa]
disco diskotéka
discount sleva
 is there a discount? je na to sleva? [yeh]
disease nemoc f [nemots]
disgusting nechutný [neHootnee]
dish (meal) jídlo [yeedlo]
 (bowl) miska
dishcloth utěrka [ootyerka]
disinfectant (noun) dezinfekční prostředek [dezinfektch-nyee prostrJedek]
disk (for computer) disketa
disposable diapers plenky na jedno použití fpl [plenki na yedno pohJi-tyee]

disposable nappies plenky na jedno použití
distance vzdálenost f [vuzdahlenost]
 in the distance v dálce [dahltseh]
distilled water destilovaná voda [−vanah]
district obvod [obvot]
disturb rušit [rooshit]/vyrušit [virooshit]
diversion (detour) odbočka [odbotchka]
diving board skákací prkno [skahkutsee purkno]
divorced rozvedený [rozvedenee]
dizzy: I feel dizzy točí se mi hlava [totchee seh mi hluva]
do dělat [dyelut]/udělat [oodyelut]
 what shall we do? co budeme dělat? [tso boodemeh]
 how do you do it? jak to děláte? [yak to dyelahteh]
 will you do it for me? uděláte to pro mě? [oo-dyelahteh − mnyeh]

•••••• DIALOGUES ••••••

how do you do? těší mě [tyeshee mnyeh]
nice to meet you těší mě
what do you do? (work) kde pracujete? [gudeh pratsoo-yeteh]
I'm a teacher, and you? (said by man/woman) já jsem učitel/ učitelka, a vy? [yah sem − vi]
I'm a student (said by man/woman) já jsem student/

studentka
what are you doing this evening?
co děláte dnes večer? [tso]
**we're going out for a drink, do you
want to join us?** jdeme na
skleničku, chcete jít s námi?
[demeh na sklenyitchkoo Hutseteh
yeet snahmi]

do you want cream? chcete
smetanu? [Hutseteh]
I do, but she doesn't já ano, ale
ona ne [yah uno uleh ona neh]

doctor (man/woman) doktor/
doktorka
we need a doctor
potřebujeme doktora
[potrJeboo-yemeh]
please call a doctor zavolejte
doktora, prosím [zuvolayteh]

In urgent cases ring 155 for an
ambulance, otherwise find the
nearest hospital (**poliklinika,
nemocnice** [nemotsnyitseh]) or
in smaller places a medical
centre (**zdravotní středisko**
[strJedyisko]). The network of
private doctors is not fully
developed yet. In the event of a
medical emergency or accident,
the reciprocal arrangement
made originally between the UK
and Czechoslovakia still applies.
But note that it only applies to
emergency treatment – for anything else you will have to pay
so it is best to take out medical
insurance before you go.

•••••• DIALOGUE ••••••

where does it hurt? kde to bolí?
[gudeh to bolee]
right here tady [tudi]
does that hurt more? bolí to ted'
víc? [ted^yeh veets]
yes ano [uno]
take this prescription to a chemist
tady máte recept [mahteh retsept]

document doklad [doklut]
dog pes
doll panenka [punenka]
domestic flight vnitrostátní let
[vunyitrostaht-nyee]
don't: don't do that! nedělejte
to! [neh-dyelayteh]
see **not**
door dveře fpl [dverJeh]
doorman vrátný [vrahtnee]
double dvojitý [dvo-yitee]
double bed manželská postel f
[munJelskah]
double room pokoj pro dvě
osoby [pokoy pro dvyeh osobi]
doughnut kobliha
down dolů [doloo]
down here tady [tudi]
put it down over there položte
to tamhle [poloshteh to
tamhleh]
it's down there on the right je
to tamhle napravo [yeh]
it's further down the road je to
dál po cestě [dahl po tses-tyeh]
downhill skiing sjezdové
lyžování [syezdoveh lizhovah-
nyee]
downmarket (restaurant etc) nižší

kategorie [nyishee kategori-eh]
downstairs v přízemí
[fprJeezemee]
dozen tucet [tootset]
   half a dozen půl tuctu [pool
   tootstoo]
drain (in sink) odtok
   (in street) kanalizace f
   [kanalizatseh]
draught beer točené pivo,
   čepované pivo [totcheneh –
   tchepovuneh]
draughty: it's draughty je tu
   průvan [yeh too proovan]
drawer zásuvka [zahsoofka]
drawing kresba
dreadful hrozný [hroznee]
dream (noun) sen
dress (noun) šaty mpl [shuti]
dressed: to get dressed obléct
   se [obletst seh]
dressing (for cut) obvaz [obvus]
   salad dressing obloha
dressing gown župan [Joopan]
drink (noun) nápoj [nahpoy]
   (verb) pít [peet]/napít
   a cold drink studený nápoj
   [stoodenee]
   can I get you a drink? dáte si
   něco k pití? [dahteh si nyetso
   kupityee]
   what would you like (to drink)?
   co si dáte? [tso]
   no thanks, I don't drink ne,
   děkuji, nepiju [neh dyekoo-yi
   nepi-yoo]
   I'll just have a drink of water
   jenom trochu vody [yenom
   troHoo vodi]

drinking water pitná voda
   [pitnah]
   is this drinking water? je to
   pitná voda? [yeh]

Tap water is perfectly drinkable,
but if you have any misgivings
there are plenty of good mineral
waters on sale.

drive řídit [rJeedyit]
   we drove here přijeli jsme
   sem autem [prJi-yeli smeh sem
   owtem]
   I'll drive you home odvezu vás
   domů [odvezoo vahs domoo]

Most foreign driving licences are
honoured in the Czech Republic – including US and Canadian
ones – but an International
Driving Licence is an easy way
to set your mind at rest. If you're
bringing your own car, you are
legally required to carry the
vehicle's registration document.
Check with your insurance
company before leaving home
whether you need a green card,
as without one you may only get
third party cover. Rules and
regulations are pretty stringent.
On-the-spot fines are still regu-
larly handed out for minor
offences. The basic rules are
driving on the right; compulsory
wearing of seat belts at all times;
and children under 12 must →

travel in the back. It's against the law to have any alcohol in your blood if you are driving. Also, don't overtake a tram when passengers are getting on and off if there's no safety island for them, and give way to pedestrians crossing the road at traffic lights, if you're turning right or left. As in other continental countries, the yellow diamond sign means you have right of way; a black line through it means you don't. Speed limits are 110kph on motorways (and if you go any faster you'll be fined), 90kph on other roads and 60kph in all cities, towns and villages.

driver (man/woman) **řidič** [rJidyitch]/**řidička**

driving licence řidičský průkaz [rJiditch-skee prookus]

drop: just a drop, please (of drink) **jenom kapku, prosím** [yenom kupkoo]

drug lék

drugs (narcotics) **droga**

drunk (adj) **opilý** [opilee]

drunken driving řízení pod vlivem alkoholu [rJeezenyee pot – alkoholoo]

dry (adj) **suchý** [sooHee]

dry-cleaner chemická čistírna [Hemitskah chistyeerna]

duck kachna [kaHna]

due: he was due to arrive yesterday **měl přijet včera** [mnyel prJi-yet ftchera]

when is the train due? **kdy má přijet vlak?** [gudi mah prJi-yet vluk]

dull (pain) **tupý** [toopee]

it's dull (weather) **oblačno** [oblutchno]

dummy (baby's) **dudlík** [doodleek]

during během [byehem]

dust prach [pruH]

dusty zaprášený [zuprahshenee]

dustbin popelnice f [popelnyitseh]

duty-free (goods) bezcelný [bestselnee]

duty-free shop duty free shop

Duty-free shops are found at the airport and at border crossings. Duty-free allowances are not the same as for EU countries. The allowances are clearly indicated in the shops and travel agencies.

duvet peřina [perJina]

E

each každý [kuJdee]

how much are they each? **kolik stojí jeden?** [sto-yee yeden]

ear ucho [oo-Ho]

earache: I have earache **bolí mě ucho** [bolee mnyeh]

early časně [chusnyeh]

early in the morning časně
ráno [rahno]

I called by earlier (said by man/
woman) byl/byla jsem tu už
dříve [bil/bila sem too oosh
drJeeveh]

earring náušnice [nah-oosh-
nyitseh]

east východ [veeHod]
  in the east na východě [veeHo-
  dyeh]

Easter Velikonoce fpl
[velikonotseh]

easy snadný [snudnee]

eat jíst [yeest]
  we've already eaten, thanks už
  jsme jedli, děkujeme [oosh
  smeh yedli dyekoo-yemeh]
  I don't eat ... nejím ...

---

eating habits

In the Czech Republic breakfast
usually consists of tea, coffee,
or cocoa with bread or rolls
accompanied by jam, marmalade, cheese or salami. Cereals
are becoming popular too.
Lunch is the main meal of the
day. Traditionally a heavy meal
consisting of potatoes, rice or
dumplings plus meat, it usually
starts with soup. Supper is
a lighter meal with tea, coffee,
bread and meat paste, for
example.

---

eau de toilette toaletní voda
[to-alet-nyee]

economy class turistickou

třídou [tooreestitskoh trJeedoh]

egg vejce n [vaytseh]

either: either ... or ... bud' ...
nebo ... [boot^yeh]
  either of them kterýkoliv z
  nich [kutereekolif znyiH]

elastic (noun) prádlová guma
[prahdlovah gooma]

elastic band gumička
[goomitchka]

elbow loket

electric elektrický [elektritskee]

electrical appliances elektrické
spotřebiče [elektritskeh
spotrJebitcheh]

electric fire elektrický krb [kurb]

electrician elektrikář
[elektrikarJ]

electricity elektřina [elektrJina]
see voltage

elevator výtah [veetuH]

else: something else něco
jiného [nyetso yineho]
  somewhere else někde jinde
  [nyegdeh yindeh]

•••••• DIALOGUE ••••••

would you like anything else? dáte
si ještě něco? [dahteh si yeshtyeh]
no, nothing else, thanks ne, už ne,
díky [neh oosh neh dyeeki]

embassy ambasáda
[umbusahda], velvyslanectví
[velvislunetstvee]

embroidery výšivka [veeshifka]

emergency naléhavý případ
[nulehavee prJeepat]
  this is an emergency! je to
  naléhavé! [yeh to nulehaveh]

emergency exit nouzový
východ [nohzovee veeHot]
empty prázdný [prahzdnee]
end (noun) konec [konets]
  at the end of the street na
  konci ulice [nah kontsi
  oolitseh]
  (verb) končit/ukončit
  [ookontchit]
  when does it end? kdy to
  končí? [gudi to kontchee]
engaged (toilet, telephone)
  obsazeno [opsuzeno]
  (to be married) zasnoubený
  [zusnohbenee]
engine (car) motor
England Anglie f [ungli-eh]
English anglický [unglitskee]
  I'm English (man/woman) jsem
  Angličan/Angličanka [sem
  unglitchun/unglitchunka]
  do you speak English? mluvíte
  anglicky? [mlooveeteh]
enjoy: to enjoy oneself bavit se
  [buvit seh]

•••••• DIALOGUE ••••••

  how did you like the film? jak se
  vám ten film líbil? [yuk seh vahm –
  leebil]
  I enjoyed it very much; did you
  enjoy it? líbil se mi moc, a vám?
  [seh mi mots]

enjoyable příjemný [prJee-
yemnee]
enlargement (of photo)
  zvětšenina [zvyetshenyina]
enormous obrovský [obrofskee]
enough dost

there's not enough to nestačí
[nestutchee]
it's not big enough není to
dost velké [nenyee – velkeh]
that's enough to stačí [to
stutchee]
entrance vchod [fHot]
envelope obálka [obahlka]
epileptic epileptický
[epileptitskee]
equipment vybavení
[vibuvenyee]
error chyba [Hiba]
especially zejména [zaymena]
essential nezbytný [nezbitnee]
  it is essential that ... je
  nezbytné, aby ... [yeh
  nezbitneh abi]
EU Evropská unie f [evropskah
ooni-eh]
Eurocheque eurošek [eh-
ooroshek]
Eurocheque card platební karta
  Eurocheque [plutebnyee kurta]
Europe Evropa
European evropský [evropskee]
even: even the ... dokonce ...
[dokontseh]
  even more ještě více [yeshtyeh
  veetseh]
  even if ... dokonce i když ...
  [gudiJ]
evening večer [vetcher]
  good evening dobrý večer
  [dobree]
  this evening dnes večer
  in the evening večer
evening meal večeře f
[vetcherJeh]

eventually nakonec [nakonets]
ever vždy [vuJdi]

•••••• D I A L O G U E ••••••

have you ever been to Karlovy
Vary? už jste někdy byl/byla v
Karlových Varech? [oosh steh
nyegdi bil/bila fkurloveeн vureн]

yes, I was there two years ago
ano, byl/byla jsem tam před
dvěma roky [uno – sem tum prJet]

every každý [kuJdee]
every day každý den
everyone každý člověk [chlo-
vyek]
everything všechno [fsheнno]
everywhere všude [fshoodeh]
exactly! přesně! [prJes-nyeh]
exam zkouška [skohshka]
example příklad [prJeeklut]
for example například
[nuprJeeklut]
excellent skvělý [skvyelee]
excellent! skvělé! [skvyeleh]
except kromě [kromnyeh]
excess baggage nadváha
[nudvah-ha]
exchange rate devizový kurz
[devizovee koors]
exciting vzrušující [vuzrooshoo-
yeetsee]
excuse me (to get past) s
dovolením [sdovoleh-nyeem]
(to get attention/say sorry)
promiňte! [promin^{yeh}teh]
exhaust (pipe) výfuk [veefuk]
exhausted (tired) vyčerpaný
[vitcherpunee]
exhibition výstava [veestuva]

exit východ [veeнot]
where's the nearest exit? kde
je nejbližší východ? [gudeh
yeh nayblishee]
expect čekat [chekut]
expensive drahý [drahee]
experienced zkušený
[skooshenee]
explain vysvětlit [vis-vyetlit]/
vysvětlovat [vis-vyetlovut]
can you explain that? můžete
to vysvětlit? [moOJeteh]
express expres
extension linka
extension 221, please linku
dvěstě dvacet jedna, prosím
[linkoo – proseem]
extension lead prodlužovačka
[prodlooJovutchka]
**extra: can we have an extra
one?** můžeme dostat jeden
navíc? [moOJemeh dostut yeden
naveets]
do you charge extra for that?
platí se to zvlášť? [plutyee seh
to zvlahsht^{yeh}]
extraordinary zvláštní [zvlahsht-
nyee]
extremely extrémně
[extremnyeh]
eye oko
will you keep an eye on my
suitcase for me? pohlídáte mi
kufr? [pohleedahteh]
eyebrow pencil tužka na obočí
[tooshka na obotchee]
eye drops oční kapky [otchnyee
kupki]
eyeglasses (US) brýle fpl

[breeleh]
eyeliner oční linky [otchnyee linki]
eye shadow oční stín [styeen]

F

face tvář f [tvarJ]
factory továrna
Fahrenheit* Fahrenhaita [fa-hrenhĭta]
faint omdlívat [omdleevut]/omdlít
  she's fainted omdlela
  I feel faint je mi slabo [yeh mi slubo]
fair (funfair) pout' f [poht^yeh]
  (trade) veletrh [veleturH]
  (adj) spravedlivý [spruvedlivee]
fairly docela [dotsela]
fake padělek [pudyelek]
fall (US) podzim
  see **autumn**
fall upadnout [oopudnoht]
  she's had a fall upadla
false falešný [faleshnee]
family rodina [ro-dyina]
famous slavný [sluvnee]
fan (electrical) ventilátor
  (hand held) vějíř [vyeh-yeerJ]
  (sports: man/woman) fanoušek [funohshek]/fanynka [funinka]
fan belt řemen ventilátoru [rJemen ventilahtoroo]
fantastic fantastický [fantastitskee]
far daleko [duleko]

•••••• DIALOGUE ••••••

  is it far from here? je to odsud daleko? [yeh to otsoot]
  no, not very far ne, není to daleko [neh nenyee]
  well how far? jak daleko? [yuk]
  it's about 20 kilometres je to asi 20 kilometrů [yeh to usi dvutset kilometroo]

fare jízdné n [yeezdneh]
farm statek [stutek]
fashionable módní [mawdnyee]
fast rychlý [riHlee]
fat (person) tlustý [tloostee]
  (on meat) sádlo [sahdlo]
father otec [otets]
father-in-law tchán [tuHahn]
faucet kohoutek [kohohtek]
fault: **sorry, it was my fault** promiňte, to byla moje chyba [promin^yehteh to bila mo-yeh Hiba]
  it's not my fault to není moje chyba [nenyee]
faulty pokažený [pokuJenee]
favourite oblíbený [obleebenee]
fax (noun) fax [fuks]
  (verb: to someone) poslat fax (+ dat) [poslut]
February únor [OOnor]
feel cítit [tsee-tyit]
  I feel hot je mi horko [yeh]
  I feel well cítím se dobře [tsee-tyeem seh dobrJeh]
  I feel unwell necítím se dobře [netsee-tyeem]
  I feel like ... chce se mi ... [Hutseh]

ENGLISH ◆ CZECH | **Fe**

I feel like going for a walk (said by man/woman) šel/šla bych se projít [shel/shla biH seh pro-yeet]

how are you feeling? jak se cítíte? [yak seh tsee-tyeeteh]

I'm feeling better cítím se lépe [lepeh]

felt-tip (pen) fix

fence plot

fender nárazník [naruznyeek]

ferry trajekt [tra-yekt]

(small) **přívoz** [prJeevos]

festival festival [festivul], **slavnost** [sluvnost]

fetch sehnat [sehunut]

I'll fetch him seženu ho [seJenoo]

will you come and fetch me later? přijdete pro mě později? [prJeedeteh pro mnyeh pozdyay-yi]

feverish horečnatý [horetchnutee]

few: a few několik [nyekolik]

a few days několik dní

few tourists málo turistů [mahlo]

fiancé snoubenec [snohbenets]

fiancée snoubenka

field pole n [poleh]

fight (noun) **rvačka** [rvutchka]

figs fíky fpl [feeki]

fill naplnit [napulnyit]

fill in vyplnit [vipulnyit]

do I have to fill this in? musím to vyplnit? [mooseem]

fill up naplnit

fill it up, please plnou nádrž,

prosím [pulno nahdrJ]

filling (in cake) **náplň** f [nahpuln^{yeh}]

(in tooth) **plomba**

film film

•••••• DIALOGUE ••••••

do you have this kind of film? máte tyto filmy? [mahteh tito filmi]

yes, how many exposures? ano, na kolik snímků? [uno – snyeemkOO]

24/36 dvacet čtyři/třicet šest

film processing vyvolání filmu [vivolahnyee filmoo]

filter coffee překapávaná káva [prJekupahvunah kahva]

filter papers filtry mpl [filtri]

filthy špinavý [shpinavee]

find najít [na-yeet]

I can't find it nemohu to najít [nemohoo]

I've found it (said by man/woman) **našel/našla jsem to** [nashel/nashla sem]

find out zjistit [zyis-tyit]

could you find out for me? (to man/woman) **mohl/mohla byste mi to zjistit?** [mohul/mo-hla bisteh]

fine (weather) **pěkný** [pyeknee]

(punishment) **pokuta** [pokoota]

•••••• DIALOGUES ••••••

how are you? jak se máte? [yuk seh mahteh]

I'm fine thanks dobře, děkuji [dobrJeh dyekoo-yi]

– and you? – a vy? [vi]

is that OK? je to v pořádku? [yeh to

fporJahtkoo]
that's fine thanks je to dobré,
děkuji [dobreh dyekoo-yi]

finger prst [purst]
finish končit [kontchit]
I haven't finished yet (said by
man/woman) ještě jsem
neskončil/neskončila
[yeshtyeh sem neskontchil]
when does it finish? kdy to
končí? [gudi to kontchee]
fire: fire! hoří! [horJee]
can we light a fire here?
můžeme tady rozdělat oheň?
[mOOJemeh tudi rozdyelut
ohen^yeh]
it's on fire hoří to
fire alarm požární poplach
[poJarnyee poplaH]
fire brigade požární sbor

In the event of a fire, phone 150.

fire escape nouzový východ
[nohzovee veeHot]
fire extinguisher hasicí přístroj
[husitsee prJeestroy]
first první [purvnyee]
(firstly) za prvé [purveh]
I was first (said by man/woman)
byl/byla jsem první [bil/bila
sem]
at first napřed [nuprJet]
the first time poprvé
[popurveh]
first on the left první nalevo
first aid první pomoc f [purvnyee
pomots]

first aid kit lékárnička [lekar-
nyitchka]
first class (travel etc) první
třídou [purvnyee trJeedoh]
first floor první poschodí
[posHodyee]
(US) přízemí [prJeezemee]
first name jméno [yumeno]
fish (noun) ryba [riba]
fishmonger's rybárna
fit (attack) záchvat [zah-Hvat]
it doesn't fit me to mně
nesedí [mnyeh nesedyee]
fitting room zkušebna
[skooshebna]
fix (repair) spravit [spruvit]
(arrange) zařídit [zarJee-dyit]
can you fix this? můžete to
spravit? [mOOJeteh]
fizzy šumivý [shoomivee]
flag prapor [prupor]
flannel flanel [flunel]
flash (for camera) blesk
flat (noun: apartment) byt [bit]
(adj) plochý [ploHee]
flat tyre prázdná pneumatika
[prahzdnah pneh-oomutika]
I've got a flat tyre mám
prázdnou pneumatiku [mahm
prahzdnoh pneh-oomutikoo]
flavour příchuť f [prJeeHoot^yeh]
flea blecha [bleHa]
flight let
flight number číslo letu [cheeslo
leetoo]
flood povodeň f [povoden^yeh]
floor (of room) podlaha [podluha]
(storey) poschodí [posHodyee]
on the floor na podlaze

[podlazeh]

florist's květinářství [kuvyeh-tyinarJ-stvee]

flour mouka [mohka]

flower květina [kvyetyina]

flu chřipka [HrJipka]

fluent: he speaks fluent Czech mluví plynně česky [mloovee plin-nyeh cheski]

fly (noun) moucha [moh-Ha]
(verb) letát [letaht]/letět [letyet]

fly in přiletět [prJiletyet]

fly out odletět [odletyet]

fog mlha [mulha]

foggy: it's foggy je mlha [yeh]

folk dancing lidové tance mpl [lidoveh tuntseh]

folk music lidová hudba [lidovah hoodba]

follow sledovat [sledovut]
follow me následujte mě [nahsledoo-iteh mnyeh]

food jídlo [yeedlo]

food poisoning otrava jídlem [otruva]

food shop/store obchod s potravinami [opHot spotruvinumi]

foot* chodidlo [Hodidlo]
on foot pěšky [pyeshki]

football (game) fotbal [fotbul]
(ball) fotbalový míč [fotbulovee meech]

football match fotbalový zápas [zahpus]

for pro (+ acc)
do you have something for ...?
(headache/diarrhoea etc) máte

něco na ...? [mahteh nyetso]

who's the goulash for? pro koho bude guláš? [boodeh]

that's for me to je pro mě [yeh pro mnyeh]

and this one? a tohle? [tohleh]

that's for her to je pro ni [nyi]

where do I get the bus for Dejvice? odkud jede autobus do Dejvic? [otkoot yedeh – dayvits]

the bus for Dejvice leaves from the square autobus do Dejvic jede z náměstí

how long have you been here for? jak jste tady dlouho? [yuk steh tudi dloh-ho]

I've been here for two days, how about you? jsem tady dva dny, a vy? [sem tudi – vi]

I've been here for a week já jsem tady týden [yah sem – teeden]

forehead čelo [chelo]

foreign cizí [tsizee]

foreigner (man/woman) cizinec [tsizinets]/cizinka [tsizinka]

forest les

forget zapomenout [zupomenoht]

I forget zapomínám [zupomeenahm]

I've forgotten (said by man/woman) zapomněl/zapomněla jsem [zupomnyel – sem]

fork (for eating) vidlička [vidlitchka]
(in road) rozcestí [rostses-tyee]

form (document) formulář [formoolarJ]

formal (dress) večerní oblek [vetchernyee]

---

formality
The Czechs are more formal than the British. They use titles much more when addressing each other and are more conscious of position. It is also customary to shake hands more often than in Britain. As a tourist you will not be expected to be fully aware of the usual forms of address.
see **name** and **you**

---

fortnight čtrnáct dní [chturnahtst dunyee]

fortunately naštěstí [nashtyestyee]

forward: could you forward my mail? posílejte prosím poštu na mou novou adresu [poseelayteh proseem poshtoo na moh novoh udresoo]

forwarding address budoucí adresa [boodohtsee]

foundation cream podkladový krém [pokludovee]

fountain fontána [fontahna]

foyer (of hotel) hala [hula] (theatre) foyer n

fracture (noun) zlomenina [zlomenyina]

France Francie f [frantsi-eh]

free svobodný [svobodnee] (no charge) bezplatný [besplutnee]

is it free (of charge)? je to bezplatné? [jeh to besplutneh]

freeway dálnice f [dahlnyitseh]

freezer mraznička [mruznyitchka]

French francouzský [fruntsohskee]

French fries hranolky mpl [hrunolki]

frequent častý [chustee]

how frequent is the bus to Olomouc? jak často jezdí autobus do Olomouce? [yuk chusto yezdyee – olomohtseh]

fresh čerstvý [cherstvee]

fresh orange čerstvý pomeranč [pomerantch]

Friday pátek [pahtek]

fridge lednička [lednyitchka]

fried smažený [smaJenee]

fried egg smažené vejce n [–neh vaytseh]

friend přítel [prJeetel]/ přítelkyně [prJeetelki-nyeh] f

friendly přátelský [prJahtelskee]

from z, od [ot]

when does the next train from Prague arrive? kdy přijede další vlak z Prahy? [gudi prJi-yedeh dalshee vluk spruhi]

from Monday to Friday od pondělí do pátku [ot pondyelee do pahtkoo]

from next Thursday od příštího čtvrtka [prJeeshtyeeho]

•••••• D I A L O G U E ••••••

where are you from? odkud jste?
[otkoot steh]

I'm from Slough jsem ze Slough
[sem zeh]

front předek [prJedek]
in front of před (+ instr) [prJet]
in front/at the front vpředu
[fprJedoo]
in front of the hotel před
hotelem

frost mráz [mrahs]

frozen mražený [mraJenee]

frozen food mražené potraviny
fpl [mraJeneh potravini]

fruit ovoce n [ovotseh]

fruit juice ovocný džus [ovotsnee
joos]

fry smažit [smaJit]

frying pan pánev f [pahnef]

full plný [pulnee]
it's full je plný [yeh]
I'm full jsem najedený [sem nī-
yedenee]
full board plná penze f [pulnah
penzeh]

fun: it was fun byla to legrace
[bila to legrutseh]
to have fun bavit se [buvit seh]

funeral pohřeb [po-hrJep]

funny (strange) **divný** [dyivnee]
(amusing) **legrační** [legrutch-
nyee]

furniture nábytek [nahbitek]

further dále [dahleh]
it's further down the road
je to dál po cestě [yeh – tses-
tyeh]

•••••• D I A L O G U E ••••••

how much further is it to Olomouc?
jak daleko je to ještě do
Olomouce? [yuk – yeh to yeshtyeh
do olomohtseh]

about 5 kilometres asi pět
kilometrů [usi pyet kilometroo]

fuse (noun) **pojistka** [po-yistka]
the lights have fused vybily se
pojistky [vibili seh po-yistki]
fuse box pojistky
fuse wire pojistkový drát
[po-yistkovee draht]
future budoucnost f
[boodohtsnost]
in future v budoucnosti

G

gallon*
game hra
(meat) **zvěřina** [zvyerJina]
garage (for fuel) **čerpací stanice**
[cherputsee stunyitseh]
(for repairs) **opravna**
automobilů [opruvna
owtomobiloo]
(for parking) **garáž** f [garahJ]

Service stations in big cities and
on main highways are usually
open 24 hours, but do not do
car repairs. They'll be able to
tell you where to find the
nearest garage for repairs.
Garages in small towns and
more remote areas are usually
open from 8 a.m. until 4 p.m.

garden zahrada [zuhruda]

garlic česnek [chesnek]

gas plyn [plin]
(US) benzín [benzeen]
see **petrol**

gas cylinder (camping gas) bomba
na plyn

gasoline (US) benzín [benzeen]
see **petrol**

gas permeable lenses gelové
kontaktní čočky [geloveh
kontaktnyee chotchki]

gas station benzínová stanice f
[benzeenovah stunyitseh]

gate vrata [vruta]
(at airport) východ [veeHot]

gay homosexuál

gears rychlosti [riHlostyi]

gearbox převodovka [prJeh-
vodofka]

gear lever řadící páka
[rJudyeetsee pahka]

general (adj) obecný [obetsnee]

gents' (toilet) páni [pahnyi],
muži [mooJi]

genuine (antique etc) originální
[originahlnyee]

German německý [nyemetskee]

German measles zarděnky fpl
[zardyenki]

Germany Německo [nyemetsko]

get (fetch) přinášet
[prJinahshet]/přinést [prJinest]
will you get me another one,
please? přinesete mi ještě
jeden, prosím [prJineseteh mi
yeshtyeh yeden]
how do I get to ...? jak se
dostanu do (+ gen) ...? [yuk

seh dostunoo]
do you know where I can get
them? nevíte, kde je mohu
sehnat? [neveeteh gudeh yeh
mohoo sehnut]

•••••• **DIALOGUE** ••••••

can I get you a drink? mohu vám
objednat něco k pití? [vahm
obyednut nyetso kupityee]
no, I'll get this one, what would
you like? ne, já to objednám, co
si dáte? [neh yah to obyednahm tso si
dahteh]
a glass of red wine sklenici
červeného vína [sklenyitsi
cherveneho veena]

get back (return) vrátit se [vrah-
tyit seh]

get in (arrive) přijet [prJi-yet]

get off vystoupit [vistohpit]
where do I get off? kde musím
vystoupit? [gudeh mooseem
vistohpit]
can you tell me how to get
to ...? můžete mi říci, jak se
dostanu do ...? [mooJeteh yuk
seh dostunoo]

get on (to train etc) nastoupit
[nustohpit]

get out (of car etc) vystoupit
[vistohpit]
get out! vypadněte! [vipud-
nyeteh]

get up (in the morning) vstávat
[fstahvut]/vstát [fstaht]

gift dárek

gift shop dárkový obchod
[darkovee opHot]

gin gin [jin]

a gin and tonic, please gin a tonic, prosím

girl dívka [dyeefka]

girlfriend přítelkyně f [prJeetelki-nyeh]

give dávat [dahvut]/dát

can you give me some change? můžete mi dát drobné? [mooJeteh – drobneh]

I gave it to him (said by man/woman) dal/dala jsem mu to [dula sem moo]

will you give this to ...? dáte to (+ dat) ...? [dahteh]

•••••• DIALOGUE ••••••

how much do you want for this? kolik chcete za tohle? [Hutseteh za tohleh]

300 crowns tři sta korun [koroon]

I'll give you 250 crowns dám vám dvě stě padesát korun [dahm vahm]

give back vracet [vrutset]/vrátit [vrah-tyit] (+ dat)

glad: I'm glad (said by man/woman) jsem rád/ráda [sem raht/rahda]

glass (material) sklo

(tumbler) sklenice [sklenyitseh]

(wine glass) sklenice na víno [veeno]

a glass of wine sklenice vína

glasses (spectacles) brýle fpl [breeleh]

glassware sklo

gloves rukavice fpl [rookavitseh]

glue (noun) lepidlo

go chodit [Hodit]/jít [yeet]

we'd like to go to the old Jewish cemetery rádi bychom šli na starý židovský hřbitov [rahdyi biHom shli na staree Jidofskee hurJbitof]

where are you going? kam jdete? [deteh]

where does this bus go? kam jede tento? [kum yedeh]

let's go! pojď'dme! [poyd^yeh'dumeh]

she's gone (left) šla pryč [shla pritch]

where has he gone? kam šel? [shel]

I went there last week (said by man/woman) šel/šla jsem tam minulý týden [sem tum]

hamburger to go (to take away) prodej hamburgerů přes ulici [proday – prJes oolitsi]

go away odejít [oday-eet]

go away! jděte pryč! [dyeteh pritch]

go back (return) vrátit se [vrahtyit seh]

go down (the stairs etc) sejít [seh-yeet]

go in vejít [veh-yeet]

go out (in the evening) jít ven [yeet]

do you want to go out tonight? chcete dnes večer jít ven? [Hutseteh]

go through projít [pro-yeet]

go up (the stairs etc) jít nahoru [yeet nahoroo]

goat koza

God Bůh [booH]

goggles potápěčské brýle fpl [potah-pyetchskeh breeleh]

gold zlato [zluto]

golf golf

golf course golfové hřiště [golfoveh hrJish-tyeh]

good dobrý [dobree]
good! dobře! [dobrJeh]
it's no good to není dobré [nenyee dobreh]

goodbye nashledanou [nus-Hledunoh]

good evening dobrý večer [dobree vetcher]

Good Friday Velký pátek [velkee pahtek]

good morning dobré ráno [dobreh rahno]

good night dobrou noc [dobroh nots]

goose husa [hoosa]

got: we've got to leave at six a.m. musíme odjet v šest ráno [mooseemeh odyet] have you got any ...? máte...? [mahteh]

government vláda [vlahda]

gradually postupně [postoop-nyeh]

grammar gramatika [grumutika]

gram* gram [grum]

granddaughter vnučka [vnootchka]

grandfather dědeček [dyedetchek]

grandmother babička [bubitchka]

grandson vnuk [vnook]

grapefruit grapefruit

grapefruit juice grapefruitový džus [–tovee joos]

grapes hrozny mpl [hrozni]

grass tráva [trahva]

grateful vděčný [vdyetchnee]

gravy omáčka [omahtchka]

great (excellent) skvělý [skyvelee]
that's great! to je skvělé! [yeh skvyeleh]
a great success velký úspěch [velkee OOspyeH]

Great Britain Velká Británie [velkah britahni-eh]

greedy nenasytný [nenusitnee]

green zelený [zelenee]

green card (car insurance) zelená karta [zelenah kurta]

greengrocer's obchod se zeleninou a ovocem [opHot seh zelenyinoh a ovotsem]

grey šedý [shedee]

grill (noun) gril

grilled grilovaný [grilovanee]

grocer's obchod s potravinami [opHot spotruvinami]

ground země f [zemnyeh]
on the ground na zemi

ground floor přízemí [prJeezemee]

group skupina [skoopina]

guarantee (noun) záruka [zarooka]
is it guaranteed? je to v záruce? [yeh to vzarootseh]

guest host m/f [hosst]

guesthouse penzión [penzi-awn] see hotel

guide (man/woman) průvodce m [proovotseh]/průvodkyně f

[pr00votki-nyeh]
guidebook průvodce m
guided tour turistický zájezd
[tooreestitskee zah-yest]
guitar kytara [kitara]
gums (in mouth) dásně fpl
[dahsnyeh]
gun (pistol) pistole f [pistoleh]
(rifle) puška [pooshka]
gypsy (male/female) cikán
[tsigahn]/cikánka
gym tělocvična [tyelotsvitchna]

H

hair vlasy mpl [vlusi]
hairbrush kartáč na vlasy
[kartahtch]
haircut ostříhání [ostrJeehah-
nyee]
hairdresser's (men's) holičství
[holitch-stvee]
(women's) kadeřnictví
[kudairJnits-tvee]

Men's hairdressers and ladies'
salons are run separately. Some
women and children prefer to go
to men's hairdressers since
there is no need to make an appointment and service is much
cheaper. Although the general
standard is good you may not be
able to obtain the latest treatment except in a few luxury
salons in bigger towns. Prices
are relatively low and a tip of 15-
20 per cent is usual.

hairdryer vysoušeč vlasů
[visohshetch vlus00], fén
hair gel gel na vlasy [gel na
vlusi]
hairgrips sponky fpl [sponki]
hair spray lak na vlasy [luk]
half půl [p00l]
half an hour půl hodiny
[ho-dyini]
half a litre půl litru
about half that asi polovina
tohoto [usi]
half board polopenze f
[polopenzeh]
half fare poloviční jízdné n
[polovitch-nyee yeezdneh]
half price poloviční cena [tsena]
ham šunka [shoonka]
hamburger hamburger
hammer (noun) kladivo [kludivo]
hand ruka [rooka]
handbag kabelka [kubelka]
handbrake ruční brzda [rootch-
nyee burzda]
handkerchief kapesník [kupes-
nyeek]
handle (on door) klika
(on suitcase etc) rukojet' f
[rooko-yet^(yeh)]
hand luggage příruční
zavazadlo [prJeerootch-nyee
zuvuzudlo]
hang-gliding závěsné létání
[zah-vyesneh lehtah-nyee]
hangover kocovina [kotsovina]
I've got a hangover mám
kocovinu [mahm kotsovinoo]
happen stát se
what's happening? co se děje?

[tso seh dyay-yeh]
**what has happened? co se
stalo?** [stulo]
happy šťastný [shtyustnee]
I'm not happy about this (said
by man/woman) nejsem tím
nadšený/nadšená [naysem
nutshenee]
harbour přístav [prJeestuf]
hard tvrdý [tvurdee]
(difficult) těžký [tyeshkee]
hard-boiled egg vejce natvrdo n
[vaytseh nutvurdo]
hard lenses tvrdé kontaktní
čočky fpl [tvurdeh kontaktnyee
chotchki]
hardly těžko [tyeshko]
hardly ever skoro nikdy
[nigdi]
hardware shop železářství
[JelezarJstvee]
hat klobouk [klobohk]
hate nenávidět [nyenahvi-dyet]
have mít [meet]
can I have a ...? mohu
dostat ...? [mohoo dostut]
do you have ...? máte ...?
[mahteh]
what'll you have? (drink) co si
dáte? [tso si dahteh]
I have to leave now musím už
jít [mooseem oosh yeet]
do I have to ...? musím ...?
can we have some ...?
můžeme dostat ...?
[mooJemeh dostut]
hayfever senná rýma [sennah
reema]
hazelnuts lískové ořechy

[leeskoveh orJeHi]
he* on
head hlava [hluva]
headache bolest hlavy f [hluvi]
headlights přední světla [prJed-
nyee svyetla]
headphones sluchátka
[slooHahtka]
health food shop prodejna
racionální výživy [prodayna
ratsi-onahl-nyee veeJivi]
healthy zdravý [zdruvee]
hear slyšet/uslyšet [ooslishet]
can you hear me? slyšíte mě?
[slisheeteh mnyeh]
**I can't hear you, could you
repeat that?** neslyším vás,
můžete to opakovat?
[neslisheem vahs, mooJeteh to
opukovut]
hearing aid naslouchátko
[nasloh-Hahtko]
heart srdce n [surtseh]
heart attack infarkt [infurkt]
heat horko
heater (in room) přenosná
kamínka npl [prJenosnah
kameenka]
(in car) topení [topenyee]
heating topení
heavy těžký [tyeshkee]
heel (of foot) pata [puta]
(of shoe) podpatek [potpatek]
could you heel these? (to man/
woman) mohl/mohla byste
tam dát podpatky? [mohul/
mo-hla bisteh tum daht potpatki]
heelbar rychloopravna [riHlo-
opruvna]

height výška [veeshka]
helicopter helikoptéra
hello dobrý den [dobree]
  (answer on phone) haló [halaw]
helmet (for motorcycle) přilba
  [prJilba], helma
help (noun) pomoc [pomots]
  (verb) pomáhat [pomah-hat]
  help! pomoc!
  can you help me? můžete mi
  pomoct? [mooJeteh mi
  pomotst]
  thank you very much for your
  help děkuji mnohokrát za
  pomoc [dyekoo-yi mnohokraht]
helpful ochotný [oHotnee]
hepatitis zánět jater [zahnyet
  yuter]
her*: I haven't seen her (said by
  man/woman) **neviděl/neviděla**
  jsem ji [nevidyel – sem yi]
  to her jí [yee]
  with her s ní [snyee]
  for her pro ni [pronyi]
  that's her to je ona [yeh]
  that's her towel to je její
  ručník [yeh-yee]
herbal tea bylinný čaj [bilinnee
  chI]
herbs byliny fpl [bilini]
here zde [zdeh], tady [tudi]
  here is/are ... zde je/jsou ...
  [yeh/soh]
  here you are (offering) **prosím**
  [proseem]
hers* její [yeh-yee]
  that's hers to je její [yeh]
hey! hej! [hay]
hi! (hello) **ahoj!** [uhoy]

hide schovat [sHovut]
high vysoký [visokee]
highchair vysoká dětská židle f
  [visokah dyetskah Jidleh]
highway dálnice f [dahlnitseh]
hill pahorek [puhorek]
him*: I haven't seen him (said by
  man/woman) **neviděl/neviděla**
  jsem ho [nevidyel – sem]
  to him jemu [yemoo]
  with him s ním [snyeem]
  for him pro něho [nyeho]
  that's him to je on [yeh]
hip bok
hire (verb) pronajmout si
  [pronImoht]
  for hire k pronajmutí
  [pronImoo-tyee]
  where can I hire a bike? kde si
  mohu pronajmout kolo?
  [gudeh si mohoo]
  see **rent**
his*: it's his car to je jeho auto
  [yeh yeho]
  that's his to je jeho
hit (verb) udeřit [ooderJit]
hitch-hike stopovat [stopovut]
hobby hobby n
hockey hokej [hokay]
hold držet [dur-Jet]
hole díra [dyeera]
holiday (work) dovolená
  [dovolenah]
  (school) prázdniny fpl [prahz-
  nyini]
  (public) státní svátek [staht-
  nyee svahtek], den pracovního
  klidu [prutsov-nyeeho klidoo]
  on holiday na prázdninách

[prahzd-nyinahH], **na dovolené**
[dovoleneh]
home domov [domof]
  at home doma
  we go home tomorrow zítra
  jedeme domů [yedemeh
  domOO]
honest čestný [chestnee]
honey med [met]
honeymoon líbánky fpl
  [leebahnki]
hood (US: of car) kapota [kupota]
hope doufat [dohfut]
  I hope so doufám, že ano
  [dohfahm Jeh uno]
  I hope not doufám, že ne
horn (of car) klakson [klukson]
horrible strašný [strushnee]
horse kůň [kOOn^yeh]
horse riding jízda na koni
  [yeezda na konyi]
hospital nemocnice f [nemots-
  nyitseh]
hospitality pohostinnost f
  thank you for your hospitality
  děkuji vám za vaši
  pohostinnost [dyekoo-yi vahm
  za vashi]
hot horký [horkee]
  (spicy) pálivý [pahlivee]
  I'm hot je mi horko [yeh mi
  it's hot today dnes je horko
hotel hotel

Some hotels are graded
according to the familiar star
system and will be corre-
spondingly expensive. Basic
→

accommodation (excluding
meals) is available in a **motel**
or a **penzión** (guesthouse).
Bed and breakfast is rarely
available. Agencies (such as
ČEDOK) can find all types of
accommodation for you be it
a hotel, a **penzión**, a **byt**
(apartment) or even a bed in
a private flat (**v soukrome**).
In summer, student hostels
(**studentské koleje**) in bigger
cities are very good value.

hotel room: in my hotel room v
  mém hotelovém pokoji
  [poko-yi]
hour hodina [ho-dyina]
house dům [dOOm]
how jak [yuk]
  how many? kolik?
  how do you do? těší mě
  [tyeshee mnyeh]

•••••• DIALOGUES ••••••

how are you? jak se máte? [yuk seh
  mahteh]
fine, thanks, and you? děkuji,
  dobře, a vy? [dyekoo-yi dobrJeh a vi]

how much is it? kolik to stojí?
  [sto-yee]
200 crowns dvě stě korun [koroon]
I'll take it vezmu si to [vezmoo si to]

humid vlhký [vul-Hkee]
Hungarian (adj) maďarský
  [mudyurskee]
  (language) maďarština
  [mudyursh-tyina]

Hungary Maďarsko
[mudyursko]

hungry hladový [hludovee]
are you hungry? máte hlad?
[mahteh hlut]

hurry spěchat [spyeHut]
I'm in a hurry spěchám
[spyeHahm]
there's no hurry není žádný
spěch [nenyee Jahdnee spyeH]
hurry up! spěchejte!
[spyeHayteh]

hurt: it hurts to bolí [bolee]
it really hurts moc to bolí
[mots]
he hurt himself zranil se
[zrunyil seh]
my leg hurts bolí mě noha
[mnyeh]

husband manžel [manJel]

I

I já [yah]

ice led [let]
with ice s ledem
no ice, thanks bez ledu,
prosím [bes ledoo]

ice cream zmrzlina [zmurzlina]

ice-cream cone kornout
zmrzliny [kornoht zmurzlini]

iced coffee mražená káva
[mruJenah kahva]

ice hockey lední hokej [lednyee
hokay]

ice lolly nanuk [nunook]

ice rink kluziště [kloozish-tyeh]

ice skates brusle fpl [broosleh]

idea myšlenka [mishlenka]

idiot idiot

if jestli [yestli]

ignition zapalování [zupulovah-
nyee]

ill nemocný [nehmotsnee]
I feel ill je mi špatně [yeh mi
shputnyeh]

illness nemoc f [nemots]

imitation (leather etc) imitace
[imitutseh]

immediately okamžitě [okumJi-
tyeh]

important důležitý [dooleJitee]
it's very important je to velmi
důležité [yeh – dooleJiteh]
it's not important není to
důležité [nenyee]

impossible nemožný
[nehmoJnee]

impressive působivý
[pOOsobivee]

improve zlepšovat [slepshovut]/
zlepšit
I want to improve my Czech
chci si zlepšit češtinu [Hutsi –
chesh-tyinoo]

in: it's in the centre je to v
centru [yeh]
in my car v mém autě
in Carlsbad v Karlových
Varech [kurloveeH vureH]
in two days from now za dva
dny
in May v květnu
in English anglicky [unglitski]
in Czech česky [cheski]
is he in? je tady? [yeh tudi]
in five minutes za pět minut

inch* inč [intch]

include zahrnovat [zuhurnovut]/ **zahrnout** [zuhurnoht]
  does that include meals? jsou v tom i jídla? [soh ftom i – yeedla]
  is that included? je to v tom zahrnuto? [yeh to ftom zahurnooto]
inconvenient nevhodný [nefhodnee]
incredible neuvěřitelný [neh-oo-vyerJitelnee]
Indian (adj) indický [inditskee]
indicator směrovka [smnyerofka], blinkr [blinkur]
indigestion špatné trávení [shpatneh travenyee]
indoor pool krytý bazén [kritee buzen]
indoors vevnitř [vevnyitrJ]
inexpensive levný [levnee]
  see **cheap**
infection infekce f [infektseh]
infectious infekční [infektch-nyee]
inflammation zánět [zahnyet]
informal neformální [neformahlnyee]
information informace f [informutseh]
  do you have any information about ...? máte nějaké informace o ...? [mahteh nyeh-yukeh]
information desk informační kancelář f [informutch-nyee kuntselarJ]
injection injekce f [inyektseh]
injured zraněný [zrunyenee]

she's been injured je zraněna [yeh zrunyena]
in-laws (husband's) příbuzní manžela [prJeebooznyee manJela]
  (wife's) příbuzní manželky [manJelki]
innocent nevinný [nevinee]
insect hmyz [humis]
insect bite štípnutí [shtyeepnoo-tyee]
insect repellent repelent
inside uvnitř [oov-nyitrJ]
  inside the hotel v hotelu
  let's sit inside sedněme si dovnitř [sednyemeh si dovnyi-turJ]
insist trvat na (+ loc) [turvut]
  I insist trvám na tom [turvahm]
insomnia nespavost f [nespuvost]
instant coffee instantní káva [instunt-nyee kahva]
instead místo [meesto]
  give me that one instead dejte mi místo toho tento [dayteh]
  instead of ... místo (+ gen) ...
insulin inzulín [inzooleen]
insurance pojištění [po-yish-tyenyee]
intelligent inteligentní [inteligent-nyee]
interested: I'm interested in ... zajímám se o (+ acc) ... [zuh-yeemahm seh]
interesting zajímavý [zuh-yeemavee]

that's very interesting to je velmi zajímavé [yeh – za-yeemaveh]

international mezinárodní [mezinarod-nyee]

interpret tlumočit [tloomotchit]

interpreter tlumočník [tloomotch-nyeek]/tlumočnice f [tloomotch-nyitseh]

intersection křižovatka [krʒiʒovutka]

interval (at theatre) přestávka [prʒestahfka]

into do (+ gen)
I'm not into ... nezajímám se moc o (+ acc) ... [neza-yeemahm seh mots]

introduce představit [prʒetstuvit]
may I introduce ...? mohu vám představit ...? [mohoo vahm prʒetstuvit]

invitation pozvání [pozvah-nyee]

invite zvát [zvaht]/pozvat [pozvut]

Ireland Irsko

Irish irský [irskee]
I'm Irish (man/woman) jsem Ir/Irka [sem]

iron (for ironing) žehlička [Jeh-hlitchka]
can you iron these for me? můžete mi to vyžehlit? [mOOJeteh – viJeh-hlit]

is* je [yeh]

island ostrov [ostrof]

it to
it is ... to je ... [yeh]
is it ...? je to ...?
where is it? kde je to? [gudeh]

it's him to je on
it was ... to byl ... [bil]

Italian (adj) italský [itahlskee]

Italy Itálie f [itahli-eh]

itch: it itches to svědí [svyedyee]

J

jack (for car) zvedák [zvedahk]

jacket sako [suko]

jar sklenice f [sklenyitseh]

jam džem [jem]

jammed: it's jammed zaseklo se to [zuseklo seh]

January leden

jaw čelist f [chelist]

jazz džez [jez]

jealous žárlivý [Jarlivee]

jeans džínsy mpl [jeensi]

jersey žerzej [Jerzay]

jetty molo

Jewish židovský [Jidofskee]

jeweller's klenotnictví [klenot-nyitstvee]

jewellery klenoty mpl [klenoti]

job zaměstnání [zumnyestnah-nyee], práce [prahtseh]

jogging kondiční běh [konditch-nyee byeн], jogging
to go jogging kondičně běhat [konditch-nyeh byeнut]

joke (noun) žert [Jert]

journey cesta [tsesta]
have a good journey! šťastnou cestu! [shtyustnoh tsestoo]

jug džbán [jubahn]
a jug of water džbán vody

juice šťáva [shtyahva]

July červenec [chervenets]
jump skákat [skahkut]/skočit [skotchit]
jumper svetr [svetur]
junction souběh cest f [sohbyeH tsest]
June červen [cherven]
just (only) jen, jenom [yen]
  just two jen dva
  just for me jen pro mě [mnyeh]
  just here právě tady [prahvyeh tudi]
  not just now ne, teď ne [neh tet^yeh]
  we've just arrived právě jsme přijeli [smeh prJi-yeli]

K

Karlsbad Karlovy Vary [kurlovi vuri]
keep nechat si [neHut]
  keep the change drobné si nechte [drobneh si neHuteh]
  can I keep it? mohu si to nechat? [mohoo]
  please keep it nechte si to, prosím
ketchup kečup [ketchoop]
kettle konvice f [konvitseh]
key klíč [kleetch]
  the key for room 201, please klíč od pokoje dvě stě jedna, prosím [otpoko-yeh]
key ring kroužek na klíče [krohJek na kleetcheh]
kidneys (in body) ledviny fpl [ledvini]

(food) ledvinky fpl
kill zabít [zubeet]
kilo* kilo
kilometre* kilometr
  how many kilometres is it to …? kolik je kilometrů do …? [yeh kilometrOO]
kind (generous) laskavý [luskavee]
  that's very kind to je velmi laskavé [yeh – luskaveh]

•••••• DIALOGUE ••••••

which kind do you want? jaký typ chcete? [yukee tip Hutseteh]
I want this/that kind chci tento/tamten typ [Hutsi – tumten]

king král [krahl]
kiosk kiosek
kiss (noun) polibek
  (verb) líbat [leebut]/políbit

It is usual to shake hands if you are introduced to a stranger, and also to say your name. Hugs and kisses are reserved for friends and relations.

kitchen kuchyně f [kooHinyeh]
kitchenette kuchyňský kout [kooHin^yeh skee koht]
Kleenex® papírové kapesníky [pupeeroveh kupes-nyeeki]
knee koleno
knickers kalhotky fpl [kulhotki]
knife nůž [nOOsh]
knitwear pletené oděvy mpl [pleteneh odyevi]
knock klepat [kleput]

knock down srazit [sruzit]
  he's been knocked down
  srazili ho
knock over (object) převrhnout
  [prJeh-vur-hunoht]
  (pedestrian) porazit [poruzit]
know (somebody, a place) znát
  [znaht]
  (something) vědět [vyedyet]
  I don't know nevím [neveem]
  I didn't know that (said by man/
  woman) nevěděl/nevěděla
  jsem to [nevyedyel – sem]
  do you know where I can
  find ...? nevíte, kde najdu
  (+ gen) ...? [neveeteh gudeh
  nīdoo]

L

label nálepka [nah–]
ladies' (toilets) dámy [dahmi],
  ženy [Jeni]
ladies' wear dámské oblečení
  [dahmskeh obletchenyee]
lady dáma [dahma]
lager ležák [leJahk]
  see **beer**
lake jezero [yezero]
lamb (meat) jehněčí n
  [yehnyetchee]
lamp lampa [lumpa]
lane (on motorway) jízdní pruh
  [yeezdnyee prooH]
  (small road) cesta [tsesta]
language jazyk [yuzik]
language course jazykový kurz
  [yuzikovee koors]
large velký [velkee]

last poslední [poslednyee]
  (previous) minulý [minoolee]
  last week minulý týden
  last Friday minulý pátek
  last night minulou noc
  [minooloh nots]
  what time is the last train to
  Pardubice? kdy jede poslední
  vlak do Pardubic? [gudi yedeh
  – purdoobits]
late pozdě [pozdyeh]
  sorry I'm late omlouvám se,
  že jdu pozdě [omlohvahm seh
  Jeh doo]
  the train was late vlak měl
  zpoždění [mnyel spoJ-dyenyee]
  we must go – we'll be late
  musíme jít – přijdeme pozdě
  [mooseemeh yeet – prJeedemeh]
  it's getting late začíná být
  pozdě [zatcheenah beet]
later později [pozdyay-yi]
  I'll come back later vrátím se
  později [vrahtyeem seh]
  see you later nashledanou
  [nus-Hledunoh]
  later on později
latest nejpozději [naypozdyay-yi]
  by Wednesday at the latest
  nejpozději ve středu
laugh smát se [smaht seh]
launderette veřejná prádelna
  [verJaynah prahdelna]
laundromat veřejná prádelna
laundry (clothes) prádlo [prahdlo]
  (place) prádelna
lavatory záchod [zah-Hot]
law zákon [zahkon]
lawn záhon

lawyer (man/woman) **právník**
[prahv-nyeek]/**právnička**
[prahv-nyitchka]

laxative **projímadlo** [pro-
yeemudlo]

lazy **líný** [leenee]

lead (electrical) **elektrická šňůra**
[elektritskah shnyOOra]
(verb) **vést**
**where does this lead to? kam
to vede?** [kum to vedeh]

leaf **list**

leaflet **leták** [letahk]

leak (of gas) **únik** [oonyik]
(verb) **unikat** [oonyikut]
(liquid) **téct** [tetst]
**the roof leaks střechou
zatéká** [strJeHoh zutekah]

learn **učit se** [ootchit seh]

least: **not in the least ani v
nejmenším** [anyi
vnaymensheem]
at least přinejmenším [prJi-
naymensheem]

leather **kůže f** [kOOJeh]

leave **odjet** [odyet]
(leave behind) **nechat** [neHut]
**I am leaving tomorrow
odjíždím zítra** [odyeeJ-dyeem]
he left yesterday odjel včera
[odyel]
**may I leave this here? mohu
to tady nechat?** [mohoo to tudi
neHut]
**I left my coat in the bar nechal
jsem kabát v baru** [neHul sem]
**when does the bus for Tábor
leave? kdy odjíždí autobus
do Tábora?** [gudi otyeeJ-dyee]

leeks **pórek** [pawrek]

left **levý** [levee]
on the left nalevo [nulevo]
to the left doleva
turn left zatočte doleva
[zutotchteh]
there's none left žádný nezbyl
[Jahdnee nezbil]

left-handed **levák** [levahk]

left luggage (office) **úschovna
zavazadel** [oosHovna zuvuzudel]

leg **noha**

lemon **citrón** [tsitrawn]

lemonade **limonáda** [limonahda]

lemon tea **čaj s citrónem** [chī s
tsitrawnem]

lend **půjčovat** [pOO-itchovut]/
půjčit [pOO-itchit]
**will you lend me your ...?
půjčíte mi váš ...?** [pOO-
itcheeteh mi vahsh]

lens (of camera) **objektiv**
[ob-yektif]

lesbian **lesbičanka**
[lesbitchunka]

less **méně** [menyeh]
less than méně než [nesh]
less expensive méně drahý
[drahee]

lesson **lekce f** [lektseh]

let: **will you let me know? dáte
mi vědět?** [dahteh mi vyedyet]
**I'll let you know dám vám
vědět** [dahm]
**let's go for something to eat
pojd'me něco sníst** [poy-
dyemeh nyetso snyeest]
flats to let byty k pronajmutí
[biti kupronīmoo-tyee]

let off nechat vystoupit [neHut vistohpit]
  will you let me off at ...? necháte mě vystoupit v (+ loc) ...? [neHahteh mnyeh]
letter dopis
  do you have any letters for me? máte pro mě nějakou poštu? [mahteh pro mnyeh nyeh-yukoh poshtoo]
letterbox poštovní schránka [poshtov-nyee suHrahnka]

> Letterboxes are small orange and blue boxes.

lettuce salát [salaht]
lever (noun) páka [pahka]
library knihovna [kunihovna]
licence povolení [povolenyee]
lid víko, poklička [poklitchka]
lie (tell untruth) lhát [luhaht]
lie down lehnout si [lenoht]
life život [Jivot]
lifebelt záchranný pás [zaHrunee pahs]
life jacket záchranná vesta
lift (in building) výtah [veetuH]
  could you give me a lift? můžete mě svézt? [mooJeteh mnyeh svest]
  would you like a lift? chcete svézt? [Hutseteh]
lift pass permanentka na vlek [permunentka]
  a daily/weekly lift pass denní/týdenní permanentka na vlek [denyee/teedenyee]
light (noun) světlo [svyetlo]

(not heavy) lehký [leHkee]
  do you have a light? máte oheň? [mahteh oHen^yeh]
light green světle zelená [svyetleh]
light bulb žárovka [Jarofka]
  I need a new light bulb potřebuji novou žárovku [potrJeboo-yi novoh Jarofkoo]
lighter (cigarette) zapalovač [zupulovutch]
lightning blesk
like mít rád [meet raht], líbit se [leebit seh]
  I like it líbí se mi to
  I like going for walks (said by man/woman) rád/ráda se procházím [raht/rahda proHahzeem]
  I like you líbíte se mi [leebeeteh seh mi]
  (stronger affection) mám tě rád/ráda [mahm tyeh]
  I don't like it nelíbí se mi to [neleebee]
  do you like ...? líbí se vám ...? [vahm]
  I'd like to go swimming (said by man/woman) šel/šla bych plavat [shel/shla biH pluvut]
  would you like a drink? dáte si něco na pití? [dahteh si nyetso na pityee]
  would you like to go for a walk? (to man/woman) šel/šla byste na procházku? [shel/shla bisteh]
  what's it like? jaké to je? [yukeh to yeh]

I want one like this chci to
samé [Hutsi to sumeh]
lime (drink) citronáda
[tsitronahda]
line linka
  could you give me an outside
  line? dejte mi linku ven,
  prosím [dayteh mi linkoo]
lips rty [ruti]
lip salve jelení lůj [yelenyee
  loo-i]
lipstick rtěnka [rutyenka]
liqueur likér
listen poslouchat [poslohHut]
litre* litr
  a litre of white wine litr bílého
  vína
little (adj) malý [mulee]
  just a little, thanks jenom
  trochu, děkuji [yenom troHoo
  dyekoo-yi]
  a little milk trochu mléka
  a little bit more trochu více
  [veetseh]
live žít [Jeet]
  we live together žijeme spolu
  [Ji-yemeh spoloo]

•••••• DIALOGUE ••••••

  where do you live? kde bydlíte?
  [gudeh bidleeteh]
  I live in London bydlím v Londýně
  [bidleem vlondeenyeh]

lively živý [Jivee]
liver játra npl [yahtra]
loaf bochník chleba [boH-nyeek
  Hleba]
lobby (in hotel) hala [hula]
lobster humr [hoomur]

local místní [meestnyee]
  can you recommend a local
  wine/restaurant? můžete nám
  doporučit místní víno/
  restauraci? [mooJeteh nahm
  doporoochit]

> To sample local wines you have
> to go to the smaller towns and
> villages of South Moravia where
> a wide variety of local wines are
> available directly from private
> cellars.
> see **wine**

lock (noun) zámek [zahmek]
  (verb) zamknout [zumknoht]
  it's locked je zamčeno [yeh
  zumtcheno]
lock in zamknout
lock out zabouchnout si dveře
  [zubohHunoht si dverJeh]
  I've locked myself out (said by
  man/woman) zabouchl/
  zabouchla jsem si dveře
  [zubohHul/zubohHla sem]
locker (for luggage etc) skříňka na
  zavazadla [skrJeen^yeh^ka na
  zuvuzudla]
lollipop lízátko [leezahtko]
London Londýn [londeen]
long dlouhý [dloh-hee]
  how long will it take to fix it?
  jak dlouho se to bude
  spravovat? [yuk dloh-ho seh to
  boodeh spruvovut]
  how long does it take? jak
  dlouho to trvá? [turvah]
  a long time dlouho

one day/two days longer o den/dva dny déle [deleh]
long-distance call meziměsto [mezimnyesto]
loo záchod [zahHot]
look dívat se [dyeevut seh]/ podívat se
　I'm just looking, thanks jen se dívám, děkuji [yen seh dyeevahm dyekoo-yi]
　you don't look well nevypadáte dobře [nevipudahteh dobrJeh]
　look out! pozor!
　can I have a look? mohu se podívat? [mohoo seh po-dyeevut]
look after starat se [sturut seh]/ postarat se o (+ acc)
look at dívat se [dyeevut seh]/ podívat se na (+ acc)
look for hledat [hledut]
　I'm looking for ... hledám ... [hledahm]
look forward to těšit se na (+ acc) [tyeshit seh]
　I'm looking forward to it těším se na to [tyesheem seh na to]
loose (handle etc) utržený [ootr-Jenee]
lorry nákladní auto [nahklud-nyee owto]
lose ztrácet [strahtset]/ztratit [strutyit]
　I'm lost, I want to get to ... (said by man/woman) zabloudil/ zabloudila jsem, chci se dostat do ... [zublohdyil – sem Hutsi seh dostut]

I've lost my bag (said by man/ woman) ztratil/ztratila jsem tašku [strutyil – tushkoo]
lost property (office) ztráty a nálezy [strahti ah nahlezi]
lot: a lot, lots spousta (+ gen) [spohsta]
　a lot of people spousta lidí
　not a lot moc ne [mots neh]
　a lot bigger o moc větší [omots vyetshee]
　I like it a lot moc se mi to líbí [seh – leebee]
lotion pleťová voda [pletyovah]
loud hlasitý [hlusitee]
lounge hala [hula]
love milovat [milovut]
　I love Prague miluji Prahu [miloo-yi prahoo]
lovely rozkošný [roskoshnee]
low nízký [nyeeskee]
luck štěstí [shtyes-tyee]
　good luck! mnoho štěstí!
luggage zavazadla npl [zuvuzudla]
luggage trolley vozík na zavazadla [vozeek]
lump (on body) boule f [bohleh]
lunch oběd [obyet]
lungs plíce fpl [pleetseh]
luxurious luxusní [looksoos-nyee]
luxury luxus

M

machine stroj [stroy]
mad (insane) bláznivý [blahz-nyivee]
　(angry) rozčilený [roztchilenee]

magazine časopis [chusopis]

maid (in hotel) pokojská [pokoyskah]

maiden name dívčí jméno [dyeeftchee yumeno]

mail (noun) pošta [poshta]
(verb) poslat poštou f [poslut poshtoh]
see **post**
is there any mail for me? mám tady nějakou poštu? [mahm tudi nyeyukoh poshtoo]

mailbox poštovní schránka [poshtov-nyee sнrahnka]
see **letterbox**

main hlavní [hluv-nyee]

main course hlavní chod [Hot]

main post office hlavní pošta [poshta]

main road (in town) hlavní třída [trJeeda]
(in country) hlavní silnice [sil-nyitseh]

mains switch hlavní vypínač [vipeenutch]

make (brand name) značka [znutchka]
(verb) dělat [dyelut]/udělat [oodyelut]
I make it 500 crowns dělá to pět set korun [dyelah – koroon]
what is it made of? z čeho to je vyrobeno? [cheho to yeh virobeno]

make-up make-up

man člověk [chlo-vyek]

manager manažer [manaJer], vedoucí m [vedohtsee]

can I see the manager? mohu mluvit s vedoucím? [mohoo mloovit svedohtseem]

manageress manažerka, vedoucí f

manual (car with manual gears) ruční řazení [rootch-nyee rJuzenyee]

many mnoho
not many moc ne [mots neh]

map mapa [mupa]

Maps of every part of the country can be bought in bookshops and travel agencies. In particular there is an extensive range of tourist maps (**turistická mapa**) which show campsites, marked foothpaths and places of interest.

March březen [brJezen]

margarine margarín [margareen]

Marienbad Mariánské Lázně fpl [mariahnskeh lahzhyeh]

market (noun) trh [turн]

marmalade marmeláda

married: I'm married (said by man/ woman) jsem ženatý/vdaná [sem Jenutee/vdunah]
are you married? (to man/woman) jste ženatý/jste vdaná? [steh]

mascara maskara [muskura]

match (football etc) zápas [zahpus]

matches zápalky fpl [zahpalki]

material (fabric) látka [lahtka]

matter: it doesn't matter na tom nezáleží [nezahleJee]

what's the matter? co se děje?
[tso seh dyay-eh]

mattress matrace f [mutrutseh]

May květen [kveten]

may: may I have another one?
mohu dostat další? [mohoo
dostut dulshee]

may I come in? mohu vejít?
[veh-yeet]

may I see it? mohu to vidět?
[vidyet]

may I sit here? mohu se tady
posadit? [seh tudi posudyit]

maybe možná [moJnah]

mayonnaise majonéza [mī-
oneza]

me*: that's for me to je pro mě
[yeh pro mnyeh]

send it to me pošlete mně to
[poshleteh]

me too já také [yah tukeh]

meal jídlo [yeedlo]

•••••• D I A L O G U E ••••••

did you enjoy your meal? chutnalo
vám? [Hootnulo vahm]

it was excellent, thank you bylo to
výborné, děkuji [bilo to veeborneh
dyekoo-yi]

mean myslet [mislet],
znamenat [znamenut]

what do you mean? co tím
myslíte? [tso tyeem misleeteh]

what does it mean? co to
znamená? [znumenah]

•••••• D I A L O G U E ••••••

what does this word mean? co
znamená to slovo?

it means ... in English v angličtině
to je ... [yunglitch-tyinyeh to yeh]

measles spalničky fpl [spal-
nyitchki]

meat maso [muso]

I don't eat meat nejím maso
[nay-yeem]

mechanic mechanik [meHanik]

medicine lék

medium (adj: size, steak) střední
[strJed-nyee]

medium-dry: a medium-dry wine
středně suché víno [strJed-
nyeh sooHeh veeno]

medium-rare středně
propečený [propetchenee]

medium-sized středně velký
[velkee]

meet potkat [potkut]

nice to meet you těší mě
[tyeshee mnyeh]

where shall I meet you? kde
se setkáme? [gudeh seh
setkahmeh]

meeting schůze f [sHoozeh]

meeting place místo schůzky
[meesto sHooski]

melon meloun [melohn]

men muži mpl [mooJi]

mend opravovat [opruvovut]/
opravit [opruvit]

could you mend this for me?
(to man/woman) mohl/mohla
byste mi to opravit? [mohul/
mo-hla bisteh]

menswear pánské oblečení
[pahnskeh obletchenyee]

mention zmínit se [zmeenyit seh]

don't mention it není zač
[nenyee zutch]
menu jídelní lístek [yeedelnyee
leestek]
  may I see the menu, please?
  mohu dostat jídelní lístek,
  prosím? [mohoo dostut]
  see Menu Reader page 203
message vzkaz [fskus]
  are there any messages for
  me? mám tady nějaké
  vzkazy? [mahm tudi nyeyukeh
  fskuzi]
  I want to leave a message
  for ... chci nechat vzkaz
  pro (+ acc) ... [Hutsi neHut]
metal (noun) kov [kof]
metre* metr
microwave (oven) mikrovlnná
  trouba [mikrovulnah trohba]
midday poledne n [poledneh]
  at midday v poledne
middle: in the middle uprostřed
  [ooprostrJet]
  in the middle of the night
  uprostřed noci
  the middle one ten
  prostřední [prostrJed-nyee]
midnight půlnoc f [poolnots]
  at midnight o půlnoci
might: I might asi ano [usi uno]
  I might not asi ne [neh]
  I might want to stay another
  day možná bych zůstal další
  den [moJnah biH zoostal
  dulshee]
migraine migréna
mild (taste) jemný [yemnee]
  (weather) mírný [meernee]

mile* míle f [meeleh]
milk mléko
milkshake mléčný koktejl
  [mletchnee koktayl]
millimetre* milimetr
minced meat sekaná [sekunah]
mind: never mind to nevadí [to
  nevudyee]
  I've changed my mind (said by
  man/woman) rozmyslel/
  rozmysela jsem si to
  [rozmislel – sem]

•••••• DIALOGUE ••••••
  do you mind if I open the window?
  bude vám vadit, když otevřu
  okno? [boodeh vahm vudyit gudiJ
  otevrJoo]
  no, I don't mind ne, nebude [neh]

mine*: it's mine to je moje [yeh
  mo-yeh]
mineral water minerálka
  [minerahlka]
mint-flavoured s příchutí máty
  [sprJeeHootyee mahti]
minute minuta [minoota]
  in a minute za chvíli [Hveeli]
  just a minute okamžik,
  prosím [okumJik]
mirror zrcadlo [zurtsudlo]
Miss slečna [sletchna]
  (speaking to someone)
  slečno
miss: I missed the bus (said by
  man/woman) zmeškal/zmeškala
  jsem autobus [sem]
missing chybí [Hibee]
  there's a suitcase missing
  chybí kufr

mist mlha [mulha]

mistake (noun) chyba [Hiba]
I think there's a mistake
myslím, že je tu nějaká
chyba [misleem Jeh yeh too
nyeh-yukah]
sorry, I've made a mistake (said
by man/woman) omlouvám se,
udělal/udělala jsem chybu
[omlohvahm seh oodyelul – sem
Hiboo]

misunderstanding
nedorozumění [nedorozoo-
mnyenyee]

mix-up: sorry, there's been a
mix-up promiňte, je to
nějaký zmatek [promin^yehteh
yeh to nyeh-yukee zmutek]

modern moderní [modernyee]

modern art gallery galerie
moderního umění f [guleri-eh
modernyeeho oo-mnyenyee]

moisturizer zvlhčovač pleti
[zvul-hutchovutch pletyi]

Moldau Vltava [vultuva]

moment: I won't be a moment
hned to bude [hnet to boodeh]

Monday pondělí [pondyelee]

money peníze mpl [penyeezeh]

month měsíc [mnyeseets]

monument památník [pumaht-
nyeek]

moon měsíc [mnyeseets]

moped moped

Moravia Morava [moruva]

Moravian (adj) moravský
[morufskee]

Moravian (man) Moravan
[moruvun]

Moravian (woman) Moravanka

more* více [veetseh]
can I have some more water,
please? mohu dostat více
vody, prosím? [mohoo dostut]
more expensive/interesting
dražší/zajímavější [drushee za-
yeemuh-vyayshee]
more than 50 více než
padesát [nesh]
more than that více než to
a lot more mnohem více

•••••• DIALOGUE ••••••

would you like some more? chcete
ješte? [Hutseteh yeshtyeh]
no, no more for me, thanks
ne, já už nechci, díky [neh yah
oosh neHutsi dyeeki]
how about you? a vy? [vi]
I don't want any more, thanks už
ne, děkuji [dyekoo-yi]

morning ráno [rahno]
this morning dnes ráno
in the morning ráno

mosquito komár

mosquito repellent repelent
proti hmyzu [protyi humizoo]

most: I like this one most of all
ten se mi líbí nejvíce [seh mi
leebee nayveetseh]
most of the time většinu času
[vyetshinoo chusoo]
most tourists většina turistů

mostly většinou [vyetshinoh]

mother matka [mutka]

motorbike motocykl [mototsikul]

motorboat motorový člun
[motorovee chlun]

motorway dálnice f [dahlnitseh]

mountain hora

  in the mountains v horách
[fhorahH]

mountaineering horolezectví
[horolezetstvee]

mountain hut horská chata
[horskah Huta]

mouse myš f [mish]

moustache knír [kunyeer]

mouth ústa n [OOsta]

mouth ulcer afta [ufta]

move: he's moved to another
room přestěhoval se do
jiného pokoje [prJes-tyehoval
seh do yineho poko-yeh]

  could you move your car? (to
man/woman) mohl/mohla byste
popojet autem? [mohul/mo-
hla bisteh popo-yet]

  could you move up a little? (to
man/woman) mohl/mohla byste
se trochu posunout? [seh
troHoo]

  where has it moved to? kam
se to přesunulo? [kum seh to
prJesoonoolo]

movie film

movie theater kino
  see cinema

Mr pan [pun]

  (speaking to someone) pane
[puneh]

Mrs paní [punyee]

Ms slečna [sletchna]

  (speaking to someone) slečno

much mnoho

  much better/worse mnohem
lépe/hůře

much hotter mnohem tepleji

not much moc ne [mots neh]

not very much ne příliš
[prJeelish]

I don't want very much nechci
moc [neHutsi]

mud bláto [blahto]

mug (for drinking) hrnek [hurnek]

I've been mugged přepadli
mě [prJepudli mnyeh]

mum maminka [muminka]

mumps příušnice [prJee-oosh-
nyitseh]

museum muzeum n [moozeh-
oom]

The majority of museums and
art galleries are closed on
Mondays. Admission charges
are relatively low, sometimes
with discounts for children
and students. Small provincial
museums or galleries dealing
with local art are often worth
visiting.

---

mushrooms houby fpl [hohbi]

music hudba [hoodba]

music festival hudební festival
[hoodeb-nyee festivul]

musician (man/woman) hudebník
m [hoodeb-nyeek]/ hudebnice f
[hoodebnyitseh]

Muslim (adj) muslimský
[mooslimskee]

mussels mušle fpl [mooshleh]

must: I must já musím [yah
mooseem]

I mustn't drink alcohol nesmím

pít alkohol [nesmeem peet]
mustard hořčice f [horJtchitseh]
my* můj [m00-i], moje [mo-yeh]
myself: I'll do it myself (said by
man/woman) udělám to sám/
sama [oodyelahm to sahm/
suma]
by myself sám/sama

N

nail (finger) nehet
(metal) hřebík [hrJebeek]
nailbrush kartáč na ruce
[kartahtch na rootseh]
nail varnish lak na nehty [luk na
neHti]
name jméno [yumeno]
my name's ... jmenuji se ...
[yumenoo-yi seh]
what's your name? jak se
jmenujete? [yuk seh yumenoo-
yeteh]
what is the name of this
street? jak se jmenuje tato
ulice? [yumenoo-yeh tuto]

Stick to Mr (pane + surname),
Mrs (paní + surname) or Miss/
Ms (slečno + surname or first
name) unless you are specifi-
cally asked to call someone by
their first name. Children, teen-
agers and students call each
other by their first names.

napkin ubrousek [oobrohsek]
nappy plenka
narrow (street) úzký [00skee]

nasty (person) zlý [zlee]
(weather, accident) ošklivý
[oshklivee]
national národní [narod-nyee]
nationality národnost f
natural (behaviour etc) přirozený
[prJirozenee]
(of nature) přírodní [prJeerod-
nyee]
nausea žaludeční nevolnost f
[Juloodetch-nyee]
navy (blue) námořnická modř f
[nahmorJ-nyitskah modurJ]
near blízko [bleesko]
is it near the city centre? je to
blízko centra? [yeh]
do you go near Wenceslas
Square? jedete blízko k
Václavskému náměstí?
[yedeteh – vahtsluvskemoo
nahmnyestyee]
where is the nearest ...? kde je
nejbližší ...? [gudeh yeh
nayblishee]
nearby sousední [sohsed-nyee]
nearly téměř [temnyerJ]
necessary nezbytný [nezbitnee]
neck krk [kurk]
necklace náhrdelník [nah-
hrudel-nyeek]
necktie vázanka [vahzunka],
kravata [kruvuta]
need: I need ... potřebuji ...
[potrJeboo-yi]
do I need to pay? musím
platit? [mooseem plutyit]
needle jehla [yehla]
negative (film) negativ [negutif]
neither: neither (one) of them

žádný z nich [Jahdnee z nyiH]
**neither ... nor ... ani ...
ani ...** [unyi]
nephew synovec [sinovets]
net (in sport) sít' f [seet^yeh]
Netherlands Nizozemí
[nizozemee]
network sít' [seet^yeh]
never nikdy [nyigdi]

•••••• DIALOGUE ••••••

have you ever been to Prague? (to
man/woman) byl/byla jste už
někdy v Praze? [bil/bila steh oosh
nyegdi fpruzeh]
no, never, I've never been there
(said by man/woman) ne, nikdy
jsem tam nebyl/nebyla [neh – sem
tum]

new nový [novee]
(brand-new) úplně nový
[OOpulnyeh]
news (radio, TV etc) zprávy fpl
[sprahvi]
newsagent's noviny-časopisy
mpl [novini-chusopisi]
newspaper noviny fpl
newspaper kiosk novinový
stánek [novinovee stahnek]
New Year Nový rok [novee]
happy New Year! št'astný
Nový rok! [shtyustnee]
New Year's Eve Silvestr
New Zealand Nový Zéland
[novee]
**New Zealander: I'm a New
Zealander** (man/woman) jsem
Novozéland'an/
Novozéland'anka [sem

novozelun-dyun]
next příští [prJeesh-tyee]
the next turning/street on the
left příští zatáčka/ulice
doleva
at the next stop na příští
zastávce
next week příští týden
next to vedle (+ gen) [vedleh]
nice (food) dobrý [dobree]
(looks, view etc) pěkný [pyeknee]
(person) milý [milee]
niece neteř f [neterJ]
night noc f [nots]
at night v noci
good night dobrou noc
[dobroh]

•••••• DIALOGUE ••••••

do you have a single room for one
night? máte jednolůžkový pokoj
na jednu noc? [mahteh
yednolOOshkovee pokoy na yednoo]
yes, madam ano, paní [punyee]
how much is it per night? kolik to
stojí na noc? [sto-yee]
it's 600 crowns for one night je to
šest set korun na noc [yehto –
koroon]
thank you, I'll take it děkuji, vezmu
si to [dyekoo-yi vezmoo]

nightclub noční klub [notch-nyee
kloop]
nightdress noční košile f
[koshileh]
night porter noční vrátný
[vrahtnee]
no ne [neh]
I've no change nemám

drobné [nemahm drobneh]

there's no ... left už žádný/
žádná není ... [oosh Jahdnee/
Jahdnah nenyee]

no way! v žádném případě!
[vJahdnem prJeepudyeh]

oh no! (upset) ach ne! [aH neh]

nobody nikdo [nyigdo]

there's nobody there nikdo
tam není [tum nenyee]

noise hluk [hlook]

noisy: it's too noisy je to moc
hlučné [yeh to mots hlootchneh]

non-alcoholic nealkoholický
[neh-ulkoholitskeh]

none žádný [Jahdnee]

nonsmoking compartment
nekuřácké kupé
[nekoorJahtskeh koopeh]

noon poledne n [poledneh]

no-one nikdo [nyigdo]

nor: nor do I ani já ne [unyi yah
neh]

normal normální [normahlnyee]

north sever

in the north na severu
[severoo]

north of Prague na sever od
Prahy [ot pruhi]

northeast severovýchod
[–veeHot]

northern severní [severnyee]

northwest severozápad
[–zahput]

Northern Ireland Severní Irsko

Norway Norsko

Norwegian norský [norskee]

nose nos

nosebleed krvácení z nosu

[krvahtsenyee znosoo]

not* ne [neh]

no, I'm not hungry ne, nemám
hlad [nemahm hlut]

I don't want any, thank you
nechci nic, děkuji [neHutsi
nyits dyekoo-yi]

it's not necessary to není
nutné [nenyee nutneh]

I didn't know that (said by man/
woman) to jsem nevěděl/
nevyděla [sem nevyedyel]

not that one – this one to ne –
toto

note (banknote) bankovka
[bunkofka]

notebook zápisník [zahpis-
nyeek]

notepaper (for letters) dopisní
papír [dopisnyee pupeer]

nothing nic [nyits]

nothing for me, thanks pro mě
nic, děkuji [mnyeh – dyekoo-yi]

nothing else nic jiného
[yineho]

novel román [romahn]

November listopad [listoput]

now nyní [ninyee]

number číslo [cheeslo]

I've got the wrong number
mám špatné číslo [mahm
shputneh]

what is your phone number?
jaké máte číslo? [yukeh
mahteh]

number plate státní poznávácí
značka [stahtnyee poznahvutsee
znutchka]

nurse (man/woman) ošetřovatel

[oshetrʌovatel]/zdravotní
sestra [zdruvot-nyee]
nursery slope cvičná louka
[tsvitchnah lohka]
nut (for bolt) **matice** f [matyitseh]
nuts (food) **ořechy** mpl [orʌeHi]

O

o'clock*: 5 o'clock **pět hodin**
[ho-dyin]
occupied (toilet) **obsazeno**
[opsazeno]
October říjen [rʌee-yen]
odd (strange) **divný** [dyivnee]
of* z (+ gen)
off (lights) **zhasnuto** [zhusnooto]
it's just off Malostranské
square **je to hned vedle**
Malostranského náměstí [yeh
to hnet vedleh]
we're off tomorrow **zítra**
jedeme pryč [zeetra yedemeh
pritch]
offensive urážlivý [oorahʌlivee]
office (place of work) **kancelář** f
[kuntselarʌ]
officer (said to policeman) **pane**
[puneh]
often často [chusto]
not often **často ne** [neh]
how often are the buses? **jak
často jezdí autobusy?** [yuk –
yezdyee]
oil (for car, for salad) **olej** [olay]
ointment mast f [must]
OK dobře [dobrʌeh]
are you OK? **jsi v pořádku?** [si
fporʌahtkoo]

is that OK with you? **souhlasíš
s tím?** [sohluseesh styeem]
is it OK to ...? **může se ...?**
[mOOJeh seh]
that's OK thanks (it doesn't
matter) **to je dobré, díky** [yeh
dobreh dyeeki]
I'm OK (nothing for me) **pro mě
nic** [mnyeh nyits]
(I feel OK) **cítím se dobře** [tsee-
tyeem seh dobrʌeh]
is this train OK for ...? **jede
tento vlak do ...?** [yedeh]
I said I'm sorry, OK? (said by man/
woman) **už jsem se omluvil/
omluvila, ne?** [oosh sem seh
omloovil – neh]
old starý [sturee]

•••••• D I A L O G U E ••••••

how old are you? **kolik vám je
roků?** [vahm yeh rokOO]
I'm twenty-five **je mi dvacet pět**
[yeh]
and you? **a vám?**

old-fashioned staromódní
[sturomawd-nyee]
old town (old part of town) **stará
část města** [sturah chahst
mnyesta]
in the old town **ve staré části
města** [veh stureh]
olive oil olivový olej [olivovee
olay]
olives olivy fpl [olivi]
omelette omeleta
on na (+ loc)
(lights) **rozsvíceno**
[rosveetseno]

on the street na ulici

is it on this road? je to na této
cestě? [yeh – tses-tyeh]

on the plane v letadle

on Saturday v sobotu

on television v televizi

I haven't got it on me nemám
to u sebe [nemahm to oo sebeh]

this one's on me (drink) to
platím já [plutyeem yah]

the light wasn't on nebylo
rozsvíceno [nebilo]

what's on tonight? co dávají
dnes večer? [tso dahvi-yee dnes
vetcher]

once (one time) jednou [yednoh]

at once (immediately) okamžitě
[okumJi-tyeh]

one* jeden [yeden], jedna,
jedno

the white one ten bílý [beelee]

one-way ticket: a one-way ticket
to … jednou do (+ gen) …
[yednoh]

onion cibule f [tsibooleh]

only jenom [yenom]

only one jenom jeden [yeden]

it's only 6 o'clock je teprve
šest hodin [yeh tepurveh]

I've only just got here (said by
man/woman) teprve jsem přijel/
přijela [sem prJi-yel]

on/off switch vypínač
[vipeenutch]

open (adj) otevřený [otevrJenee]

(verb: door) otevřít [otevrJeet]

when do you open? kdy máte
otevřeno? [gudi mahteh
otevrJeno]

I can't get it open nemohu to
otevřít [nemohoo]

in the open air venku [venkoo]

opening times otvírací doba
[otveerutsee]

open ticket (plane) otevřená
letenka [otevrJenah]

opera opera

operation (medical) operace f
[operutseh]

operator (telephone: man/woman)
spojovatel [spo-yovutel]/
spojovatelka

opposite proti (+ dat) [protyi]

the bar opposite bar naproti

opposite my hotel proti
mému hotelu

optician optik

or nebo

orange (fruit) pomeranč
[pomeruntch]

(colour) oranžový [orunJovee]

orange juice pomerančová
šťáva [pomeruntchovah
shtyahva]

orchestra orchestr [orHestur]

order: can we order now?
můžeme si objednat?
[mooJemeh si ob-yednut]

I've already ordered, thanks
(said by man/woman) už jsem si
objednal/objednala, díky
[oosh sem si ob-yednul – dyeeki]

I didn't order this (said by man/
woman) toto jsem si
neobjednal/neobjednala
[sem si]

out of order mimo provoz
[provos]

ordinary obyčejný [obitchaynee]

other jiný [yinee]

  the other one ten druhý [droohee]

  the other day nedávno [nedahvno]

  I'm waiting for the others čekám na ostatní [chekahm na ostut-nyee]

  do you have any others? máte nějaké jiné? [mahteh nyeh-yukeh yineh]

otherwise jinak [yinuk]

our* náš [nahsh], naše [nusheh]

ours* náš, naše

out: she's out šla ven [shla]

  three kilometres out of town tři kilometry od města [ot mnyesta]

outdoors venku [venkoo]

outside: can we sit outside? můžeme sedět venku? [mOOJemeh sedyet]

  outside the church před kotelem [prJet]

oven kamna n [kumna]

over: over here tady [tudi]

  over there tamhle [tum-hleh]

  over 500 nad pět set

  it's over skončilo to [skontchilo]

overcharge: you've overcharged me (to man/woman) účtoval/účtovala jste mi moc vysokou cenu [OOtchtovul – steh mi mots visokoh tsenoo]

overcoat kabát [kubaht]

overlook: I'd like a room overlooking the courtyard (said by man/woman) chtěl/chtěla bych pokoj s okny do dvora [Hutyel – biH pokoy sokni]

overnight (travel) přes noc [prJes nots]

overtake předjet [prJedyet]

owe: how much do I owe you? kolik vám dlužím? [vahm dlooJeem]

own: my own ... můj vlastní ... [mOO-i vlustnyee]

  are you on your own? (to man/woman) jste sám/sama? [steh sahm/suma]

  I'm on my own (said by man/woman) jsem sám/sama [sem]

owner (man/woman) majitel [mī-yitel]/majitelka

P

pack (verb: suitcase) balit [bulit]

package (small parcel) balík [buleek]

package holiday turistický zájezd [tooristitskee zah-yest]

packed lunch balíček s obědem [buleetchek sob-yedem]

packet: a packet of cigarettes krabička cigaret [krubitchka tsigaret]

padlock (noun) visací zámek [visutsee zahmek]

page (of book) strana [struna]

  could you page Mr ...? můžete předat zprávu na kapesní přijímač na jméno ...? [mOOJeteh prJedut sprahvoo na

kupesnyee prJeemutch na
yumeno]

pain bolest f
  I have a pain here bolí mě
  tady [bolee mnyeh tudi]

painful bolestivý [bolestivee]

painkillers lék proti bolesti
  [protyi bolestyi]

paint (noun) barva [burva]

painting obraz [obrus]

pair: a pair of ... pár (+ gen) ...

Pakistani (adj) pakistánský
  [pukistahnskee]

palace palác [palahts]

pale bledý [bledee]
  pale blue bledě modrý
  [bledyeh]

pan pánev f [pahnef]

panties kalhotky fpl [kulhotki]

pants (underwear: men's) spodky
  mpl [spotki]
  (women's) **kalhotky** fpl
  (US: trousers) **kalhoty** fpl

pantyhose punčocháče fpl
  [poontchoHahtcheh]

paper papír [pupeer]
  (newspaper) noviny fpl [novini]
  a piece of paper kus papíru
  [koos pupeeroo]

paper handkerchiefs papírové
  kapesníky [pupeeroveh
  kupesnyeeki]

parcel balík [buleek]

pardon (me)? prosím? [proseem]

parents: my parents moji rodiče
  [mo-yi rodyitcheh]

parents-in-law rodiče manželky
  [manJelki]

park (noun) park [purk]

(verb) **parkovat** [purkovut]
  can I park here? mohu tady
  parkovat? [mohoo tudi]

parking parkování [purkovah-
  nyee]

Parking is often prohibited in
the centre of major cities, where
special local rules often apply.
Unauthorized parking is pun-
ished by the police clamping the
car or towing it away. Car parks
are scarce. The tube and local
transport offer a speedier and
more convenient alternative in
the centre of Prague.

parking lot parkoviště n
  [parkovish-tyeh]

part (noun) část f [chahst]

partner (boyfriend, girlfriend etc)
  partner [partner]

party (group) skupina
  [skoopina]
  (celebration) oslava [osluva],
  party

pass (in mountains) průsmyk
  [prOOsmik]

passenger (man/woman) pasažér
  [pusuJer]/pasažérka

passport cestovní pas [tsestov-
  nyee pus]

past: in the past v minulosti
  [vminoolostyi]
  just past the information office
  hned za informační
  kanceláří [hnet]

path pěšina [pyeshina]

pattern vzor

pavement chodník [Hod-nyeek]
  on the pavement na chodníku
  [Hodnyeekoo]
pavement café venkovní
  kavárna [venkov-nyee kuvarna]
pay (verb) platit [plutyit]
  can I pay, please? mohu
  zaplatit, prosím? [mohoo]
  it's already paid for to už je
  zaplaceno [oosh yeh
  zuplutseno]

•••••• DIALOGUE ••••••

who's paying? kdo platí? [gudo
plutyee]
I'll pay platím já [plutyeem yah]
no, you paid last time, I'll pay
ne, ty jsi platil posledně, já
platím [neh tisi plutyil posled-nyeh]

payphone telefon na mince
  [mintseh]
peaceful pokojný [pokoynee]
peach broskev f [broskef]
peanuts burské oříšky
  [boorskeh orJeeshki]
pear hruška [hrooshka]
peas hrášek (m sing) [hrahshek]
peculiar (taste, custom) divný
  [dyivnee]
pedestrian crossing přechod
  pro chodce [prJeHot pro
  Hotseh]
pedestrian precinct pěší zóna
  [pyeshee zawna]
peg (for washing) kolíček na
  prádlo [koleetchek na prahdlo]
  (for tent) stanový kolík
  [stunovee koleek]
pen pero

pencil tužka [tooshka]
penfriend (male/female) známý/
  známá na dopisování
  [snahmee/snahmah na
  dopisovahnyee]
penicillin penicilín [penitsileen]
penknife kapesní nůž
  [kupesnyee nOOsh]
pensioner (man/woman)
  důchodce [dOOHotseh]/
  důchodkyně [dOOHotki-nyeh]
people lidé [lideh]
  the other people in the hotel
  ostatní lidé v hotelu
  [ostutnyee]
  too many people příliš
  mnoho lidí [prJeelish mnoho
  lidyee]
pepper (spice) pepř [pepurJ]
  (vegetable) paprikový lusk
  [paprikovee loosk]
peppermint (sweet) mentol
per: per night za noc [nots]
  per week za týden [teeden]
  how much per day? kolik za
  den?
  per cent procento [protsento]
perfect perfektní [perfektnyee]
perfume parfém [purfem]
perhaps možná [moJnah]
  perhaps not možná ne [neh]
period (of time) období [obdobee]
  (menstruation) menstruace f
  [menstroo-utseh]
perm trvalá [turvulah]
permit (noun) povolení
  [povolenyee]
person osoba
personal stereo walkman

petrol benzín [benzeen]

> There are three kinds of petrol:
> **special** – lower grade petrol
> **super** – equal to four star
> **Natural** – lead-free
> **nafta** – diesel

petrol can kanystr [kunistr]
petrol station benzínová
  stanice f [benzeenovah
  stunyitseh]
pharmacy lékárna
  see **chemist's**
phone (noun) telefon
  (verb) telefonovat [telefonovut]

> In Prague and major cities,
> phonecard phones are common
> and you can make international
> calls from them. Phonecards can
> be bought from the post office.
> Elsewhere call boxes in the
> street are generally only for calls
> within the same town or city. If
> you want to make a long-
> distance or international call,
> use any private phone, your
> hotel phone or go to the post
> office where you will have to go
> to the desk to book the phone
> call and leave a deposit. Inter-
> national calls are expensive.
> The dialling tone is a repeated
> long and short tone; the engaged
> tone is a repeated short tone;
> and the connecting tone is a very
> fast repeated short tone telling →

> you to wait for the connection.
> Three consecutive tones of vary-
> ing pitch mean that the number
> is out of service or that there is
> a technical problem.
> see **speak**

phone book telefonní seznam
  [telefonyee seznum]
phone box telefonní budka
  [bootka]
phonecard telefonní karta
  [kurta]
phone number telefonní číslo
  [cheeslo]
photo fotografie f [fotografi-eh]
  **excuse me, could you take a
  photo of us?** (to man/woman)
  promiňte, mohl/mohla byste
  nás vyfotografovat?
  [promin^yehteh mohul – bisteh
  nahs vifotografovut]
phrase book konverzační
  příručka [konverzutch-nyee
  prJeerootchka]
piano piano
pickpocket (man/woman) kapesní
  zloděj [kupesnyee zlodyay]/
  kapesní zlodějka
**pick up: will you be there to pick
  me up?** vyzvednete mě tam?
  [vizvedneteh mnyeh tum]
picnic (noun) piknik
picture obraz [obrus]
pie (meat) pečivo plněné
  masem [petchivo pulnyeneh
  musem]
  (fruit) pečivo plněné

ovocem [ovotsem]

piece kus [koos]

a piece of ... kus ... (+ gen)

pill pilulka [piloolka]

I'm on the pill užívám antikoncepci [ooJeevahm untikontseptsi]

pillow polštář [polshtarJ]

pillow case povlak na polštář [povluk]

Pilsen Plzeň [pulzen^{yeh}]

pin (noun) špendlík [shpendleek]

pineapple ananas [ununus]

pineapple juice ananasový džus [ununusovee joos]

pink růžový [rooJovee]

pipe (for smoking) dýmka [deemka]

(for water) trubka [troopka]

pipe cleaners čistič dýmky [chistitch deemki]

pity: it's a pity to je škoda [yeh shkoda]

pizza pizza

place (noun) místo [meesto]

is this place taken? je toto místo obsazené? [yeh – meesto opsuzeneh]

at your place u tebe/vás [oo tebeh/vahs]

at his place u něho [nyeho]

plain (not patterned) jednobarevný [yednoburevnee]

plane letadlo [letudlo]

by plane letadlem [letudlem]

plant rostlina

plaster cast sádra [sahdra]

plasters náplasti fpl [nahplustyi]

plastic umělá hmota [oomnyelah

humota]

(credit cards) platební karty [plutebnyee karti]

plastic bag igelitová taška [igelitovah tushka]

plate talíř [tuleerJ]

platform nástupiště n [nahstoopish-tyeh]

which platform is for Plzeň, please? z kterého nástupiště jede vlak na Plzeň? [skutereho – jedeh vluk na pulzen^{yeh}]

play (noun: in theatre) hra (verb) hrát [hraht]

playground hřiště n [hrJishtyeh]

pleasant příjemný [prJee-yemnee]

please prosím [proseem]

yes, please ano, prosím [uno]

could you please ...? (to man/ woman) mohl/mohla byste ..., prosím? [mohul/mo-hla bisteh]

please don't prosím vás, ne [vahs neh]

pleased to meet you těší mě [tyeshee mnyeh]

pleasure: it's a pleasure je mi potěšením [yeh mi pot-yeshenyeem]

my pleasure potěšení je na mé straně [potyeshenyee yeh na meh strunyeh]

plenty: plenty of ... spousta (+ gen) ... [spohsta]

there's plenty of time je dost času [yeh dost chusoo]

that's plenty, thanks to je až moc, děkuji [yeh ush mots dyekoo-yi]

pliers kleště fpl [kleshtyeh]

plug (electrical) zástrčka [zahsturtchka]
(for car) svíčka [sveetchka]
(in sink) zátka [zahtka]

plumber instalatér [instuluter]

p.m.*: 11 p.m. jedenáct hodin v noci [ho-dyin vnotsi]
2 p.m. dvě hodiny odpoledne [ho-dyini otpoledneh]
7 p.m. sedm hodin večer [vetcher]

poached egg ztracené vejce n [strutseneh vaytseh]

pocket kapsa [kupsa]

point: two point five dvě celé pět [dvyeh tseleh pyet]
there's no point nemá to smysl [nemah to smisul]

poisonous jedovatý [yedovutee]

Poland Polsko

police policie f [politsi-eh]
call the police! volejte policii! [volayteh politsi-i]

Phone 158 for the police.

policeman policista m [politsista]

police station policejní stanice f [politsay-nyee stunitseh]

policewoman policistka [politsistka]

polish (noun) leštidlo [leshtyidlo]

Polish (adj) polský [polskee]

polite zdvořilý [zdvorʃilee]

polluted znečištěný [znetchish-tyenee]

pony pony m

pool (for swimming) bazén [buzen]

poor (not rich) chudý [Hoodee]
(quality) špatný [shputnee]

pop music populární hudba [popoolar-nyee hoodba]

pop singer (man/woman) zpěvák/zpěvačka (populárních písní) [spyevahk/spyevutchka popoolar-nyeeH peesnyee]

population populace f [popoolatseh]

pork vepřové maso [veprʃoveh muso]

port (for boats) přístav [prʃeestuf]
(drink) portské víno [portskeh veeno]

porter (in hotel) nosič [nositch]

portrait portrét

posh (restaurant) luxusní [looksoosnyee]

possible možný [moʃnee]
is it possible to ...? je možné ...? [yeh moʃneh]
as ... as possible tak ... jak to jen bude možné [tuk ... yuk to yen boodeh moʃneh]

post (noun: mail) pošta [poshta]
(verb) poslat poštou [poslut poshtoh]
could you post this for me? (to man/woman) mohl/mohla byste to dát na poštu? [mohul/mohla bysteh to daht na poshtoo]

postbox poštovní schránka [poshtov-nyee sHrahnka]

postcard pohlednice f [pohled-nyitseh]

poster plakát [plakaht]

post office pošta [poshta]

Post offices are open Monday to Friday from 7 a.m. to 7 p.m. and on Saturdays until noon. In major cities there is a main post office with a 24-hour telephone, telegram and fax service. Expect airmail to take about four days to Britain and the United States. Parcels are expensive to mail. Courier services are becoming available in bigger cities.

---

poste restante poste restante

potato brambora [brumbora]

potato chips (US) lupínky mpl [loopeenki]

pots and pans nádobí [nahdobee]

pottery keramika [kerumika]

pound* (money, weight) libra

power cut výpadek elektřiny [veepudek elektrJini]

power point zásuvka [zahsoofka]

practise: I want to practise my Czech chci si procvičit češtinu [Hutsi si protsvitchit chesh-tyinoo]

Prague Praha [pruha]

prefer: I prefer ... preferuji ... [preferoo-yi]

pregnant těhotná [tyehotnah]

prescription recept [retsept]
see **chemist's**

present (gift) dárek

president (of country: man/woman) prezident/prezidentka

pretty pěkný [pyeknee]
it's pretty expensive to je

pěkně drahé [yeh pyeknyeh draheh]

price cena [tsena]

priest kněz [kunyes]

prime minister (man/woman) premiér [premyer]/premiérka

printed matter tiskoviny fpl [tyiskovini]

priority (in driving) přednost f [prJednost]

prison vězení [vyezenyee]

private soukromý [sohkromee]

private bathroom soukromá koupelna [sohkromah kohpelna]

private room soukromý pokoj [sohkromee pokoy]

probably asi [usi]

problem problém
no problem! to není problém! [nenyee]

program(me) program

promise: I promise slibuji [sliboo-yi]

pronounce: how is this pronounced? jak se to vyslovuje? [yuk seh to vislovoo-yeh]

properly (repaired, locked etc) pořádně [porJahd-nyeh]

protection factor (of suntan lotion) ochranný faktor [oHrunnee fuktor]

Protestant protestant [protestunt]

pub hospoda
(in country) hostinec [hostinets]
see **bar**

public convenience veřejné

záchody [verJayneh zah-Hodi]
public holiday den pracovního
klidu [prutsov-nyeeho klidoo]
pudding (dessert) pudink
[poodink]
pull táhnout [tah-hunoht]
pullover pulovr [poolovur]
puncture (noun) defekt
purple fialový [fi-alovee]
purse (for money) peněženka
[penyeJenka]
(US) kabelka [kubelka]
push tlačit [tlatchit]
pushchair skládací dětská
sedačka [sklahdutsee dyetskah
sedutchka]
put položit [poloJit]
where can I put ...? kam můžu
položit ...? [kum mooJoo]
could you put us up for the
night? (to man/woman) mohl/
mohla byste nás na noc
ubytovat? [mohul/mo-hla bisteh
nahs na nots oobitovut]
pyjamas pyžamo [piJamo]

Q

quality kvalita [kvulita]
quarantine karanténa
[kuruntena]
quarter čtvrt f [chutvurt]
question otázka [otahska]
queue (noun) fronta, řada
[rJuda]
quick rychlý [riHlee]
that was quick to bylo rychlé
[bilo riHleh]
what's the quickest way there?

jaká je tam nejrychlejší
cesta? [yuka yeh tum
nayriHlayshee]
fancy a quick drink? dáte si
skleničku? [dahteh si
sklenyichkoo]
quickly rychle [riHleh]
quiet (place, hotel) tichý [tyiHee]
quiet! ticho! [tyiHo]
quite (fairly) docela [dotsela]
(very) úplně [OOpulnyeh]
that's quite right to je pravda
[yeh pruvda]
quite a lot docela hodně
[ho-dnyeh]

R

rabbit králík [krahleek]
race (for runners, cars) závod
[zahvot]
racket (tennis, squash etc) raketa
[ruketa]
radiator radiátor [rudi-ahtor]
radio rádio [rahdi-o]
on the radio v rádiu [rahdi-oo]
rail: by rail vlakem [vlukem]
railway železnice f [Jelez-nyitseh]
rain (noun) déšť [dehsht^yeh]
in the rain v dešti [fdeshtyi]
it's raining prší [purshee]
raincoat plášť do deště
[plahsht^yeh do deshtyeh]
rape (noun) znásilnění [znahsil-
nyenyee]
rare (steak) krvavý [kurvahvee]
rash (on skin) vyrážka [virahshka]
raspberry malina [mulina]
rat krysa [krisa]

rate (for changing money) kurz
[koors]

rather: it's rather good to je
docela dobré [yeh dotsela
dobreh]

I'd rather ... radši bych ...
[rutshi biH]

razor (dry) břitva [brJitva]
(electric) holicí strojek
[holitsee stro-yek]

razor blades žiletky fpl [Jiletki]

read číst [cheest]

ready připravený [prJipruvenee]

are you ready? (to man/woman)
jste připravený/připravená?
[steh – prJipruvenah]

I'm not ready yet (said by man/
woman) ještě nejsem
připravený/připravená
[yeshtyeh naysem]

•••••• DIALOGUE ••••••

when will it be ready? kdy to bude
hotové? [gudi to boodeh hotoveh]

it should be ready in a couple of
days mělo by to být hotové za
několik dní [mnyelo bi to beet
hotoveh za nyekolik dnyee]

real skutečný [skootetchnee]

really opravdu [opruvdoo]

that's really great to je
opravdu výborné [veeborneh]
really? opravdu?

rearview mirror zpětné zrcátko
[spyetneh zurtsahtko]

reasonable (prices etc) rozumný
[rozoomnee]

receipt potvrzení [potuvrzenyee]

recently v poslední době
[fposled-nyee dobyeh]

reception recepce f [retseptseh]
at reception na recepci

reception desk recepce

receptionist recepční m/f
[retseptch-nyee]

recognize poznat [poznut]

recommend: could you
recommend ...? (to man/woman)
mohl/mohla byste
doporučit ...? [mohul/mo-hla
bisteh doporootchit]

record (music) gramofonová
deska [grumofonovah]

red červený [chervenee]

red wine červené víno
[cherveneh veeno]

refund (noun) peněžitá náhrada
[penyeJitah nah-hruda]
can I have a refund? mohu
dostat zpět peníze? [mohoo
dostut spyet penyeezeh]

region region [regi-on]

registered: by registered mail
doporučeně [doporootchenyeh]

registration number státní
poznávací značka [staht-nyee
poznahvtsee znutchka]

relative (man/woman) příbuzný
[prJeebooznee]/příbuzná
[prJeebooznah]

religion náboženství
[nahboJenstvee]

remember: I don't remember
nepamatuji si [nepumatoo-yi]
I remember pamatuji si
[pumatoo-yi]
do you remember? pamatu-
jete si? [pumatoo-yeteh]

rent (noun: for apartment etc)
nájemné n [nah-yemneh]
(verb: car, apartment etc) najmout
si [nīmoht]
to/for rent k pronajmutí
[pronīmoo-tyee]

•••••• DIALOGUE ••••••

I'd like to rent a car (said by man/
woman) rád/ráda bych si
pronajal/pronajala auto [raht/
rahda biH si pronī-yal – owto]

for how long? na jak dlouho? [yuk
dloh-ho]

two days dva dny

this is our range to je naše
nabídka [yeh nasheh nabeetka]

I'll take the ... vezmu si ...
[vezmoo]

is that with unlimited mileage? je
to bez omezení ujetých
kilometrů? [bes omezenyee oo-
yeteeH kilometroo]

it is ano [uno]

can I see your licence please?
můžete mi, prosím, ukázat váš
řidičský průkaz? [mooJeteh mi
proseem ookahzut vahsh rJi-dyichskee
prookus]

and your passport? a váš pas?
[vahsh pus]

is insurance included? je v tom
pojištění? [yeh ftom po-yish-
tyenyee]

yes, but you pay the first 2,000
crowns ano, ale se spoluúčastí
dva tisíce korun [uleh seh spoloo-
oochustyee – koroon]

can you leave a deposit of 100

crowns? dáte mi zálohu sto
korun? [dahteh mi zahlohoo]

rented car pronajaté auto
[pronī-uteh owto]

repair (verb) opravovat
[opruvovut]/opravit [opruvit]

can you repair it? můžete to
opravit? [opruvit]

repeat opakovat [opukovut]/
zopakovat

could you repeat that? (to man/
woman) mohl/mohla byste to
opakovat? [mohul/mo-hla
bisteh]

reservation rezervace f
[rezervutseh]

I'd like to make a reservation
(said by man/woman) rád/ráda
bych si rezervoval/
rezervovala místo [raht/rahda
biH si rezervovul – meesto]

•••••• DIALOGUE ••••••

I have a reservation mám
rezervaci [mahm rezervutsi]

yes sir, what name please? ano,
pane, na jaké jméno, prosím?
[uno puneh na yukeh yumeno]

reserve rezervovat [rezervovut]

•••••• DIALOGUE ••••••

can I reserve a table for tonight?
můžu si na dnes večer
rezervovat stůl? [mooJoo – vetcher
– stool]

yes madam, for how many people?
ano, paní, pro kolik osob? [uno
punyee]

for two pro dva

and for what time? a na kolik
hodin? [ho-dyin]
for eight o'clock na osm hodin
and could I have your name
please? a na jaké jméno, prosím?
[yukeh yumeno]
see **alphabet** for spelling

rest: I need a rest potřebuju si
odpočinout [potrJeboo-yoo si
otpotchinoht]
the rest of the group zbytek
skupiny [zbitek skoopini]
restaurant restaurace f
[restowratseh]

The distinction between pubs
and restaurants is not precise in
the Czech Republic. If you
want a full meal you can go to
a **restaurace** (restaurant), a
hospoda/pivnice/hostinec
(pub), **vinárna** (wine bar) or a
jídelna (canteen/cafeteria). If
your main concern is price,
the local **pivnice**, **hospoda**, or
hostinec are the ones to go for
though some of those offer a
rather limited menu. Nearly all
of them will serve meals from
mid-morning until 2-3 p.m., and
some continue serving until 8 or
9 p.m. A **vinárna** – though not
necessarily its kitchen – will
sometimes stay open until after
11 p.m.
see **bill**

restaurant car jídelní vůz

[yeedel-nyee vOOs]
rest room toaleta [to-uleta]
see **toilet**
retired: I'm retired jsem v
důchodu [sem fdOOHodoo]
return (come back) návrat
[nahvrut]
(give back) vrátit [vrahtyit]
return ticket zpáteční (lístek)
[spahtetchnyee leestek]
reverse charge call hovor na
účet volaného [OOchet
voluneho]
reverse gear zpátečka
[spahtetchka]
revolting odpudivý [otpoo-
dyivee]
rib žebro [Jebro]
rice rýže f [reeJeh]
rich (person) bohatý [bo-hutee]
(food) sytý [sitee]
ridiculous směšný [smnyeshnee]
right (correct) správně [sprahv-
nyeh]
(not left) pravý [pravee]
you were right měl jste
pravdu [mnyel steh pruvdoo]
that's right! správně! [sprahv-
nyeh]
this can't be right to nemůže
být správně [nemooJeh beet]
right! dobře! [dobrJeh]
is this the right road for ...? (on
foot) jdu dobře na
(+ acc) ...? [doo dobrJeh]
is this the right road for ...?
(by car) jedu dobře na
(+ acc) ...? [yedoo]
on the right napravo [nupruvo]

turn right zabočte doprava
[zubotchteh dopruva]

right-hand drive pravé řízení
[pruveh rJeezenyee]

ring (on finger) prsten [prusten]

I'll ring you zavolám vám
[zuvolahm vahm]

ring back zavolat zpět [zuvolut
spyet]

ripe (fruit) zralý [zrulee]

rip-off: it's a rip-off to je
zlodějna [yeh zlodyayna]

rip-off prices zlodějské ceny
[zlodyayskeh tseni]

risky riskantní [riskant-nyee]

river řeka [rJeka]

road ulice f [oolitseh]

is this the road for ...? je to
cesta na (+ acc) ...? [yeh to
tsesta]

down the road po cestě [tses-
tyeh]

road accident dopravní nehoda
[dopruv-nyee]

road map silniční mapa
[silnitch-nyee mupa]

roadsign dopravní značka
[znutchka]

rob: I've been robbed (said by
man/woman) byl/byla jsem
oloupen/oloupena [bil/bila
sem olohpen]

rock skála [skahla]

(music) roková hudba [rokovah
hoodba]

on the rocks (with ice) s ledem

rock climbing horolezectví
[horolezetstvee]

roll (bread) rohlík [ro-hleek]

roof střecha [strJeHa]

roof rack zahrádka na
automobil [zuhrahtka na
owtomobil]

room pokoj [pokoy]

in my room v mém pokoji
[poko-yi]

see hotel

•••••• DIALOGUE ••••••

do you have any rooms? máte
nějaký volný pokoj? [mahteh nyeh-
yukee volnee]

for how many people? pro kolik
osob?

for one/for two pro jednoho/pro
dva [yednoho]

yes, we have rooms free ano,
máme volné pokoje [uno mahmeh
volneh poko-yeh]

for how many nights will it be? na
kolik nocí? [notsee]

just for one night jen na jednu noc
[yen nah yednoo]

how much is it? kolik to stojí?
[sto-yee]

... with bathroom and ... without
bathroom ... s koupelnou a ... bez
koupelny [skohpelnoh a ... bes
kohpelni]

can I see a room with bathroom?
mohu se podívat na pokoj s
koupelnou? [mohoo seh podyeevut]

OK, I'll take it dobře, vezmu to
[dobrJeh vezmoo]

room service hotelová obsluha
[hotelovah opslooha]

rope provaz [provus]

rosé (wine) růžové víno

[rooJoveh veeno]

roughly (approximately) **zhruba**
[zhrooba]

**round: it's my round ted' platím
já** [tet^yeh plutyeem yah]

roundabout (for traffic) **kruhový
objezd** [kroo-hovee ob-yest]

**round trip ticket: a round trip
ticket to ... zpáteční
do** (+ gen) **...** [spahtetch-nyee]

route trasa [trusa]
  **what's the best route? jaká je
nejlepší trasa?** [yukah yeh
naylepshee]

rubber (material, eraser) **guma**
[gooma]

rubber band gumička
[goomitchka]

rubbish (waste) **odpadky mpl**
[otputki]
  (poor quality goods) **krámy**
[krahmi]

rubbish! (nonsense) **nesmysl!**
[nesmisul]

rucksack ruksak [rooksuk]

rude drzý [durzee]

ruins trosky fpl [troski]

rum rum [room]
  **rum and coke rum a
kokakola**

run (verb) **běhat** [byehut]
  **how often do the buses run?
jak často jezdí autobusy?**
[yuk chusto yezdye]
  **I've run out of money došly mi
peníze** [doshli]

rush hour dopravní špička
[shpitchka]

Russia Rusko [roosko]

Russian (adj) **ruský** [rooskee]

S

sad smutný [smootnee]

saddle (for bike, horse) **sedlo**

safe (not in danger) **v bezpečí**
[vbespetchee]
  (not dangerous) **bezpečný**
[bespetchnee]

safety pin zavírací špendlík
[zuveerutsee shpendleek]

sail (noun) **plachta** [pluHta]

sailboard (noun) **surf** [soorf]

sailboarding surfování
[soorfovah-nyee], **windsurfing**

salad salát [salaht]

salad dressing zálivka [zahlifka]

sale (reduced price) **výprodej f**
[veeproday]
  for sale na prodej [proday]

salmon losos

salt sůl f [sool]

same: the same to samé
[sumeh]
  **the same as this to samé jako
toto** [yuko]
  **the same again, please ještě
jednou to samé, prosím**
[yeshtyeh yednoh]
  **it's all the same to me mně je
to jedno** [mnyeh yeh to yedno]

sand písek [peesek]

sandals sandály mpl [sandahli]

sandwich obložený chléb
[obloJenee Hlep]

**sanitary napkins dámské vložky
fpl** [dahmskeh vloshki]

sanitary towels dámské

vložky fpl

sardines sardinky fpl [sardinki]

Saturday sobota

sauce omáčka [omahtchka]

saucepan pánev f [pahnef]

saucer talířek [tuleerJek]

sauna sauna [sowna]

sausage párek

say: how do you say ... in Czech? jak řeknete česky ...? [yuk rJekneteh cheski]

what did he say? co říkal? [tso rJeekal]

I said ... (said by man/woman) říkal/říkala jsme, že ... [rJeekal – smeh Jeh]

he said ... řikal, že ...

could you say that again? (to man/woman) mohl/mohla byste to říct ještě jednou? [mohul/mo-hla bisteh to rJeetst yeshtyeh yednoh]

scarf (for neck) šála [shahla]

(for head) šátek [shahtek]

scenery krajina [krī-ina]

schedule (US: train, bus) jízdní řád [yeezd-nyee rJaht]

scheduled flight plánovaný let [plahnovunee]

school škola [shkola]

scissors: a pair of scissors nůžky [nOOshki]

scotch whisky f

Scotch tape® izolepa

Scotland Skotsko

Scottish skotský [skotskee]

I'm Scottish (man/woman) jsem Skot/Skotka [sem]

scrambled eggs míchaná vajíčka npl [meeHanah vī-yeetchka]

scratch (noun) škrábanec [shkrahbunets]

screw (noun) šroub [shrohb]

screwdriver šroubovák [shrohbovahk]

sea moře n [morJeh]

search (verb) hledat [hledut]

seat sedadlo [sedudlo]

is this anyone's seat? je to něčí sedadlo? [yeh to nyetchee]

seat belt bezpečnostní pás [bespechnost-nyee pahs]

secluded odloučený [odlohtchenee]

second (adj) druhý [droohee]

(of time) sekunda [sekoonda], vteřina [fterJina]

just a second! jen vteřinu! [yen fterJinoo]

second class (travel) druhou třídou [droohoh trJeedoh]

second floor druhé poschodí [droohee posHodyee]

(US) první poschodí [purv-nyee]

second-hand z druhé ruky [zdrooheh rooki]

see vidět [vidyet]/uvidět [oovidyet]

can I see? mohu se podívat? [mohoo seh po-dyeevut]

have you seen ...? (to man/woman) viděl/viděla jste ...? [vidyel – steh]

see you! nashle! [nus-Hleh]

I see (I understand) rozumím [rozoomeem]

I saw him this morning (said by man/woman) viděl/viděla jsem ho dopoledne [sem ho dopoledneh]

self-catering apartment byt bez stravování [bit bes struvovah-nyee]

self-service samoobsluha [samo-opslooha]

sell prodávat [prodahvut]
do you sell ...? prodáváte ...? [prodahvahteh]

Sellotape® izolepa

send posílat [poseelut]/poslat [poslut]
I want to send this to England chci to poslat do Anglie [Hutsi – ungli-eh]

senior citizen (man/woman) starší občan [starshee opchun]/starší občanka

separate oddělený [od-dyelenee]

separated: I'm separated (from wife) nežiji s manželkou [neJi-yi s munJelkoh]
(from husband) nežiji s manželem

separately (pay, travel) zvlášť [zvlahsht^yeh]

September září [zarJee]

septic hnisavý [hunyisavee]

serious vážný [vahJnee]

service station autoservis [owtoservis]

serviette ubrousek [oobrohsek]

set menu menu [meni]

several několik [nyekolik]

sew šít [sheet]/našít [nusheet]
could you sew this back on?

(to man/woman) mohl/mohla byste to našít zpátky? [mohul/mo-hla bisteh – nahsheet spahtki]

sex sex

sexy sexy

shade: in the shade ve stínu [veh styeenoo]

shake: let's shake hands podejme si ruce [podaymeh si rootseh]

shallow (water) mělký [mnyelkee]

shame: what a shame! to je škoda! [yeh shkoda]

shampoo (noun) šampón [shumpawn]
shampoo and set vodovou [vodovoh]

share (verb: room, table etc) dělit se [dyelit seh]/rozdělit se o (+ acc)

sharp ostrý [ostree]

shattered (very tired) zničený [znyitchnee]

shaver holicí strojek [holitsee stro-yek]

shaving foam pěna na holení [pyena na holenyee]

shaving point zásuvka pro holicí strojek [zahsoofka pro holitsee]

she* ona
is she here? je tady ona? [yeh tudi]

sheet (for bed) prostěradlo [pros-tyerudlo]

shelf polička [politchka]

sherry šery n [sheri]

ship loď f [lot^yeh]

by ship lodí [lodyee]
shirt košile f [koshileh]
shit! do prdele! [prudeleh]
shock (noun) šok [shok]
 **I got an electric shock from
 the ...** (said by man/woman)
 dostal/dostala jsem ránu ze
 (+ gen) ... [dostul – sem rahnoo
 zeh]
shock-absorber nárazník [naruz-
 nyeek]
shocking šokující [shokoo-
 yeetsee]
shoe bota
 a pair of shoes boty [boti]
shoelaces tkaničky fpl [tku-
 nyitchki]
shoe polish krém na boty
shoe repairer opravář obuvi
 [oprvahrJ oboovi]
shop obchod [opHot]

Most shops open between about
7.30 and 9 a.m. and close
around 6 or 7 p.m. Some have a
lunch hour some time between
12 and 2 p.m. Shops used to be
closed on Saturday afternoon,
but now some are open. Most
are closed on Sunday. In bigger
towns there are late-night
grocery stores (**večerka**) and in
bigger villages along the main
roads there are shops open on
Saturdays and Sundays.

shopping: I'm going shopping
 jdu nakupovat: [yudoo
 nukoopovut]

shopping centre nákupní
 středisko [nahkoopnyee
 strJedyisko]
shop window výklad [veeklut]
shore (of lake) břeh [brJeH]
short krátký [krahtkee]
shortcut zkratka [skrutka]
shorts šortky fpl [shortki]
should: what should I do? co
 mám dělat? [tso mahm dyelut]
 he shouldn't be long nemělo
 by mu to trvat dlouho
 [nemnyelo bi moo to turvut
 dloh-ho]
 you should have told me (to
 man/woman) měl/měla jsi mi to
 říct [mnyel – si mi to rJeetst]
shoulder rameno [rumeno]
shout (verb) křičet [krJitchet]
show (in theatre) představení
 [prJetstuvenyee]
 could you show me? (to man/
 woman) mohl/mohla byste mi
 to ukázat? [mohul/mo-hla
 bisteh – ookahzut]
shower (in bathroom) sprcha
 [spurHa]
 (rain) přeháňka
 [prJehahn^(yeh)ka]
 with shower se sprchou [seh
 spurHoh]
shut (verb) zavírat [zuveerut]/
 zavřít [zuvrJeet]
 when do you shut? kdy
 zavíráte? [gudi zuveerahteh]
 when do they shut? kdy
 zavírají? [zuveerI-ee]
 they're shut mají zavřeno
 [mI-yi zuvrJeno]

I've shut myself out (said by man/woman) **zabouchl/zabouchla jsem si dveře** [zubohHul – sem si dverJeh]

shut up! buď zticha! [boot^{yeh} styiHa]

shutter (on camera) **závěrka** [zahvyerka]
(on window) **okenice fpl** [okenyitseh]

shy ostýchavý [osteeHuvee]

sick (US) **nemocný** [nemotsnee]
see **ill**
I'm going to be sick (vomit) **budu zvracet** [boodoo zvrutset]

side strana [struna]
the other side of town druhá strana města [droohah – mnyesta]

side lights boční světla [botchnyee svyetla]

side salad salát [salaht]

side street boční ulice [botchnyee oolitseh]

sidewalk chodník [Hod-nyeek]
see **pavement**

sight: the sights of ... turistické atrakce (+ gen) ... [tooristitskeh utruktseh]

sightseeing: we're going sightseeing jdeme na prohlídku [yudemeh na prohleetkoo]

sightseeing tour prohlídka [prohleetka]

sign (roadsign etc) **značka** [znutchka]

signal: he didn't give a signal (driver, cyclist) **neukazoval**

směr [neh-ookuzoval smnyer]

signature podpis [potpis]

signpost ukazatel [ookazatel]

silence ticho [tyiHo]

silk hedvábí [hedvahbee]

silly hloupý [hlohpee]

silver (noun) **stříbro** [strJeebro]

silver foil alobal [ulobul]

similar podobný [podobnee]

simple (easy) **jednoduchý** [yednodooHee]

since: since yesterday od včerejška [ot fcherayshka]
since I got here (said by man/woman) **co jsem přijel/přijela** [tso sem prJi-yel]

sing zpívat [speevut]/**zazpívat** [zuspeevut]

singer (man/woman) **zpěvák** [spyevahk]/**zpěvačka** [spyevutchka]

single: a single room jednolůžkový pokoj [yednolOOshkovee pokoy]
a single to ... jednou do (+ gen) ... [yednoh]
I'm single (said by man/woman) **jsem svobodný/svobodná** [sem svobodnee/svobodnah]

sink (in kitchen) **dřez** [drJes]

sister sestra

sister-in-law švagrová [shvugrovah]

sit: can I sit here? mohu se tady posadit? [mohoo seh tudi posudyit]
is anyone sitting here? sedí tady někdo? [sedyee tudi nyegdo]

sit down posadit se [posudyit seh]
  sit down! posad'te se! [posud^yeh teh]
size velikost
ski (noun) lyže fpl [liJeh]
  (verb) lyžovat [liJovut]
  a pair of skis lyže [liJeh]
ski boots lyžařské boty [liJurJskeh boti]
skiing lyžování [liJovah-nyee]
  we're going skiing jedeme lyžovat [yedemeh liJovut]
ski instructor lyžařský instruktor [liJurJskee instrooktor]/lyžařská instruktorka [liJurJskah]
ski-lift lyžařský vlek
skin kůže f [kOOJeh]
skin-diving sportovní potápění [sportov-nyee potah-pyenyee]
skinny vyhublý [vihooblee]
ski-pants šponovky fpl [shponofki]
ski-pass permanentka na vlek [permunentka]
ski pole lyžařská hůl f [liJarJskah hOOl]
skirt sukně f [sook-nyeh]
ski slope lyžařský svah [liJurJskee svuH]
ski trail lyžařská stopa [liJurJskah]
ski wax lyžařský vosk
sky obloha
sleep spát [spaht]
  did you sleep well? (to man/woman) spal/spala jste dobře? [spul – steh dobrJeh]

I need a good sleep potřebuji se pořádně vyspat [potrJeboo-yi seh porJahd-nyeh visput]
sleeper (on train) lůžkový vůz [lOOshkovee vOOs]
sleeping bag spací pytel [sputsee pitel]
sleeping car lůžkový vůz [lOOshkovee vOOs]
sleeping pill prášek na spaní [prahshek nah spunyee]
sleepy: I'm feeling sleepy (said by man/woman) jsem ospalý/ospalá [sem ospulee/ospulah]
sleeve rukáv [rookahf]
slide (photographic) diapozitiv
slip (under dress) kombiné n [kombineh]
slippery kluzký [klooskee]
Slovak (adj) slovenský [slovenskee]
  (language) slovenština [slovensh-tyina]
  (man) Slovák [slovahk]
  (woman) Slovenka
  the Slovaks Slováci [slovahtsi]
Slovakia Slovensko
Slovak Republic Slovenská republika [slovenskah repooblika]
slow pomalý [pomulee]
  slow down! (driving, speaking) zpomal! [spomul]
slowly pomalu [pomuloo]
  could you say it slowly? (to man/woman) mohl/mohla byste to říct pomalu? [mohul/mo-hla bisteh to rJeetst]

very slowly velmi pomalu
small malý [mulee]
smell: it smells (smells bad) smrdí
to [smurdyee]
smile (verb) usmívat se
[oosmeevut seh]/usmát se
[oosmaht]
smoke (noun) kouř [kohrJ]
do you mind if I smoke? bude
vám vadit, když budu
kouřit? [boodeh vahm vudyit
gudiJ boodoo kohrJit]
I don't smoke já nekouřím
[yah nekohrJeem]
do you smoke? kouříte?
[kohrJeeteh]
snack: I'd just like a snack chci
jen něco malého [Hutsi yen
nyetso muleho]
sneeze (noun) kýchat [keeHut]
snow (noun) sníh [snyeeH]
it's snowing sněží [snyeJee]
so: it's so good je to moc
dobré [yeh to mots dobreh]
not so fast ne tak rychle [neh
tuk riHleh]
so am I já také [yah tukeh]
so do I já také
so-so tak tak [tuk]
soaking solution (for contact
lenses) fyziologický roztok
[fizi-ologitskee rostok]
soap mýdlo [meedlo]
soap powder mýdlový prášek
[meedlovee prahshek]
sober střízlivý [strJeezlivee]
sock ponožka [ponoshka]
socket (electrical) zásuvka
[zahsoofka]

soda (water) soda
sofa pohovka [pohofka]
soft (material etc) měkký
[mnyekee]
soft-boiled egg vejce naměkko
n [vaytseh numnyeko]
soft drink nealkoholický nápoj
[neh-ulkoholitskee nahpoy]
soft lenses měkké kontaktní
čočky fpl [mnyekeh
kontuktnyee chotchki]
sole podrážka [podrahshka]
**could you put new soles on
these?** můžete tam dát nové
podrážky? [mooJeteh tum daht
noveh podrahshki]
**some: can I have some water/
rolls?** mohu dostat trochu
vody/nějaké rohlíky? [mohoo
dostut troHoo – nyayukeh]
can I have some? mohu
trochu dostat? [mohoo troHoo
dostut]
somebody, someone někdo
[nyegdo]
something něco [nyetso]
something to drink něco k pití
[nyetso kupityee]
sometimes někdy [nyegdi]
somewhere někde [nyegdeh]
son syn [sin]
song píseň [peesen^{yeh}]
son-in-law zeť [zet^{yeh}]
soon brzy [burzi]
I'll be back soon brzy budu
zpátky [burzi boodoo spahtki]
as soon as possible co
nejdříve [tso naydrJeeveh]
sore: it's sore je to bolavé [yeh

to bolaveh]

sore throat bolest v krku f
[fkurkoo]

sorry: (I'm) sorry (apology)
prominte [prominᵞᵉʰteh]
(sympathy) je mi to moc líto
[yeh mi to mots leeto]

sorry? (didn't understand)
prosím? [proseem]

sort: what sort of ...? jaké ...?
[yukeh]

soup polévka [polefka]

sour (taste) kyselý [kiselee]

south jih [yiн]
in the south na jihu [yihoo]

South Africa Jižní Afrika [yiჯnyee
ufrika]

South African (adj) jihoafrický
[yiho-ufritskee]
I'm South African (man/woman)
jsem Jihoafričan/
Jihoafričanka [sem yiho-
ufritchun]

southeast jihovýchod
[yihoveeнot]

southwest jihozápad
[yihozahpat]

souvenir suvenýr [sooveneer]

spa lázně fpl [lahznyeh]

Spain Španělsko [shpanyelsko]

spanner klíč na matice [kleetch
na mutyitseh]

spare part náhradní díl [nah-
hrudnyee dyeel]

spare tyre rezervní pneumatika
[rezerv-nyee pneh-oomutika]

spark plug zapalovací svíčka
[zupalovutsee sveetchka]

speak mluvit [mloovit]

do you speak English? mluvíte
anglicky? [mlooveeteh
unglitski]

I don't speak ... nemluvím ...
[nemlooveem]

•••••• DIALOGUE ••••••

can I speak to Vlasta? mohu
mluvit s Vlastou? [mohoo –
svlastoh]

who's calling? kdo volá? [gudo
volah]

it's Patricia Patricia

**I'm sorry, she's not in, can I take a
message?** bohužel, není doma,
mám jí něco vzkázat? [bo-hooჯel
nenyee – mahm yee nyetso fskahzut]

no thanks, I'll call back later ne,
díky, zavolám později [neh dyeeki
zuvolahm pozdyay-i]

please tell her I called prosím vás,
řekněte jí, že jsem volala
[proseem vahs rჯek-nyeteh yee ჯeh
sem volula]

speciality specialita [spetsi-ulita]

spectacles brýle fpl [breeleh]

speed (noun) rychlost f [riнlost]

speed limit omezení rychlosti f
[omezenyee]

speedometer tachometr
[taнometur]

spell: how do you spell it? jak se
to hláskuje? [yuk seh to
hlahskoo-yeh]
see alphabet

spend utrácet [ootrahtset]/
utratit [ootrutyit]

spider pavouk [pavohk]

spin-dryer ždímačka

[Jdyeemutchka]
splinter tříska [trJeeska]
spoke (in wheel) špice f [shpitseh]
spoon lžíce f [luJeetseh]
sport sport
sprain: I've sprained my ankle
mám výron v kotníku [mahm
veeron fkotnyeekoo]
spring (season) jaro [yuro]
(of car, seat) pero
square (in town) náměstí
[nahmnyes-tyee]
stairs schody mpl [sHodi]
stale (bread) oschlý [osHlee]
stall: the engine keeps stalling
motor zhasíná [zhuseenah]
stamp (noun) známka [znahmka]

Stamps can be bought at post
offices, tobacconists and newspaper kiosks.

•••••• DIALOGUE ••••••
a stamp for England, please
známku do Anglie, prosím
[znahmkoo do ungli-eh proseem]
is it for a postcard or letter? na
pohlednici nebo na dopis? [po-
hled-nyitsi]
a postcard pohlednici

standby (flight) standby
star hvězda [hvyezda]
(in film) filmová hvězda
[filmovah]
start (noun) začátek [zutchahtek]
(verb) začít [zutcheet]/začínat
[zutcheenut]
when does it start? kdy to

začíná? [gudi to zutcheena]
the car won't start auto
nestartuje [owto nestartoo-yeh]
starter (of car) startér [sturter]
(food) předkrm [prJetkurm]
starving: I'm starving umírám
hlady [oomeerahm hludi]
state (in country) stát [staht]
the States (USA) Spojené státy
[spo-yeneh stahti]
station nádraží [nahdruJee]
statue socha [soHa]
stay: where are you staying? kde
bydlíte? [gudeh bidleeteh]
I'm staying at ... bydlím v
(+ loc) ... [bidleem]
I'd like to stay another two
nights (said by man/woman) rád/
ráda bych zůstal/zůstala
další dvě noci [rahd/rahda biH
zoostul – dulshee dvyeh notsi]
steak biftek
steal krást [krahst]
my bag has been stolen
ukradli mi tašku [ookrudli mi
tushkoo]
steep (hill) prudký [prootkee]
steering řízení [rJeezenyee]
step: on the steps na schodech
[sHodeH]
stereo stereo
sterling (currency) libra šterlinků
[shterlinkoo]
steward (on plane) stevard
[stevurd]
stewardess letuška [letooshka]
sticking plaster náplast f
[nahplust]
still: I'm still waiting ještě

čekám [yeshtyeh chekahm]
is he still there? je ještě tady?
[yeh – tudi]
keep still! nehýbej se!
[neheebay seh]
sting: I've been stung něco mě
píchlo [nyetso mnyeh peeHlo]
stockings punčochy
[poontchoHi]
stomach žaludek [Juloodek]
stomach ache bolest žaludku f
[Julootkoo]
stone (rock) kámen [kahmen]
stop (verb) zastavovat
[zustuvovut]/zastavit [zustuvit]
  please, stop here (to taxi driver
  etc) zastavte tady, prosím
  [zustufteh tudi proseem]
  do you stop near ...? stavíte
  blízko (+ gen) ...? [stuveeteh
  bleesko]
  stop doing that! nech toho!
  [neH]
stopover mezipřistání
[meziprJistah-nyee]
storm bouře f [bohrJeh]
straight: it's straight ahead je to
přímo před vámi [yeh to
prJeemo prJet vahmi]
  a straight whisky čistá whisky
  [chistah]
straightaway rovně [rovnyeh]
strange (odd) divný [dyivnee]
stranger (man/woman) cizinec
[tsizinets]/cizinka
  I'm a stranger here jsem tu
  cizí [sem too tsizee]
strap pásek [pahsek]
strawberry jahoda [yuhoda]

stream proud [proht]
street ulice f [oolitseh]
  on the street na ulici [oolitsi]
streetmap mapa města
[mnyesta]
string provázek [provahzek]
strong silný [silnee]
stuck zaseklý [zuseklee]
  the key's stuck klíč se zasekl
  [kleetch seh zusekul]
student (male/female) student
[stoodent]/studentka
stupid hloupý [hlohpee]
suburb předměstí [prJed-
mnyestyee]
subway (US: railway) metro
suddenly najednou [nĭ-yednoh]
suede jemný semiš [yemnee
semish]
sugar cukr [tsookr]
suit (noun) oblek
  it doesn't suit me (jacket etc)
  nesedí mi to [nesedyee]
  it suits you sluší ti to [slooshee
  tyi]
suitcase kufr [koofr]
summer léto
  in the summer v létě [vletyeh]
sun slunce n [sloontseh]
  in the sun na slunci
  out of the sun ve stínu [veh
  styeenoo]
sunbathe opalovat se [opulovut
seh]/opálit se [opahlit]
sunblock (cream) krém s
ochranným faktorem
[soHruneem fuktorem]
sunburn spálenina (sluncem)
[spahlenyina sloontsem]

sunburnt spálený sluncem
[spahlenee]

Sunday neděle f [nedyeleh]

sunglasses sluneční brýle
[sloonech-nyee breeleh]

sun lounger lehátko [lehahtko]

sunny: it's sunny svítí slunce
[sveetyee sloontseh]

sun roof (in car) střešni okno
[strJesh-nyee]

sunset západ slunce n [zahpaht
sloontseh]

sunshade slunečník [sloonech-
nyeek]

sunshine sluneční svit
[sloonetch-nyee]

sunstroke úpal [oopul]

suntan opálení f [opahlenyee]

suntan lotion emulze na
opalování [emoolzeh na
opulovah-nyee]

suntanned opálený [opahlenee]

suntan oil olej na opalování
[olay na opulovah-nyee]

super super [sooper]

supermarket velká
samoobsluha [velkah samo-
opslooha]

supper večeře f [vetcherJeh]

supplement (extra charge)
doplatek [doplutek]

sure: are you sure? (said to man/
woman) jste si tím jistý/jistá?
[stesi tyeem yistee/yistah]

sure! jistě! [yistyeh]

surname příjmení [prJee-
yumenyee]

swearword nadávka [nadahfka]

sweater pulovr [poolovur]

sweatshirt mikina

Sweden Švédsko [shvetsko]

Swedish (adj) švédský
[shvetskee]

sweet (taste) sladký [slutkee]
(noun: dessert) dezert [dezert],
moučník [mohtch-nyeek]

sweets bonbóny mpl [bonbawni]

swelling opuchlina [opooHlina]

swim (verb) plavat [pluvut]
I'm going for a swim jdu si
zaplavat [yudoo si zupluvut]
let's go for a swim pojd'me si
zaplavat [poyd[yeh]meh si
zupluvut]

swimming costume plavky fpl
[plufki]

swimming pool plavecký bazén
[pluvetskee buzen]

swimming trunks plavky fpl
[plufki]

switch (noun) vypínač
[vipeenutch]

switch off (lights) zhasnout
[zhusnoht]
(TV, engine) vypnout [vipnoht]

switch on (lights) rozsvítit
[rosveetyit]
(TV, engine) zapnout [zupnoht]

swollen opuchlý [opooHlee]

T

table stůl [stool]
a table for two stůl pro dva

tablecloth ubrus [oobroos]

table tennis stolní tenis
[stolnyee]

table wine stolní víno [veeno]

tailback (of traffic) šňůra aut
[shnyoora owt]
tailor krejčí m [kraytchee]
take (lead) brát [braht]/vzít
[vzeet]
  (accept) přijmout [prJeemoht]
  can you take me to the airport?
  můžete mě vzít na letiště?
  [moozheteh mnyeh – letyish-
  tyeh]
  do you take credit cards?
  berete platební karty?
  [plutebnyee kurti]
  fine, I'll take it dobře, beru to
  [dobrJeh beroo]
  can I take this? (leaflet etc)
  mohu si to vzít? [mohoo si]
  how long does it take? jak
  dlouho to trvá? [yuk dloh-ho to
  turvah]
  it takes three hours trvá to tři
  hodiny [turvah]
  is this seat taken? je toto
  místo obsazeno? [yeh –
  meesto opsuzeno]
  can you take a little off here?
  (to hairdresser) můžete mi
  to tady trochu sestřihnout?
  [moozheteh – tudi troHoo
  sestrJihnoht]
  hamburger to take away
  prodej hamburgerů přes
  ulici [proday – prJes oolitsi]
talcum powder pudr [poodur]
talk (verb) mluvit [mloovit]
tall vysoký [visokee]
tampons tampóny mpl
[tumpawni]
tan (noun) opálení [opahlenyee]

to get a tan opálit se [opahlit
seh]
tank (of car) nádrž f [nahdursh]
tap kohoutek [kohohtek]
tape (for cassette) páska [pahska]
  (sticky) izolepa
tape measure krejčovský metr
[kraytchofskee metur]
tape recorder magnetofon
[mug–]
taste (noun) chuť f [Hoot^{yeh}]
  can I taste it? mohu to
  ochutnat? [mohoo to oHootnut]
taxi taxi [tuksi] n
  will you get me a taxi?
  zavoláte mi taxi? [zuvolahteh]
  where can I find a taxi? kde
  mohu najít taxi? [gudeh
  mohoo nī-eet]

Taxis are expensive and in
Prague particularly there is a
risk of being ripped off. Make
sure the meter is switched on.
In fact, it might be best to avoid
taxis altogether in Prague. It is
possible to get a bus from
the airport to an underground
station and then take the underground to the centre of town.

•••••• DIALOGUE ••••••

to the airport/to the Forum Hotel,
please na letiště/do hotelu
Forum, prosím [letyish-tyeh/do
hoteloo – proseem]
how much will it be? kolik to bude
stát? [boodeh staht]
... crowns ... korun [koroon]

that's fine, right here, thanks to je
dobré, tady, děkuji [yeh dobreh
tudi dyekoo-yi]

taxi-driver taxikář [tuksikarJ]
taxi rank stanoviště taxi n
[stunovishtyeh]
tea čaj [tchī]
one tea/two teas, please jeden
čaj/dva čaje, prosím [chī-eh
proseem]
teabags porcovaný čaj
[portsovanee]
teach: could you teach me? (to
man/woman) mohl/mohla byste
mě učit? [mohul/mo-hla bisteh
mnyeh ootchit]
teacher (man/woman) učitel
[ootchitel]/učitelka
team družstvo [drooshstvo]
teaspoon čajová lžička [tchī-
ovah luJitchka]
tea towel utěrka [ootyerka]
teenager teenager
telegram telegram [telegrum]
telephone telefon
see phone
television televize f [televizeh]
tell: could you tell him ...? (to
man/woman) mohl/mohla byste
mu říct ...? [mohul/mo-hla
bisteh moo rJeetst]
temperature (weather) teplota
(fever) horečka [horetchka]
tennis tenis
tennis ball tenisový míč [–ovee
meech]
tennis court tenisový kurt
[koort]

tennis racket tenisová raketa
[–ovah ruketa]
tent stan [stun]
term (at university, school) semestr
terminus (rail) konečná stanice
f [konetchnah stunyitseh]
terrible strašný [strushnee]
terrific fantastický [fantastitskee]
than* než [nesh]
smaller than menší než
[menshee]
thank: thanks díky [dyeeki]
thank you děkuji vám [dyekoo-
yi vahm]
thank you very much děkuji
mockrát [motskraht]
thanks for the lift díky za
svezení
no thanks ne, díky [neh]
•••••• DIALOGUE ••••••
thanks díky
that's OK, don't mention it to je v
pořádku, není zač [yeh fporJahtkoo
nenyee zutch]

that: that man ten muž
that woman ta žena
that one tamten [tumten]
I hope that ... doufám, že ...
[dohfahm Jeh]
that's nice to je pěkné [yeh
pyekneh]
is that ...? je to ...?
that's it (that's right) to je ono
the*
theatre divadlo [divudlo]
their* jejich [yeh-yiH]
theirs* jejich
them* jim [yim]

for them pro ně [nyeh]

with them s nimi [snyimi]

I gave it to them (said by man/ woman) dal/dala jsem jim to [dul – sem yim]

who? - them kdo? – oni [gudo onyi]

then potom

there tam [tum]

over there tamhle [tum-hleh]

up there tamhle

is there ...? je tady ...? [yeh tudi]

are there ...? jsou tady ...? [soh]

there is ... tady je ...

there are ... tady jsou ...

there you are (giving something) prosím [proseem]

thermal springs termální prameny mpl [termahlnyee prumeni]

thermometer teploměr [teplomnyer]

thermos flask termoska

these*: these men ti muži [tyi]

these women ty ženy [ti]

can I have these? mohu dostat tyto? [mohoo dostut tito]

they* oni [onyi], ony [oni], ona

thick silný [silnee]

(stupid) hloupý [hlohpee]

thief (man/woman) zloděj [zlodyay]/zlodějka

thigh stehno

thin tenký [tenkee]

thing věc f [vyets]

my things mé věci [meh]

think myslet [mislet]

I think so myslím, že ano [misleem Jeh uno]

I don't think so myslím, že ne [neh]

I'll think about it budu o tom přemýšlet [boodoo – prJemeeshlet]

third party insurance pojištění zákonné odpovědnosti [poyish-tyenyee zahkonneh otpovyednostyi]

thirsty: I'm thirsty mám žízeň [mahm Jeezen^yeh]

this: this man tento muž

this woman tato žena [tuto]

this one tento

this is my wife to je moje manželka [yeh mo-yeh munJelka]

is this ...? je to ...?

those: those men ti muži [tyi]

those women ty ženy [ti]

which ones? – those kteří? – ti [kuterJee – tyi]

thread nit f [nyit]

throat hrdlo [hurdlo]

throat pastilles pastilky fpl [pustilki]

through skrz [skurs]

does it go through ...? (train, bus) projíždí to ...? [pro-yeeJdyee]

throw (verb) házet [hahzet]/hodit [ho-dyit]

throw away zahodit [zuho-dyit]

thumb palec [pulets]

thunderstorm bouře f [bohrJeh]

Thursday čtvrtek [chutvurtek]

ticket lístek [leestek]

(for plane) **letenka**

•••••• DIALOGUE ••••••

a return ticket to Tábor zpáteční do Tábora [spahtetch-nyee]

coming back when? kdy se vracíte? [gudi seh vrutseeteh]

today/next Tuesday dnes/v úterý

that will be 64 crowns šedesát čtyři korun [koroon]

ticket office pokladna [pokludna]

tie (necktie) **vázanka** [vahzunka], **kravata** [kruvuta]

tight (clothes etc) **těsný** [tyesnee]

it's too tight je to příliš těsné [yeh to prJeelish tyesneh]

tights punčocháče fpl [poontchoHahtcheh]

till (cash desk) **pokladna** [pokludna]

time* čas [chus]

what's the time? kolik je hodin? [yeh ho-dyin]

this time tentokrát [tentokraht]

last time posledně [posled-nyeh]

next time příště [prJeesh-tyeh]

four times čtyřikrát [chtirJikraht]

timetable jízdní řád [yeezd-nyee rJaht]

tin (can) **plechovka** [pleHofka]

tinfoil staniol [stuni-ol]

tin opener otvírák konzerv [otveerahk konzerf]

tiny malinký [mulinkee]

tip (for waiter etc) **spropitné** n [spropitneh]
see **bill**

tired unavený [oonuvenee]

I'm tired (said by man/woman) **jsem unavený/unavená** [sem]

tissues papírové kapesníky [pupeeroveh kupesnyeeki]

to: to Prague do Prahy [pruhi]

to the Czech Republic do České republiky [cheskeh repoobliki]

to the post office na poštu [poshtoo]

toast (bread) **topinka**

today dnes

toe palec [pulets]

together společně [spoletch-nyeh]

we're together (in shop etc) **jsme spolu** [smeh spoloo]

can we pay together? můžeme platit dohromady? [mooJemeh plutyit dohromudi]

toilet toaleta [to-uleta]

where is the toilet? kde je toaleta? [gudeh yeh]

I have to go to the toilet musím jít na toaletu [mooseem yeet]

Public toilets are not a common phenomenon in the Czech Republic. You will have to take advantage of toilets in restaurants and bars or at railway/bus stations and in museums etc. In public toilets, it is customary to pay on the way in. Anything up to 5 crowns is usual.

toilet paper toaletní papír [to-ulet-nyee pupeer]

tomato rajče jablko [rītcheh yubulko]

tomato juice rajčatová šťáva [rītchutovah shtyahva]

tomato ketchup kečup [ketchoop]

tomorrow zítra [zeetra]

tomorrow morning zítra ráno [rahno]

the day after tomorrow pozítří [pozeetrJee]

toner (cosmetic) toner

tongue jazyk [yuzik]

tonic (water) tonik

tonight dnes večer [vetcher]

tonsillitis zánět mandlí [zahnyet mundlee]

too (excessively) příliš [prJeelish]

(also) také [tukeh]

too hot příliš horko

too much příliš mnoho

me too já také [yah tukeh]

tooth zub [zoop]

toothache bolest zubu f [zooboo]

toothbrush kartáček na zuby [kartahtchek na zoobi]

toothpaste pasta na zuby [pusta]

top: on top of it k tomu [tomoo]

at the top nahoře [nuhorJeh]

top floor horní patro [hornyee putro]

topless nahoře bez

torch baterka f [buterka]

total (noun) celek [tselek]

tour (noun) prohlídka [prohleetka]

is there a tour of ...? existuje prohlídka (+ gen) ...? [existoo-yeh]

tour guide průvodce [proOvotseh]

tourist (man/woman) turista [toorista]/turistka

tourist information office turistická informační kancelářf [tooristitskah informuchnyee kuntselarJ]

tour operator cestovní agentura [tsestovnyee ugentoora]

towards směrem k (+ dat) [smnyerem]

towel ručník [roochnyeek]

town město n [mnyesto]

in town ve městě [veh mnyes-tyeh]

just out of town hned za městem [hnet]

town centre střed města [strJet mnyesta], centrum města [tsentroom]

town hall radnice f [rudnitseh]

toy hračka [hrutchka]

track (US) nástupiště n [nahstoopish-tyeh]

see platform

tracksuit teplákova souprava [teplahkovah sohpruva]

traditional tradiční [truditch-nyee]

traffic provoz [provos]

traffic jam dopravní zácpa [dopravnyee zahtspa]

traffic lights semafor [semufor]

trailer (for carrying tent etc) přívěs

[prJeevyes]
(US) karavan [kuruvun],
obytný přívěs [obitnee]
trailer park kemp pro přívěsy
[prJeevyesi]
train vlak [vluk]
  by train vlakem

•••••• D I A L O G U E ••••••

is this the train for Brno? jede to
do Brna? [yedeh to do burna]
sure ano [uno]
no, you want that platform there
ne, musíte jet z tamtoho
nástupiště [neh mooseeteh yet
stumtoho nahstoopish-tyeh]

trainers (shoes) tenisky fpl
[teniski]
train station železniční stanice
[zheleznitch-nyee stunyitseh]
tram tramvaj f [trumvī]
  see bus
tram stop tramvajová zastávka
[trumvī-ovah zustahfka]
translate překládat
[prJeklahdut]/přeložit
[prJeloJit]
could you translate that? (to
man/woman) mohl/mohla byste
to přeložit? [mohul/mo-hla
bisteh to]
translation překlad [prJeklut]
translator (man/woman)
překladatel [prJekludutel]/
překladatelka
trashcan popelnice f
[popelnitseh]
travel cestovat [tsestovut]
  we're travelling around jen tak

cestujeme [yen tuk tsestoo-
yemeh]
travel agent's cestovní
agentura [tsestov-nyee
ugentoora]
travellers' cheque cestovní šek
[shek]
tray podnos
tree strom
tremendous obrovský
[obrofskee]
trendy módní [mawd-nyee]
trim: just a trim please (to
hairdresser) jen zarovnat,
prosím [yen zarovnut]
trip (excursion) výlet [veelet]
  I'd like to go on a trip to …
  (said by man/woman) rád/ráda
  bych jel/jela na výlet do
  (+ gen) … [raht/rahda biн yel/
  yela na veelet]
trolley vozík [vozeek]
trolleybus trolejbus [trolayboos]
trouble (noun) problém
  I'm having trouble with …
  mám problém s (+ instr) …
  [mahm]
trousers kalhoty fpl [kulhoti]
true skutečný [skootetchnee]
  that's not true to není pravda
  [nenyee pruvda]
trunk (of car) zavazadlový
  prostor [zuvuzudlovee], kufr
  [koofr]
trunks (swimming) plavky fpl
  [plufki]
try zkusit [skoosit]
  can I have a try? mohu to
  zkusit? [mohoo]

ENGLISH ❖ CZECH Tr

try on zkusit si
can I try it on? mohu si to
zkusit?
T-shirt tričko [tritchko]
Tuesday úterý n [00teree]
tuna tuňák [toonyahk]
tunnel tunel [toonel]
turn: turn left/right zabočte
doleva/doprava [zubotchteh]
turn off: where do I turn off? kde
musím odbočit? [gudeh
mooseem odbotchit]
can you turn the heating off?
můžete vypnout topení?
[m00Jeteh vipnoht topenyee]
turn on: can you turn the heating
on? můžete zapnout topení?
[zupnoht]
turning (in road) zatáčka
[zutahtchka]
TV televize [televizeh]
tweezers pinzeta
twice dvakrát [dvukraht]
twice as much dvakrát tolik
twin beds manželské postele
[munJelskeh posteleh]
twin room dvoulůžkový pokoj
[dvohl00shkovee pokoy]
twist: I've twisted my ankle (said
by man/woman) zvrtl/zvrtla jsem
si kotník [zvurtul/zvurtula sem
si kotnyeek]
type (noun) typ [tip]
a different type of ... jiný typ
(+ gen) ... [yinee]
typical typický [tipitskee]
tyre pneumatika [puneh-
oomutika]

U

ugly škaredý [shkaredee]
UK Spojené království [spo-
yeneh krahlofstvee]
Ukraine Ukrajina [ookrī-ina]
Ukrainian (adj) ukrajinský
[ookrī-inskee]
ulcer vřed [vrJet]
umbrella deštník [desht-nyeek]
uncle strýc [streets]
unconscious v bezvědomí [vbez-
vyedomee]
under pod (+ instr)
underdone (meat) nedopečený
[nedopetchenee]
underground (railway) metro
underpants spodky fpl [spotki]
understand: I understand
rozumím [rohzoomeem]
I don't understand nerozumím
do you understand? rozumíte?
[rozoomeeteh]
unemployed nezaměstnaný
[nezuh-mnyestnunee]
United States Spojené státy
[spo-yeneh stahti]
university univerzita
[ooniverzita]
unleaded petrol bezolovnatý
benzín [bezolovnutee benzeen],
Natural [nutoorul]
unlimited mileage bez omezení
kilometrů [omezenyee
kilometr00]
unlock odemknout [odemknoht]
unpack vybalit [vibalit]
until do (+ gen)
unusual neobyčejný

[neobitchaynee]
up nahoře [nahorJeh]
(upwards) **nahoru** [nahoroo]
up there tam nahoře [tum
nahorJeh]
he's not up yet (not out of bed)
ještě není vzhůru [yeshtyeh
nenyee vzhOOroo]
what's up? (what's wrong?) **co se
děje?** [tso seh dyay-eh]
upmarket (restaurant etc) **vyšší
kategorie** [vishee kutegori-eh]
**upset stomach pokažený
žaludek** [pokuJenee Juloodek]
upside down vzhůru nohama
[vzhOOroo nohuma]
upstairs nahoře [nahorJeh]
urgent naléhavý [nuleh-huvee]
us* nás [nahs], **nám** [nahm],
námi
with us s námi
for us pro nás
USA Spojené státy americké
[spo-yeneh stahti umeritskeh]
use používat [pohJeevut]/**použít**
[pohJeet]
**may I use ...? mohu
použít ...?** [mohoo pohJeet]
useful užitečný [ooJitetchnee]
usual obvyklý [obviklee]
the usual (drink etc) **jako
obyčejně** [yuko obitchay-nyeh]

V

**vacancy: do you have any
vacancies?** (hotel) **máte něco
volného?** [mahteh nyetso
volneh-ho]
see **room**

vacation (from school, university)
prázdniny fpl [prahzd-nyini]
(work) **dovolená** [dovolenah]
see **holiday**
vaccination očkování
[otchkovah-nyee]
vacuum cleaner vysavač
[visuvutch]
valid (ticket etc) **platný** [plutnee]
**how long is it valid for? jak
dlouho to platí?** [yuk dloh-ho
to plutyee]
valley údolí [OOdolee]
valuable (adj) **cenný** [tsennee]
**can I leave my valuables here?
mohu tady nechat své
cennosti?** [mohoo tudi neHut
sveh tsenostyi]
value (noun) **hodnota**
van dodávkové auto
[dodahfkoveh owto]
vanilla vanilka [vunilka]
**a vanilla ice cream vanilková
zmrzlina** [vunilkovah zmurzlina]
vary: it varies to je různé [yeh
rOOzneh]
vase váza [vahza]
veal telecí maso [teletsee muso]
vegetables zelenina [zelenyina]
vegetarian (noun: man/woman)
vegetarián [vegeturiahn]/
vegetariánka
**vending machine prodejní
automat** [proday-nyee owtomut]
very velmi
**very little for me pro mě jen
velmi málo** [mnyeh yen –
mahlo]
I like it very much moc se mi

to líbí [mots seh – leebee]

vest (under shirt) tričko [tritchko]

via přes [prJes]

video (noun: film) video
(recorder) videorekordér

Vienna Vídeň [veeden^yeh]

view výhled [vee-hlet]

villa vila

village vesnice f [ves-nyitseh]

vinegar ocet [otset]

vineyard vinice f [vi-nyitseh]

visa vízum n [veezoom]

visit (verb) navštívit [nufsh-
tyeevit]/navštěvovat [nufsh-
tyevovut]

I'd like to visit ... (said by man/
woman) rád/ráda bych
navštívil/navštívila ... [raht/
rahda biн nufsh-tyeevil]

vital: it's vital that ... je
nezbytné, aby ... [yeh
nezbitneh ubi]

vodka vodka [votka]

voice hlas [hlus]

voltage napětí [nupetyee]

The supply is 220V, though anything requiring 240V will work.
Most plugs have two round
pins; a travel plug is necessary
for British appliances.

vomit zvracet [zvrutset]

W

waist pás [pahs]

waistcoat vesta

wait čekat [chekut]/počkat

[potchkut]

wait for me počkejte na mě
[potchkayteh na mnyeh]

don't wait for me nečekejte
na mě [netchekayteh]

can I wait until my wife/partner
gets here? mohu počkat, až
přijde má žena/můj partner?
[mohoo – ush prJi-yudeh]

can you do it while I wait?
můžete to udělat na
počkání? [mooJeteh to oo-
dyelut na potchkah-nye]

could you wait here for me? (to
man/woman) mohl/mohla byste
tady na mě počkat? [mohul/
mo-hla bisteh tudi na mnyeh
potchkut]

waiter číšník [cheesh-nyeek]

waiter! pane vrchní! [puneh
vurн-nyee]

waitress číšnice f [cheesh-
nyitseh]

waitress! paní vrchní! [punyee
vurн-nyee]

(to a younger one) slečno!
[sletchno]

wake: can you wake me up at
5.30? můžete mě vzbudit v
pět třicet? [mooJeteh mnyeh
vzboo-dyit]

wake-up call buzení telefonem
[boozenyee]

Wales Wales

walk: is it a long walk? je to
pěšky daleko? [yeh to pyeshki
duleko]

it's only a short walk není to
pěšky daleko [nenyee]

I'll walk půjdu pěšky [poo-yudoo pyeshki]

I'm going for a walk jdu se projít [yudoo seh pro-yeet]

Walkman® walkman

wall stěna [styena], zeď f [zet^{yeh}]

wallet náprsní taška [nahprus-nyee tushka]

wander: I like just wandering around líbí se mi jen tak se procházet [leebee seh mi yen tuk seh proHahzet]

want: I want a ... chci ... [Hutsi]

I don't want any ... nechci žádný ...[neHutsi Jahdnee]

I want to go home chci jít domů [yeet domoo]

I don't want to ... nechci ... [Hutseh]

he wants to ... chce ... [Hutseh]

what do you want? co chcete? [tso Hutseteh]

ward (in hospital) oddělení [od-dyelenyee]

warm teplý [teplee]

I'm so warm je mi moc teplo [yeh mi mots]

was*: it was ... bylo to ...

wash (verb) mýt [meet]/umýt [oomeet]

(oneself) mýt se [seh]

can you wash these? můžete tyhle umýt? [mooJeteh ti-hleh oomeet]

washer (for bolt etc) těsnění [tyes-nyenyee]

washhand basin umývadlo [umeevudlo]

washing (clothes) prádlo

[prahdlo]

washing machine pračka [prutchka]

washing powder prášek na praní [prahshek na prunyee]

washing-up liquid mycí prostředek na nádobí [mitsee prostrJedek na nahdobee]

wasp vosa

watch (wristwatch) hodinky fpl [ho-dyinki]

will you watch my things for me? pohlídáte mi věci? [po-hleedahteh mi vyetsi]

watch out! pozor! [pozor]

watch strap řemínek na hodinky [rJemeenek na ho-dyinki]

water voda

may I have some water? můžu dostat trochu vody? [mooJoo dostut troHoo vodi]

waterproof (adj) vodotěsný [vodo-tyesnee]

waterskiing vodní lyžování [vod-nyee liJovah-nyee]

way: it's this way je to tudy [yeh to toodi]

it's that way je to tamtudy [tumtoodi]

is it a long way to ...? je daleko do (+ gen) ...? [yeh duleko]

no way! v žádném případě! [vJahdnem prJee-pudyeh]

•••••• DIALOGUE ••••••

could you tell me the way to ...?
(to man/woman) mohl/mohla byste mi říct, kudy se jede do ...?

[mohul/mo-hla bisteh mi rJeetst koodi seh yedeh]

go straight on until you reach the traffic lights jed'te rovně, až na křižovatku se semaforem [yedyeteh rovnyeh ush na krJiJovutkoo seh semuforem]

turn left zabočte doleva [zabotchteh]

take the first on the right zabočte první doprava [purvnyee dopruva]

see where

we* my [mi]

weak slabý [slubee]

weather počasí [potchusee]

• • • • • • DIALOGUE • • • • • •

what's the weather forecast? jaká je předpověď počasí? [yukah yeh prJetpo-vyet^yeh]

it's going to be fine bude hezky [boodeh heski]

it's going to rain bude pršet [purshet]

it'll brighten up later později se vyjasní [pozdyay-i seh vi-yusnyee]

wedding svatba [svutba]

wedding ring snubní prsten [snoob-nyee pursten]

Wednesday středa [strJeda]

week týden [teeden]

a week (from) today za týden

a week (from) tomorrow od zítřka za týden [ot zeetrJka]

weekend víkend [veekend]

at the weekend o víkendu [veekendoo]

weight váha [vah-ha]

weird podivný [podyivnee]

weirdo podivín [podyiveen]

welcome: welcome to ... vítejte v ... (+ loc) [veetayteh]

you're welcome (don't mention it) prosím [proseem]

well: I don't feel well necítím se dobře [netsee-tyeem seh dobrJeh]

she's not well necítí se dobře [netsee-tyee]

you speak English very well mluvíte moc dobře anglicky [mlooveeteh mots dobrJeh unglitski]

well done! výborně! [veebornyeh]

this one as well tento také [tukeh]

well well! (surprise) ale, ale! [uleh]

• • • • • • DIALOGUE • • • • • •

how are you? jak se vám daří? [yuk seh vahm darJee]

very well, thanks děkuji, dobře [dyekoo-yi dobrJeh]

– and you – a vám [vahm]

well-done (meat) dobře propečený [dobrJeh propetchenee]

Welsh velšský [velshskee]

I'm Welsh (man/woman) jsem Velšan/Velšanka [sem velshun]

were* byl [bil], byli, byly [bili]

west západ [zahpat]

in the west na západě [zahpudyeh]

West Indian (adj)
  západoindický [zahpado-
  inditskee]
wet mokrý [mokree]
what? cože? [tsoJeh]
  what's that? co je tohle? [tso
  yeh to-hleh]
  **what should I do? co bych
  měl dělat?** [tso biH mnyel
  dyelut]
  what a view! to je podívaná!
  [po-dyeevunah]
  **what bus is it? který je to
  autobus?** [kuteree yeh to
  owtobus]
wheel kolo
wheelchair invalidní křeslo
  [invulid-nyee krJeslo]
when? kdy? [gudi]
  **when we get back když se
  vrátíme** [gudish seh vrah-
  tyeemeh]
  **when's the train? kdy jede
  vlak?** [yedeh vluk]
where? kde? [gudeh]
  **I don't know where it is
  nevím, kde to je** [neveem –
  yeh]

  **where is the cathedral? kde
  je katedrála?** [gudeh]
  it's over there je to tamhle [yeh to
  tum-hleh]
  **could you show me where it is on
  the map?** (to man/woman) **mohl/
  mohla byste mi to ukázat na
  mapě?** [mohul/mo-hla bisteh mi to
  ookahzut na mupyeh]

it's just here je to přesně tady [yeh
  to prJes-nyeh tudi]
  see way

**which: which bus? který
  autobus?** [kuteree owtoboos]

  which one? který/ktera? [kuteree]
  that one tamten/tamta [tumten]
  this one? ten/ta?
  no, that one ne, tamten/tamtu
  [neh]

**while: while I'm here zatímco
  jsem tady** [zutyeemtso sem
  tudi]
whisky whisky f
white bílý [beelee]
white wine bílé víno [beeleh
  veeno]
who? kdo? [gudo]
  who is it? kdo je to? [yeh]
  **the man who ... ten muž,
  který ...** [kuteree]
**whole: the whole week celý
  týden** [tselee teeden]
  the whole lot všechno
  [fsheHno]
whose: whose is this? čí je to?
  [chee yeh]
why? proč? [protch]
  why not? proč ne? [neh]
wide široký [shirokee]
wife: my wife moje manželka
  [mo-yeh munJelka]
**will*: will you do it for me?
  uděláte to pro mě?** [oo-
  dyelahteh to pro mnyeh]
wind (noun) **vítr** [veetr]

window (of house) okno
(of shop) výklad [veeklut]
near the window blízko okna
[bleesko]
in the window (of shop) ve
výkladě [veh veekludyeh]
window seat místo u okna
[meesto oo]
windscreen čelní okno [chel-
nyee]
windscreen wiper stěrač
čelního skla n [styerutch]
windsurfing windsurfing
windy: it's so windy hodně
fouká [hod-nyeh fohkah]
wine víno [veeno]
can we have some more wine?
můžeme dostat ještě víno?
[mOOJemeh dostut yeshtyeh
veeno]

South Moravia is the principal
wine-growing region. Central
Bohemia boasts some fine white
wines. Bohemia's wine-growing
region consists of only 1,000
acres around the town of
Mělník, but it produces at least
one good red wine, Ludmila,
and a couple of whites. Burčák,
a misty, slightly alcoholic wine,
is drunk in the autumn soon
after the harvest.

wine bar vinárna
see bar
wine list nápojový lístek
[nahpo-yovee leestek]
winter zima

in the winter v zimě
[zimnyeh]
winter holiday zimní
prázdniny [zimnyee prahzd-
nyini]
wire drát [draht]
wish: best wishes všechno
nejlepší [fsheHno naylepshee]
with s (+ instr)
I'm staying with ... bydlím s
(+ instr) ... [bidleem]
without bez (+ gen)
witness (man/woman) svědek
[svyedek]/svědkyně
[svyetkinyeh]
will you be a witness for me?
budete můj svědek?
[boodeteh mOO-yuh svyedek]
woman žena [Jena]
wonderful nádherný
[nahdhernee]
won't*: it won't start nechce to
nastartovat [neHutseh to
nusturtovut]
wood (material) dřevo [drJevo]
woods (forest) les
wool vlna [vulna]
word slovo
work (noun) práce f [prahtseh]
it's not working nefunguje to
[nefoongoo-yeh]
I work in ... pracuju v
(+ loc) ... [prutsoo-yoo]
world svět [svyet]
worry: I'm worried mám starosti
[mahm sturostyi]
worse: it's worse je to horší
[yeh to horshee]
worst nejhorší [nayhorshee]

**worth: is it worth a visit? stojí to
za návštěvu?** [sto-yee – nahfsh-
tyevoo]
**would: would you give this
to ...?** (to man/woman) **dal/dala
byste to** (+ dat) **...?** [dul/dula
bisteh]
wrap: could you wrap it up? (to
man/woman) **mohl/mohla byste
to zabalit?** [mohul/mo-hla
zubulit]
wrapping paper balicí papír
[bulitsee pupeer]
wrist zápěstí [zahpyes-tyee]
write psát [psaht]/**napsat**
[nupsut]
  could you write it down? (to
  man/woman) **mohl/mohla byste
  to napsat?** [mohul/mo-hla
  bisteh]
  **how do you write it? jak to
  píšete?** [yuk to peesheteh]
writing paper psací papír
[psutsee pupeer]
**wrong: it's the wrong key to je
špatný klíč** [yeh shpahtnee]
  **this is the wrong train to je
  špatný vlak**
  the bill's wrong účet je špatně
  [OOchet yeh shpaht-nyeh]
  **sorry, wrong number
  promiňte, to je omyl** [omil]
  sorry, wrong room (said by man/
  woman) **promiňte, spletl/
  spletla jsem si pokoj** [spletul
  – sem si pokoy]
  **there's something wrong
  with ... něco je v
  nepořádku ...** [nyetso yeh

fneporJahtkoo]
  what's wrong? co se děje? [tso
  seh dyay-eh]

X

X-ray rentgen

Y

yacht jachta [yaHta]
yard* yard
year rok
yellow žlutý [Jlutee]
yes ano [uno]
yesterday včera [fchera]
yesterday morning včera ráno
[rahno]
  **the day before yesterday
  předevčírem** [prJedefcheerem]
yet nicméně [nitsmenyeh], **už**
[oosh]

•••••• **DIALOGUE** ••••••

  is it here yet? už je tady? [yeh tudi]
  no, not yet ne, ještě ne [neh yesh-
  tyeh]
  **you'll have to wait a little longer yet
  budete muset ještě chvíli počkat**
  [boodeteh mooset yeshtyeh Hveeli
  potchkut]

yobbo klacek [klutsek]
yoghurt jogurt [yogoort]
  **natural yoghurt přírodní
  jogurt** [prJeerod-nyee]
you* (sing, fam) **ty** [ti]
  (pl or pol) **vy**
  **this is for you to je pro tebe/
  vás** [yeh pro tebeh/vahs]

with you s tebou/vámi [teboh/vahmi]

> There are two ways of saying 'you' in Czech: **ty** is the singular, familiar form used when speaking to friends, family and children – it's also used among young people and students; **vy** is the singular, polite form and is used to speak to strangers or older people; **vy** is also the form to use when addressing more than one person.

young mladý [mludee]
your* (sing, fam) tvůj [tvoo-i], tvoje [tvo-yeh]
(pl or pol) váš [vahsh], vaše [vahsheh]
yours* (sing, fam) tvůj, tvoje
(pl or pol) váš, vaše
youth hostel (turistická) ubytovna mládeže [tooristitskah oobitovna mlahdeJeh]

Z

zero nula [noola]
zip zip
could you put a new zip on?
(to man/woman) mohl/mohla byste našít nový zip? [mohul/mo-hla nusheet novee]
zoo zoologická zahrada [zo-ologitskah]

Czech-English

A

a [a] and

ačkoliv [utchkolif] although

adaptér [udapter] adaptor

adresář [udresahrJ] address book

adresát [udresaht] addressee

advokát m [udvokaht], advokátka f lawyer

agentura [agentoora] agency

agresivní [ugresiv-nyee] aggressive

ahoj [uhoy] hello, hi; cheerio

aktovka [uktofka] briefcase

aktuální [uktoo-ahl-nyee] recent

ale [uleh] but

ale ano! [uno] oh yes I do!

alergický na [ulergitskee] allergic to

amatérský [umaterskee] non-professional

ambiciózní [umbitsi-awz-nyee] ambitious

ambulance f [umbooluntseh] out-patients' department

americký [umeritskee] American (adj)

Američan m [umeritchun], Američanka f American

ampér amp

anglický [unglitskee] English

Angličan [unglitchun] Englishman

Angličanka Englishwoman

angličtina [unglitch-tyina] English (language)

Anglie f [ungli-eh] England

ani ... ani ... [unyi] neither ...

nor ...

ano [uno] yes

antikoncepce f [untikontsep-tseh] contraception

antikoncepční prostředek [untikontseptch-nyee prostrJyedek] contraceptive

antikvariát [untikvariaht] secondhand bookshop/bookstore

apartmá n [upurtmah] suite

archeologický výzkum m sing [–gitskee veeskoom] archaeological excavations

architekt m [arHitekt], architektka f architect

architektura [arHitektoora] architecture

arkýř [arkeerJ] bay window

asi [usi] about; probably

astma [ustma] asthma

atletika [utletika] athletics

atraktivní [utruktiv-nyee] attractive

Australan m [owstrulun] , Australanka f Australian

Austrálie f [owstrahli-eh] Australia

australský [owstrulskee] Australian (adj)

auto m [owto] car

autobus [owtoboos] bus; coach

autobusová zastávka [–sovah zustahfkah] bus stop

autobusové nádraží m [–soveh nahdruJee] bus station/coach station

autokempink [owtokempink] motel and campsite

automatický [owtomutitskee] automatic

automobil [owtomobil] car

automobilové závody mpl [–loveh zahvodi] motor racing

B

babička [bubitchka] grandmother

bahnitý [buh-nyitee] muddy

balení [balen-yee] package size

balet [balet] ballet

balicí papír [balitsee pupeer] wrapping paper

balíček [buleetchek] package

balík [buleek] parcel

balíková přepážka [buleekovah prjepahshka] parcels counter

balíky mpl parcels

balit/zabalit [zubulit] to pack; to wrap

balkón [bulkawn] balcony

balón [bulawn] ball

banka [bunka] bank

bankokarta [bunkokurta] card used at a cash dispenser/automatic teller

bankomat [bunkomut] cash dispenser, automatic teller

bankovka [bunkofka] banknote, (US) bill

barevný [burevnee] coloured, colour (adj)

barmanka [burmunka] barmaid

barva [burva] colour

barva na vlasy [vlusi] hair dye

barvy fpl [burvi] colours, hues

barvy-laky fpl [luki] paints

baterie f [buteri-eh] battery

baterka [buterka] torch

batoh [butoн] backpack

bát se [baht seh] to be afraid of

bavlna [buvulna] cotton

bazén f [buzen] swimming pool

bázlivý [bahzlivee] timid

běhat [byeh-hut] to run; to jog

během [byeh-hem] during

Belgie f [belgi-eh] Belgium

bělovlasý [byelo-vlusee] white-haired

benzín [benzeen] petrol, (US) gasoline

benzínová stanice f [benzeenovah stunyitseh] petrol station, gas station

berle fpl [berleh] crutches

berte ... tablety najednou take ... pills/tablets at a time

beton concrete

betonový [betonovee] concrete

bez [bes] without

bezbarvý [bezburvee] colourless

bezbolestný [bezbolestnee] painless

bezbranný [bezbrunee] defenceless

bezcelný [bes-tselnee] duty-free

bezcenný [bestsenee] worthless

bez konzervačních přísad no preservatives

beznadějný [beznudyay-nee] hopeless

bezolovnatý [bezolovnutee] lead-free

bezpečnostní pás [bespetchnost-nyee pahs] seat belt

bezpečnostní zóna [zawna]

safety zone
bezpečný [bespetchnee] safe
bezplatný [besplutnee] free (of charge)
bezprostřední [besprostrJed-nyee] immediate
bezradný [bezrudnee] puzzled
bezvadný [bezvudnee] perfect
bezvětří [bez-vyetrJee] mild weather
bezvízový styk f [bezveezovee stik] no visa required
bezvýsledný [bezveeslednee] fruitless
běžet [byeJet] to run, to go for a run
běžný [byeJnee] common
béžový [beh-Jovee] beige
bicí npl [bitsee] drums
bílý [beelee] white
bít [beet] to beat up
blahopřeji! [bluhoprJay-i] congratulations!
bláto [blahto] mud
bláznivý [blah-znyivee] mad
blbče! [bulptcheh] you idiot!
blbec [bulbets] idiot
bledý [bledee] pale
blecha [bleh-Ha] flea
blesk flash; lightning
bleskový [bleskovee] very fast
blinkr [blinkur] indicator
blízký [bleeskee] near
blížit se [bleeJit seh] to approach, to near
blondýna f [blondeena] blonde
blýskat se [bleeskut seh] to lighten
boční světla npl [botch-nyee

svyetla] sidelights
bohatý [bohutee] rich
bojácný [boy-ahtsnee] timid
bok hip
bolest f pain
bolestivý [bolestyivee] painful
bolet to ache
bonbón [bonbawn] sweet, candy
borovice f [borovitseh] pine tree
bosý [bosee] barefoot
bota m [bota] boot (shoe)
botanická zahrada [botunitskah zuhruda] botanical garden
bouře f [boh-rJeh] storm
brada [bruda] chin
bradka [brutka] beard
branka [brunka] goal
brát/vzít* [braht/vuzeet] to take
bratr [brutur] brother
bratranec [brutrunets] cousin (male)
Brit m Briton
britský British
brouk [brohk] beetle
broušené sklo n [brohsheneh] cut glass
brož f [brosh] brooch
brožura [broJoora] brochure
bruneta f [brooneta] brunette
brusle fpl [broosleh] skates
bruslení [brooslenyee] skating
brutální [brootahlnyee] brutal
brýle fpl [breeleh] glasses, (US) eyeglasses
brzda [burzda] brake
brzdová kapalina [burzdovah kupulina] brake fluid
brzy [burzi] soon
břeh [brJeH] river bank

březen [brJezen] March

břitva [brJitva] razor

bříza m [brJeeza] birch

buben [booben] drum

bude [boodeh] he/she/it will be

budeme [boodemeh] we will be

budeš [boodesh] you will be

budete [boodete] you will be

budík [boo-dyeek] alarm clock

budit [boo-dyit] to wake
  (someone)

bud'... nebo [boot^(yeh)] either ...
  or ...

budou [boodoh] they will be

budoucí [boodohtsee] future

budoucnost f [boodohtsnost]
  future

budova [boodova] building

budu [boodoo] I will be

bufet [boofet] snack bar

Bůh [booH] God

Bulhar m [boolhur], Bulharka f
  Bulgarian

Bulharsko [boolhursko] Bulgaria

bulharský [boolhurskee]
  Bulgarian (adj)

bulharština [boolhursh-tyina]
  Bulgarian (language)

bunda [boonda] jacket

butan [bootan] camping gas

bydlet [bidlet] to live; to stay

býk [beek] bull

byl [bil] he was

byla [bila] she was; they were

byla jsem [sem] I was

byla jsi [si] you were

byli [bili] they were

byli jsme [smeh] we were

byli jste [steh] you were

byl jsem [sem] I was

byl jsi [si] you were

bylina [bilina] herb

bylo [bilo] it was

byly [bili] they were

byly jsme [smeh] we were

byly jste [steh] you were

bystrý [bistree] bright

byt [bit] flat, apartment

být* [beet] to be

byt a strava [bit a struva] board
  and lodging

být na dně [beet na-dnyeh] to be
  down, to be depressed

být vzhůru [vuz-hooroo] to be
  awake

C

celkem [tselkem] altogether

celkový [tselkovee] complete

celnice f [tsel-nyitseh] customs

celní kontrola [tsel-nyee]
  customs control

celní prohlášení [pro-hlahshen-
  nyee] customs declaration

celodenní [tselodenyee] all day
  long

celý [tselee] all; whole

cena [tsena] price

v ceně [ftsenyeh] included

ceník holičských prací price list
  (in barber's)

ceník kadeřnických prací price
  list (in hairdresser's)

cenný [tsenee] valuable

cenová: I./II./III./IV. cenová
  skupina restaurant price
  categories 1/2/3/4, 1 being

the most expensive
centrum [tsentrum] town centre
cesta [tsesta] journey; road
cestovat [tsestovut] to travel
cestovní kancelář f [tsestov-nyee kuntselarJ] travel agency
cestovní pas [tsestov-nyee pus] passport
cestovní šek [tsestov-nyee shek] travellers' cheque
cestující m/f [tsestoo-yeetsee] passenger
cigareta [tsigureta] cigarette
cihla [tsi-hla] brick
cikán m [tsikahn], **cikánka** f gypsy
cimbál [tsimbahl] dulcimer
cimbálová muzika [tsimbahlovah moozika] fiddle and dulcimer folk band
církevní [tseerkev-nyee] church (adj)
cítit [tsee-tyit] to smell
cítit se [seh] to feel
citlivý [tsitlivee] sensitive
cizí [tsizee] foreign; strange
cizinec m [tsizinets] **cizinka** f foreigner; stranger
clo [tslo] customs
co?* [tso] what?
co je to? [yeh] what's this?
cože? [tsoJeh] what?
cukrárna [tsookrarna] cake shop; café; confectionery shop
cyklista m [tsiklista], **cyklistka** f cyclist
cyklistika [tsiklistika] cycling

Č

čajová konvice f [chī-ovah konvitseh] teapot
čas [chus] time
časně [chus-nyeh] early
časopis [chusopis] magazine
část f [chahst] part
často [chusto] often
častý [chustee] frequent
ČD Czech Railways
ČEDOK [chedok] Czech travel agency
Čech m [cheH] Czech, Bohemian (man)
Čechy fpl [cheHi] Bohemia
čekárna [chekarna] waiting room
čekat [chekut] to wait
čelist f [chelist] jaw
čelní sklo [chel-nyee sklo] windscreen
čelo [chelo] forehead
čepice f [chepitseh] cap
černý [chernee] black
černý kašel [chernee kashel] whooping cough
čerstvě natřeno wet paint
čerstvý [cherstvee] fresh
červen [cherven] June
červenec [chervenets] July
červený [chervenee] red
česat se [chesut seh] to comb one's hair
Česká republika [cheskah repooblika] Czech Republic
České dráhy Czech Railways
český Czech; Bohemian
čestný [chestnee] honest

Češi mpl [cheshi] the Czechs

Češka f [cheshka] Czech;
Bohemian (woman)

čeština [chesh-tyina] Czech
(language)

četl he read

čí [chee] whose

čilý [chilee] active

činohra [chino-hra] drama

čínský [cheenskee] Chinese

číslo n [cheeslo] number

číslo pasu [pasoo] passport
number

jaké je to číslo? [yukeh yeh to
cheeslo] what number is it?

číst* [cheest] to read

čistírna [chis-tyeerna] dry
cleaner's

čistý [chistee] clean

číšnice f [cheesh-nyitseh]
waitress

číšník [cheesh-nyeek] waiter

člověk [chlo-vyek] man

čokoláda [chokolahda] chocolate

čokoládový [chokolahdovee]
chocolate (adj)

ČR [cheh er] Czech Republic

ČSA Czech Airways

ČSAD Czech transport
company

čtrnáct [chturnahtst] fourteen

čtrnáctý [chturnahtstee]
fourteenth

čtvrt f [chut-vurt] quarter

čtvrtek [chut-vurtek] Thursday

čtvrtý [chut-vurtee] fourth

čtyři [chtirɈi] four

čtyřicet [chtirɈitset] forty

D

dále! [dahleh] come in!

daleko [duleko] far (away)

dálkový spoj [dahlkovee spoy]
long-distance bus

dálnice f [dahl-nyitseh]
motorway, highway,
freeway

další! [dulshee] next one please!

dáma [dahma] lady

dámská vložka [dahmskah
vloshka] sanitary towel/
napkin

dámské oděvy mpl [dahmskeh
odyevi] ladies' wear

dámy fpl [dahmi] ladies'
(toilet), ladies' room

Dán m [dahn], Dánka f Dane

Dánsko [dahnsko] Denmark

dánský [dahnskee] Danish

dánština [dahn-shtyina] Danish
(language)

daň f [dun^yeh] tax

dárek present (gift)

dáseň f [dahsen^yeh] gum (in
mouth)

dát [daht] to give

datum n [dahtoom] date (time)

datum narození [narozenyee]
date of birth

dav [duf] crowd

dávat/dát [dahvut] to give

dávat/dát přednost [prɈednost] to
prefer; to give way to

dcera [tsera] daughter

dědeček [dyedetchek]
grandfather

dědičný [dyeh-dyitchnee]

hereditary
dějiny fpl [dyay-ini] history
dej přednost give way
deka blanket
děkovat/poděkovat [dyekovut] to thank
děkuji (vám) [dyekoo-yi (vahm)] thank you
dělat/udělat [oodyelut] to make; to do
dělej! [dyelay] move!
dělit se/podělit se [dyelit seh] to share
délka length
delší [delshee] longer
demise f [demiseh] resignation
den day
deník [denyeek] diary
denní krém [denyee] day cream
denní sazba [suzba] daily rate
denní teplota daily temperature
denní tisk [tyisk] dailies
denní vinárna wine-bar open during the day
desátý [desahtee] tenth
deset ten
děsivý [dyesivee] appalling
deska board; record
déšť [desht^yeh] rain
deštivý [desh-tyivee] rainy
deštník [desht-nyeek] umbrella
detailní [deta-il-nyee] detailed
děťátko n [dyeh-tyahtko] baby
děti [dyetyi] children
dětská postýlka [dyetskah posteelka] cot
dětský [dyetskee] child's
dětství n [dyet-stvee] childhood

devadesát [devudesaht] ninety
devatenáct [devutenahtst] nineteen
devatenáctý [devutenahtstee] nineteenth
devátý [devahtee] ninth
děvčátko n [dyefchahtko] little girl
děvče n [dyeftcheh] girl
devět [devyet] nine
devizový kurs [devizovee koors] exchange rate
devizy mpl [devizi] hard currency
diabetický [di-abetitskee] diabetic (adj)
diapozitiv [di-apozitif] slide (film)
díky [dyeeki] thanks
diplomatický [-titskee] diplomatic
díra [dyeera] hole
dirigent m, **dirigentka** f conductor
diskrétní [-nyee] discreet
dítě n [dyeetyeh] child
divadlo [dyivudlo] theatre
dívat se/podívat se [po-dyeevut seh] to look
dívka [dyeefka] girl
divný [dyivnee] funny; strange
divoký [dyivokee] wild
dlouho [dloh-ho] a long time
dlouhý [dloh-hee] long; tall
dnes today
dnes večer [vetcher] tonight
do* until; to
dobírka [dobeerka] cash on delivery
dobré ráno [dobreh rahno]

good morning

dobrodružný [dobro-drooJnee] adventurous

dobrou chuť [dobroh Hoot^yeh] enjoy your meal!

dobrou noc [nots] good night

dobrovolný [dobrovolnee] voluntary

dobrý [dobree] good

dobrý den [den] hello

dobrý večer [vetcher] good evening

dobře! [dobrJeh] good!

dobře, děkuji [dyekoo-yi] very well thank you

dočasný [dochusnee] temporary

do data na obalu before date on the package

dodatečný [dodutetchnee] supplementary

dodávkové auto [dodahfkoveh owto] van

dodržet [dodurJet] to keep one's word

dohoda agreement

dojatý [do-yutee] moved

dojemný [do-yemnee] touching

dojet [do-yet] to arrive

dojíst [do-yeest] to eat up

doklad [doklut] document

dokonalý [dokonulee] perfect

dokonce [dokontseh] even

doktorka f doctor (woman)

doletět [doleh-tyet] to fly to (one's destination)

doma home; at home

domácí potřeby fpl [domahtsee potrJebi] domestic appliances

dopis letter

doporučeně [doporootcheh-nyeh] by registered mail

doporučené dopisy registered letters

doporučit [dopo-rootchit] to recommend

doprava (f) [dopruva] transport; to the right

dopravní podnik transport company

do prčic! [purtchits] hell!

do prdele! [purdeleh] shit!

doprovázet/doprovodit [doprovahzet/doprovo-dyit] to accompany

dopředu [doprJedoo] forward

dospělá f [dos-pyelah] adult

dospělí mpl [dos-pyelee] adults

dospělý m [dos-pyelee] adult

dost enough

dostávat/dostat [dostahvut/dostut] to get, to obtain

dostihová dráha [dos-tyihovah drah-hah] race course

dostihy mpl [dos-tyihi] races

dostupný [dostoopnee] accessible

dotýkat se/dotknout se [doteekut seh/dotkunoht] to touch

doufat [dohfut] to hope

doutník [doht-nyeek] cigar

dovolená leave (noun)

s dovolením [zdovolenyeem] excuse me

dovoleno allowed

dovolovat/dovolit [dovolovut] to allow

drahocenný [druhotsenee] precious

drahokam [druhokum] precious stone

drahý [druhee] dear, expensive

dramatický [drumutitskee] dramatic

drát [draht] wire

drobné mpl [drobneh] change (money)

droga drug

drogerie f [drogeri-eh] shop selling toiletries

drogy fpl [drogi] drugs

drsný [dursnee] rough

druhé: z druhé ruky [zdrooheh rooki] second-hand

druhé poschodí [posHodyee] second floor, (US) third floor

druhý [droohee] second

družstvo [droosh-stvo] team

držet [durJet] to hold; to keep

drzý [durzee] rude

dřevěný [drJevyenee] wooden

dřevo [drJevo] wood

dřez [drJes] sink

dub [doop] oak

duben [dooben] April

dudy fpl [doodi] bagpipes

duha [dooha] rainbow

duchaplný [dooHapulnee] witty

důchodce m [dooHotseh], **důchodkyně** f [dooHotkin-yeh] pensioner, senior citizen

důležitý [dooleJitee] important

dům [doom] house

Dunaj f [doonï] Danube

důrazný [dooruznee] emphatic

dusný [doosnee] stuffy

duše f [doosheh] soul

duše pneumatiky f [doosheh puneh-oomutiki] inner tube

duševní [dooshev-nyee] mental

dutý [dootee] hollow (adj)

důvěrný [doovyer-nee] intimate

důvěřivý [doo-vyerJivee] trustful

důvěřovat [doovyerJovut] to trust

dvacátý [dvutsahtee] twentieth

dvacet [dvutset] twenty

dvacetikoruna [–tyi-koroona] 20-crown coin or banknote/ bill

dvakrát denně [dvukraht denyeh] twice a day

dvanáct [dvunahtst] twelve

dvanáctý [dvunahtstee] twelfth

dvě [dvyeh] two

dveře fpl [dverJeh] door

dvojčata npl [dvoytchuta] twins

dvojdílné plavky fpl [dvoy-dyeelneh plufki] bikini

dvojitý [dvo-yitee] double

dvoudenní [dvohdenyee] two-day long

dvoulůžkový pokoj [dvohl00shkovee pokoy] twin room

dvousetkoruna [dvohsetkoroona] 200-crown banknote/bill

dvůr [dvoor] yard

dýchat [deeHut] to breathe

dýmka [deemka] pipe (for smoking)

džbán [jubahn] jug

džez [jes] jazz

džínsy mpl [jeensi] jeans

E

ekonomický [ekonomitskee]
economic
elastický [elustitskee] elastic
(adj)
elegantní [elegunt-nyee] elegant
elektrikář [elektrikarJ]
electrician
elektrické spotřebiče mpl
[elektritskeh spotrJebitcheh]
electrical appliances
elektrický [elektritskee] electric
elektrický krb [krub] electric fire
elektřina [elek-trJina] electricity
elementární [elementar-nyee]
elementary
eurošek [eh-ooroshek]
Eurocheque
evangelický [evungelistkee]
evangelical
Evropa Europe
Evropan m [evropun], **Evropanka** f
European
expozimetr light meter
expres express train; first
class

F

falešný [fuleshnee] false
fantastický [funtustitskee]
fantastic
fén hair-dryer
fialový [fi-ulovee] purple
Finsko Finland
flirtovat [flirtovut] to flirt
folklórní [folklor-nyee] folk (adj)
fontána [fontahna] fountain

forma form; shape
  ve formě [veh formnyeh] fit, in
  good shape
formální [formahl-nyee] formal
formulář [formoolarJ] form
fotbal [fodbul] soccer
fotbalové hřiště n [fodbuloveh
  hrJish-tyeh] football pitch
fotoaparát [–upuraht] camera
fotografie f [fotogrufi-eh]
  photograph
fotografovat/vyfotografovat
  [vifotogrufovut] to photograph
foukaná [fohkunah] blow-dry
  (noun)
Francie f [fruntsi-eh] France
francouzský [fruntsohskee]
  French (adj)
francouzský klíč [kleetch]
  wrench
franština [frunsh-tyina] French
  (language)
freska fresco
fritovací hrnec [fritovutsee
  hurnets] deep-fat fryer
fronta queue
fungovat [foongovut] to work

G

galanterie f [gulunteri-eh]
  fashion accessories
galerie f [galeri-eh] art gallery
garáž [gurahsh] garage (shelter)
garsoniéra [gurzoni-era] flatlet,
  small apartment
geniální [geniahl-nyee] ingenious
gramofon record player
gramofonová deska [–ovah]

record (music)
guma [gooma] rubber; eraser
gumový [goomovee] rubber (adj)
gymnázium [gimnahzi-oom]
 secondary school
gynekolog [ginekolok]
 gynaecologist

H

habsburský [hapsboorskee]
 Habsburg
had [hut] snake
hádat se/pohádat se [hahdut
 seh] to argue
hadr [hudur] rag
hala [hula] lounge; hall
halenka [hulenka] blouse
halíře mpl [huleerJeh] hellers
haló [hulo] hello
hasicí přístroj [husitsee prJee-
 stroy] fire extinguisher
hasič [husitch] fireman
havarijní pojištění [huvahri-nyee
 po-yishtyen-nyee] insurance
házet/hodit [hahzet/ho-dyit] to
 throw
hedvábí n [hedvahbee] silk
herna gambling room
hezký [heskee] handsome
historický [historitskee] historic,
 historical
hlad [hlut] hunger
 mám hlad [mahm hlut] I'm
 hungry
hladina [hluh-dyina] surface
hladina oleje oil level
hladký [hlutkee] smooth
hladový [hludovee] hungry

hlas [hlus] voice
hlasatel [hlusutel], hlasatelka f
 announcer, newscaster
hlasitý [hlusitee] loud
hlava [hluva] head
hlavní [hluv-nyee] main (adj)
hlavní nádraží n [nahdruJee]
 main station
hledáček [hledahtchek]
 viewfinder
hledat [hledut] to look for
hlídané parkoviště n car park/
 parking lot with attendant
hlína [hleena] soil, earth
hloupý [hlohpee] stupid
hluboký [hloobokee] deep
hlučný [hlootchnee] noisy
hluchý [hlooHee] deaf
hluk [hlook] noise
hmyz [humis] insect
hnědý [hnyedee] brown
hnout [hnoht] to move (change
 position)
hnusný [hnoosnee] disgusting
hodina [ho-dyina] hour
 kolik je hodin? [yeh ho-dyin]
 what time is it?
hodinářství n [ho-dyinahrJ-stvee]
 watch repairer's
hodinky fpl [ho-dyinki]
 wristwatch
hodiny fpl [ho-dyini] clock
hodit [ho-dyit] to throw
hodnotný [hodnotnee] valuable
hodný [hodnee] kind
hoch [hoH] boy
hokej [hokay] ice-hockey
Holandsko [holuntsko] Holland
holič m [holitch], holička f men's

hairdresser

holičství [holitch-stvee] barber's, men's hairdresser's

holínky fpl [holeenki] wellingtons

holit to shave

hora mountain

horečka [horetchka] fever

horko heat

horký [horkee] hot

horolozectví [horolozets-tvee] rockclimbing

horší [horshee] worse

Horská služba [horskah slooJba] mountain rescue service

horské kolo [horskeh] mountain bike

horský hřeben [horskee hrJeben] mountain ridge

hořet [horJet] to burn

hoří! [horJee] fire!

hořká čokoláda [horJkah chokolahda] plain chocolate

hořký [horJkee] bitter

hořlavý [horJluvee] inflammable

hospoda pub

host m/f [hosst] guest

hostinec [hos-tyinets] pub

hotelová obsluha [–lovah op-slooha] room service

hotovost f cash

v hotovosti [hotovos-tyi] in cash

housle fpl [hohsleh] violin

hovorný [hovornee] talkative

hovořit to speak; to talk

hra game; play

hrací [hrutsee] playing

hráč m [hrahtch], hráčka f player

hračka [hrutchka] toy

hračky fpl [hrutchki] toys

hradby fpl [hrudbi] city walls

hradní [hrud-nyee] castle (adj)

hranice f [hrunyitseh] border

hraniční přechod border crossing

hrát [hraht] to play

hravý [hruvee] playful

hrdlo [hurdlo] throat

hrdý [hurdee] proud

hrnec [hurnets] pot

hrom n thunder

hromadný [hromudnee] mass (adj)

hromobití [hromobi-tyee] thunderstorm

hrozný [hroznee] awful

hruď f [hroot^yeh] chest

hřbitov [hurJbitof] cemetery

hřeben [hrJeben] comb

hřebík [hrJebeek] nail (in wall)

hřiště n [hrJish-tyeh] playground

hubený [hoobenee] thin

hudba [hoodba] music

hudebnice f [hoodeb-nyitseh] musician

hudební festival [hoodeb-nyee festivul] music festival

hudebník m [hoodeb-nyeek] musician

hudební nástroj m [hoodeb-nyee nahstroy] musical instrument

hustý [hoostee] dense

hvězda [hvyezda] star

hýbat [heebut] to move (change position)

hymna [himna] anthem

CH

chata [Huta] chalet
chce [Hutseh] he/she/it wants
chceme [Hutsemeh] we want
chceš [Hutsesh] you want
chcete [Hutseteh] you want
chci [Hutsi] I want
chirurg [Hiroorg] surgeon
chirurgie f [Hiroorgi-eh] surgery
chládek [Hlahdek] (cool) shade
chladič [Hluh-dyitch] radiator
chladicí kapalina [Hludyitsee
  kupulina] coolant
chladný [Hludnee] cool
chlapec [Hlupets] boy
chlazený [Hluzenee] cooled
chléb-pečivo [Hlep-petchivo]
  baker's shop
chmel [Humel] hops
chobot [Hobot] trunk
chodba [Hodba] corridor
chodidlo [Ho-dyidlo] foot
chodit/jít* [Ho-dyit/yeet] to go; to
  walk
chodník [Hod-nyeek] pavement,
  sidewalk
choroba [Horoba] disease
choulostivý [Hohlos-tyivee]
  delicate
chráněný [Hrah-nyenee]
  protected
chránit [Hrah-nyit] to protect
chrápat [Hrahput] to snore
chřipka [HrJipka] flu
chtějí [Hutyay-ee] they want
chtěl [Hutyel] he wanted
chtít* [Huh-tyeet] to want
chudý [Hoodee] poor

chuť f [Hoot^yeh] appetite; taste
chutný [Hootnee] tasty
chyba [Hiba] mistake
chybět [Hi-byet] to miss
chytnout/chytit [Hitnoht/Hi-tyit] to
  catch
chytrý [Hitree] clever

I

i as well as
ideální [ideh-ahlnyee] ideal
igelitový [igelitovee] plastic
imunní [imoonyee] immune
indický [inditskee] Indian (adj)
Indie f [indi-eh] India
infarkt [infurkt] heart attack
infekce f [infektseh] infection
infekční [infektchnyee] infectious
informace f [informutseh]
  information; directory
  enquiries
informační [informutchnyee]
  information (adj)
informační kancelář f·
  [kuntselahrJ] information
  desk
injekce f [inyektseh] injection
instalatér [instuluter] plumber
inteligentní [inteligent-nyee]
  intelligent
intenzivní [intenziv-nyee]
  intensive
invalida m/f [invulida] invalid;
  disabled person
invalidní [invulid-nyee] disabled
invalidní vozík [vozeek]
  wheelchair
inventura closed for

stocktaking
Ir Irishman
Irka Irishwoman
Irsko Ireland
irský [irskee] Irish
Itálie f [itahli-eh] Italy
italský [itulskee] Italian (adj)
italština [itulshtyina] Italian (language)
izolepa Sellotape®, Scotch tape®

J

já* [yah] I
jachta [yuHta] yacht
jachtink [yuHtink] yachting
jak [yuk] how; what; the way; as
  jak se máš? [seh mahsh] how are you?
  jak se máte? [mahteh] how are you?
  jak se vám daří? [vahm darJee] how are you?
jaké: jaké je to ...? [yukeh yeh] what ... is it?
jako [yuko] as, like; in the way (of)
jaký [yukee] what; what sort
jakž-takž [yuksh-tuksh] so-so
jaro [yuro] spring (season)
jasný [yusnee] clear
játra npl [yahtra] liver
jazyk [yuzik] tongue; language
jazyková škola [yuzikovah shkola] language school
jdi k čertu! [yudee ktchertoo] go to hell!

je* [yeh] he/she/it is; it; them
  to je ... [yeh] it is·...
  je mi špatně [shput-nyeh] I feel sick
  je tady ...? [tudi] is there ...?
jed [yet] poison
jeden [yeden] one
jedenáct [yedenahtst] eleven
jedenáctý [yedenahtstee] eleventh
jedí [yedyee] they eat
jedinečný [yedyinetchnee] unique
jediný [yedyinee] (the) only
jedl [yedul] he ate
jedle f [yedleh] fir
jedlý [yedlee] edible
jedna [yedna], **jedno** [yedno] one
jednodenní [yednodenyee] one-day long, a day's
jednoduchý [yednodooHee] simple
jednolůžkový pokoj [yednolooshkovee pokoy] single room
jednosměrná silnice/ulice f [yedno-smnyernah seelnyitseh/oolitseh] one way street
jednotlivý [yednotlivee] individual
jednou [yednoh] once
jednou denně [denyeh] once a day
jedovatý [yedovutee] poisonous
jehla [yehla] needle
jeho* [yeho] (of) him/it; his
jehož [yehosh] whose
její* [yeh-yee] her; hers
jejich* [yeh-yeeH] their; theirs
jelen [yelen] red deer

jemný [yemnee] gentle; soft

jemu* [yemoo] (to) him/it

jen [yen] just; only

jen do … kg up to … kg only

jen na lékařský předpis only on prescription

jenom před spaním only when you go to bed

jen ve svátky on public holidays only

jen ve všední dny on weekdays only

jen v neděli on Sundays only

jeskyně f [yeski-nyeh] cave

jestli [yestli] if

ještě [yeshtyeh] still

ještě! more!

ještě ne [neh] not yet

jezdit/jet [yezdyit/yet] to travel; to go (by car, by sea etc)

jezero [yezero] lake

ji* [yi] her

jí* [yee] her; of her; to her; by her; he/she/it eats

jídelna [yeedelna] dining room

jídelní vůz [yeedel-nyee voos] restaurant car

jídlo [yeedlo] food; meal

jih [yiH] south

Jihoafrická republika [yiho-ufritskah repooblika] South Africa

jihoafrický [jiho-ufritskee] South African (adj)

Jihoafričan m [yiho-ufritchun], Jihoafričanka f South African

jich* [yiH] (of) them

jim* [yim] (to) them

jím* [yeem] (by) him/it; I eat

jíme* [yeemeh] we eat

jimi* [yimi] (by) them

jinak [yinuk] otherwise

jinde [yindeh] elsewhere

jiný [yinee] other

jíst* [yeest] to eat

jistý [yistee] sure

jíš [yeesh] you eat

jít* [yeet] to go; to walk

jít domů [domoo] to go home

jít nahoru [nuhoroo] to go upstairs

jít nakupovat [nukoopovut] to go shopping

jít na procházku [proHahskoo] to go for a walk

jít na záchod [zah-Hot] to go to the toilet/bathroom

jít spát [spaht] to go to bed

jíte [yeeteh] you eat

jízda [yeezda] ride

jízda na koni [konyi] horse-riding

jízdenka [yeezdenka] ticket

jízdenky, prosím [yeezdenki proseem] tickets please

jízdní kolo [yeezd-nyee] bicycle

jízdní řád [rJaht] timetable, (US) schedule

jízlivý [yeezlivee] malicious

jižně [yiJnyeh] south

jižně od [ot] south of

jižní [yiJ-nyee] southern

jméno [yumeno] name

jmenovat se [yumenovut seh] to be called

jak se jmenujete? [yuk seh yumenoo-yeteh] what's your name?

jsem [sem] I am

jsi [si] you are

jsme [smeh] we are

jsou [soh] they are

  jsou tady ...? [tudi] are
there ...?

jste [steh] you are

K

k* to; towards

kabát [kubaht] coat

kabel [kubel] cable

kabelka [kubelka] handbag, (US)
purse

kadeřnice f [kuderɟnyitseh]
hairdresser

kadeřnictví [kuderɟnyits-tvee]
ladies' hairdresser's

kadeřník [kuderɟ-nyeek]
hairstylist, hairdresser

kajuta [kī-oota] cabin

kalendář [kulendarɟ] calendar

kalhotky fpl [kulhotki] panties

kalhoty fpl [kulhoti] trousers,
(US) pants

kalkulačka [kulkoolutchka]
calculator

kámen [kahmen] stone

kamenný [kumenee] stone (adj)

kamera [kumera] movie camera

kamna npl [kumna] oven

Kanaďan m [kunuh-dyun],
Kanaďanka f Canadian

kanadský [kunutskee] Canadian
(adj)

kanál [kunahl] channel; canal

kancelář f [kuntselarɟ] office

kanoe n [kuno-eh] canoe

kanoistika [kuno-istika]
canoeing

kapalný [kupulnee] liquid

kapat [kuput] to drip; to leak

kapesník [kupes-nyeek]
handkerchief

kapesní nůž [kupes-nyee nOOsh]
penknife

kapesní zloděj m [zlodyay],
kapesní zlodějka f pickpocket

kapitán [kupitahn] captain

kapka [kupka] drop

kaple f [kupleh] chapel

kapota [kupota] bonnet (car),
(US) hood

kapsa [kupsa] pocket

kapuce f [kupootseh] hood (on
coat)

karburátor [kurburahtor]
carburettor

kartáč [kurtahtch] brush

kartáček na zuby [kurtahtchek na
zoobi] toothbrush

kartón [kurton] cardboard

karty fpl [kurti] cards

kašel [kushel] cough

kašlat/zakašlat [kushlut] to
cough

kašna [kushna] fountain

katedrála [kutedrahla] cathedral

katolický [kutolitskee] Catholic

kaučuk [kowtchook] rubber
(material)

kavárna [kuvarna] coffee bar

kazeta [kuzeta] cassette

kazetový magnetofon [kuzetovee
mug–] cassette player

každodenní [kuɟdodenyee] every
day

každý [kuJdee] every

Kč Czech Crown

kde [gudeh] where

kdekdo [gudeh-gudo] almost
  everybody

kdo [gudo] who

kdokoli [gudokoli] whoever

kdy? [gudi] when?

když [gudiJ] when

keramický [kerumitskee] ceramic

keř f [kerJ] bush

kino cinema, movie theater

kladivo m [kludyivo] hammer

klakson [klukson] horn (in car)

klasický [klusitskee] classical

klavír [kluveer] piano

klenotnictví [klenot-nyitstvee]
  jeweller's

klenoty mpl [klenoti] jewellery

kleště fpl [klesh-tyeh] pliers

klíč [kleetch] key

klíč na matice [mutyitseh]
  spanner

klidný [klidnee] calm

klika [klika] door handle

klimatizace f [klimutizutseh] air-
  conditioning

klimatizovaný [klimutizovunee]
  air-conditioned

klinika clinic

klobouk [klobohk] hat

kloub [klohp] joint

klub [kloop] club

kluzký [klooskee] slippery

kněz [kunyes] priest

kněžna [kunyeJna] duchess

kniha [kunyiha] book

knihkupec [kunyiнkoopets]
  bookseller

knihkupectví [kunyiнkoopets-tvee]
  bookshop, bookstore

knihovna [kunyihovna] library

knihovnice f [kunyi-hovnyitseh],
  knihovník m [kunyi-hovnyeek]
  librarian

knihy fpl [kunyihi] books

knír [kunyeer] moustache

kníže n [kunyeeJeh] duke

knoflík [kunofleek] button

koberec [koberets] carpet

kocovina [kotsovina] hangover

kočárek [kohtchahrek] pram

kočka [kotchka] cat

kohoutek [ko-hohtek] tap, (US)
  faucet

kojit [ko-yit] to breastfeed

kolečkové brusle [koletchkoveh
  broosleh] roller skates

kolej f [kolay] platform, (US)
  track; university hall of
  residence

kolek f stamp (on form)

koleno knee

kolik? how many?; how much?
  kolik je hodin? [yeh ho-dyin]
  what time is it?

kolínská voda [koleenskah] eau-
  de-toilette

kolky mpl [kolki] duty stamps

kolmý [kolmee] vertical

kolo bicycle; wheel

komár mosquito

komedie f [komedi-eh] comedy

komerční [komertch-nyee]
  commercial, advert

komora closet; larder;
  chamber

kompas [kompus] compass

komplikovaný [–ovanee] complicated

končit/skončit [konchit] to finish

kondice f [konditseh] form

kondicionér conditioner

kondiční běh [konditch-nyee byeH] jogging

konec [konets] end

konec dálnice end of motorway/highway/freeway

konečná [konetchnah] terminus

konečná, vystupovat! terminus, all change!

konečně [konetch-nyeh] at last

kontaktní čočky fpl [kontuktnyee tchotchki] contact lenses

kontaktovat [kontuktovut] to contact

konto bank account

kontrola jízdenek [yeezdenek] ticket inspection

kontrolovat/zkontrolovat [–lovut] to check

konverzace f [konvairzutseh] conversation

konverzační příručka [–zutch-nyee prJeerootchka] phrasebook

konvice f [konvitseh] kettle

konzerva tin

kopací míč [koputsee meetch] football (ball)

kopat/kopnout [koput/kopnoht] to kick

koruna [koroona] crown; tree top

kořen [korJen] root

kosmetika cosmetics; ladies' salon; beauty parlour

kost f bone

kostel church

kostka cube

kostnatý [kostnutee] skinny

košík [kosheek] basket

košíková [kosheekovah] basketball

košile f [koshileh] shirt

koště n [koshtyeh] broom

kotník [kot-nyeek] ankle

koupací čepice f [kohputsee chepitseh] bathing cap

koupaliště n [kohpulish-tyeh] swimming pool

koupat se/vykoupat se [vikohput seh] to take a bath

koupel f [kohpel] bath

koupelna [kohpelna] bathroom

koupit [kohpit] to buy

kouř [kohrJ] smoke

kouření zakázáno no smoking

kouřit [kohrJit] to smoke

kousat [kohsut] to bite

kousek [kohsek] a little bit

kousnout/kousat [kohsnoht/kohsut] to bite

kouzelný [kohzelnee] magic

kov [kof] metal

kovový [kovovee] metal (adj)

koza goat

kožená bunda [koJenah boonda] leather jacket

kožená galanterie f [gulunteri-eh] leather goods

kožešina [koJeshina] fur

kožešnictví [koJesh-nyits-tvee] fur shop

krabice f [krubitseh] box

krabička [krubitchka] packet

krádež f [krahdesh] theft

krajina [krī-yina] countryside

krajka [krīka] lace

král [krahl] king

královna [krahlovna] queen

kraslice f [kruslitseh] Easter egg

krásný [krahsnee] beautiful

krást [krahst] to steal

krátkodobý [krahtkodobee] short time

krátkozraký [krahtkozrukee] shortsighted

krátký [krahtkee] short

kráva [krahva] cow; stupid woman

kravata [kruvuta] tie, necktie

krejčí [kraytchee] tailor

krém cream

krém na boty [boti] shoe polish

krev f [kref] blood

krevní skupina [krevnyee skoopina] blood group

krevní tlak [tluk] blood pressure

krk [kurk] neck

kroj [kroy] traditional folk costume

kromě [kromnyeh] except

kromě neděle Sundays excepted

kroupy fpl [krohpi] hail

krucifix! [krootsifiks] damn!

krutý [krootee] cruel

krvácet [kurvahtset] to bleed

krysa [krisa] rat

křeč [krJetch] cramp

křeslo [krJeslo] arm-chair

křestní jméno [krJest-nyee yumeno] Christian name

křičet [krJitchet] to shout

křída [krJeeda] chalk

křídlo [krJeedlo] wing

křiklavý [krJikluvee] loud

křišťálové sklo [krJish-tyahloveh] crystal

křivý [krJivee] crooked

křižovatka [krJiJovutka] crossroads, intersection

křižovatka s kruhovým objezdem [kroohoveem ob-yezdem] roundabout

kšiltovka [kshiltofka] peak cap

který [kuteree] which; that

kufr [koofr] car boot, (US) trunk; suitcase

kuchař m [kooHurJ], kuchařka f cook

kuchyň f [kooHin^yeh] kitchen

kulatý [koolutee] round (circular)

kuličkové pero [koolitchkoveh] biro®

kulma [koolma] curling tongs

kulturní [kooltoornyee] cultural

kůň [kOОn^yeh] horse

kupé n [koopeh] compartment

kupovat/koupit [koopovut/kohpit] to buy

kurs [koors] exchange rate

kursy pro turistiku mpl tourist exchange rates

kurva [koorva] whore

kurva! fuck!

kurzovní lístek [koorzovnyee leestek] exchange rates

kuřáci mpl [koorJahtsi] smokers

kuřácké kupé n [koorJaht-skeh koopeh] smoking compartment

kuřák m [koorJahk], kuřačka f [koorJutchka] smoker

kus [koos] piece

kůže f [kooJeh] skin; leather

kuželky fpl [kooJelki] ninepins

květen [kvyeten] May

květina [kvyetyina] flower

květinářství [kvyetyinarJ-stvee] florist's

květiny fpl [kvyetyini] flowers

kvůli [kvooli] because of

kýchat/kýchnout [keeHut/ keeHnoht] to sneeze

kyselý [kiselee] sour

kytara [kitura] guitar

L

laciný [lutsinee] cheap, inexpensive

láhev f [lah-hef] bottle

lahodný [lah-hodnee] delicious

lahůdky fpl [luhOOtki] delicatessen

lak na nehty [luk na neHti] nail polish

lak na vlasy [vlusi] hair spray

lampa [lumpa] lamp

lano [luno] rope

lanovka [lunofka] cablecar

láska [lahska] love (noun)

laskavý [luskuvee] kind

látka [lahtkah] material

lavice f [luvitseh] bench

lázeňský [lahzen^{yeh}skee] spa (adj)

lázně f [lahznyeh] spa

lebka [lepka] skull

led [let] ice

leden January

lednička [led-nyitchka] fridge

lední hokej [led-nyee hokay] ice-

hockey

ledviny fpl [ledvini] kidneys (in body)

legální [legahl-nyee] legal

legrační [legrutch-nyee] funny

lehátko [lehahtko] deckchair

lehátkový vůz [lehahtkovee vOOs] couchette

lehkomyslný [leHkomiselnee] careless

lehký [leHkee] light

lehnout si [lehnoht] to lie down

lék medicine

lékárenská služba [lekarenskah slooJba] duty pharmacy

lékárna pharmacy

lékař m [lekurJ], lékařka f doctor

lékařský předpis [lekurJskee prJetpis] prescription

lekce f [lektseh] lesson

lepidlo glue

lepší [lepshee] better

lepší než [nesh] better than

les wood, forest

lesbička [lesbitchka] lesbian

lesklý [lesklee] shiny

lesní [les-nyee] forest (adj)

let flight

letadlo [letudlo] aircraft, plane

leták [letahk] leaflet

letecká linka [letetskah] airline

letecky [letetski] by air/airmail

letenka plane ticket

letět [letyet] to fly

letiště n [letyish-tyeh] airport

letní výprodej [letnyee veeproday] summer sale

léto summer

letuška [letooshka] air hostess,

stewardess

leukoplast f [leh-ookoplust] (sticking) plaster

lev [lef] lion

levák [levahk] left-handed person

levné zboží low-priced goods

levný [levnee] cheap, inexpensive

levý [levee] left

ležet si/lehnout si [leJet si/lenoht] to lie down

lhář m [luharJ], **lhářka** f liar

lhát [luhaht] to lie (tell a lie)

lhostejný [luhostaynee] indifferent

líbánky fpl [leebahnki] honeymoon

líbat/políbit [leebut] to kiss

líbit se [leebit seh] to like **líbí se mi to** I like it

libra pound (weight, money)

lidé mpl [lideh] people

lidová hudba [lidovah hoodba] folk music

lichý [liHee] odd (number)

límec [leemets] collar

líný [leenee] lazy

list leaf

lístek [leestek] ticket; single/ one-way ticket

lístek na autobus [owtoboos] bus ticket

lístek na metro underground/ subway ticket

listopad [listoput] November

listovní přepážka [listov-nyee prJepahshka] letter counter

liška [lishka] fox

lítost f [leetost] sorrow

litovat [litovut] to regret **to je mi líto** [leeto] I am very sorry

lízátko [leezahtko] lollipop

loď f [lot^(yeh)] boat; ship

loket elbow

lokomotiva engine (train)

loutka [lohtka] puppet

ložnice f [loJnitseh] bedroom

ložní prádlo [lohJnyee prahdlo] bed linen

lunapark [loonuh-purk] funfair

luxus [looksoos] luxury

luxusní [looksoosnyee] luxurious

lůžko [looshko] bed

lůžkový vůz [looshkovee vOOs] sleeper, sleeping car

lyžař m [liJurJ], **lyžařka** f skier

lyžařské boty fpl [liJurJskeh boti] ski boots

lyžařské vázání [vahzah-nyee] ski binding

lyžařský svah [liJurJskee svuH] ski slope

lyžařský výtah [veetuH] ski-lift

lyže f [liJeh] ski

lyžování [liJovah-nyee] skiing

lyžovat [liJovut] to ski

lžíce f [luJeetseh] spoon

lžička [luJitchka] teaspoon

M

má* [mah] my; mine; he/she/it has

Maďar m [mudyur], **Maďarka** f Hungarian

Maďarsko [mudyursko] Hungary

maďarský [mudyurskee] Hungarian (adj)

maďarština [mudyur-shtyina] Hungarian (language)

magnetofon [mug–] tape recorder

majitel m [mī-yitel], majitelka f owner

malíř m [muleerJ], malířka f painter

malířský [muleerJskee] artist's

málo [mahlo] few

malovat/namalovat [mulovut/ numulovut] to paint

malý [mulee] small

maminka [muminka] mum

manažer [munuJer] manager

manažerka manageress

manžel [munJel] husband

manželka [munJelka] wife

manželská postel f [munJelskah] double bed

mapa [mupa] map

masírovat/namasírovat [numuseerovut] to massage

maso-uzeniny [muso-oozenyini] butcher's

mast f [must] ointment

mastný [mustnee] greasy

máš: jak se máš? [yuk seh mahsh] how are you?

máte [mahteh] you have

máte ...? have you got ...?, do you have ...?

jak se máte? [yuk seh mahteh] how are you?

mateřská škola [muterJskah shkola] kindergarten

matice f [mutyitseh] nut (for bolt)

matka [mutka] mother

matrace f [mutrutseh] mattress

max. výška maximum height

mdlý [mudlee] tasteless

mé* [meh] my; mine

mě* [mnyeh] (of) me

mechanik [meHunik] mechanic

medvěd [med-vyet] bear

medvídek [medveedek] teddy bear

mého* [meho] (of) my; (of) mine

měkký [mnyekee] soft

měl [mnyel] he had

melír [meleer] highlights (in hair)

mělký [mnyelkee] shallow

mém* [mehm] my; mine

mému* [memoo] (to) my; (to) mine

méně [menyeh] less

méně než [nesh] less than

měnit/vyměnit [vimnyenyit] to change

menstruace f [mentsroo-utseh] period (menstruation)

menší [menshee] smaller

měrka [mnyerka] oil gauge

měsíc [mnyeseets] month; moon

měsíčník [mnyeseetch-nyeek] monthly

město [mnyesto] town

městská brána [mnyestskah brahna] town gate

městský [mnyestskee] municipal

městský úřad [OOrJut] municipal office

mezi among; between

meziměstský hovor [mezi-mnyestskee] long-distance

call

mezinárodní [mezinarod-nyee]
international

mezinárodní hovor
international call

mezipřistání [meziprJistahnyee]
intermediate stop

mi* [mi] (to) me

mí* [mee] my; mine

míč [meetch] ball (large)

míček [meetchek] ball (small)

míchat/zamíchat [zumeeHut] to
mix

mikrovlnná trouba [mikrovulnah
trohba] microwave

milión [mili-yawn] million

milovat [milovut] to love
milovat se [seh] to make love

milý [milee] nice (person)

miminko baby

mimo provoz out of order

ministerstvo ministry

mínit [mee-nyit] to mean

minuta [minoota] minute

mírný svah [meernee svuH]
gentle slope

miska bowl

místa pro invalidy for the
disabled

místenka [meestenka] seat
reservation ticket

místenková pokladna
[meestenkovah pokludna]
reservation office

místenkový vůz reserved seats
only

místenky fpl reservations

místní čas [meest-nyee chus]
local time

místní hovor local call

místo [meesto] seat; place

místo narození [nurozenyee]
place of birth

místo u okna [oo] window seat

mistrovství [mistrofstvee]
championship

mít* [meet] to have

mít rád [raht] to like

mít strach [meet struH] to be
scared

mladí [mluh-dyee] youth, young
age

mladík [mluh-dyeek] young man

mladý [mludee] young

mléčná čokoláda [mletchnah
chokolahda] milk chocolate

mléčné výrobky mpl [mletchneh
veeropki] dairy products

mléčný [mletchnee] milky

mlékárna dairy shop

mlha [mulha] fog

mluvit [mloovit] to speak
mluví [mloovee] the line is
engaged
mluvíte ...? [mlooveeteh] do you
speak ...?

mne* [mneh] me; of me; to me

mně* [mnyeh] (to) me

mnoho many

mnohokrát [mnohokraht] many
times
mnohokrát děkuji [dyekoo-yi]
thank you very much

mnoho štěstí [shtyest-tyee] good
luck!

mnou* [mnoh] (with) me

moc [mots] a lot
moc ne [neh] not too much

moci [motsi] can; to be able

móda [mawda] fashion

moderní [modernyee] modern

módní [mawdnyee] fashionable

modrý [modree] blue

modřina [modrJina] bruise

mohl [mohul] I was able to; you were able to; he was able to; it was able to

mohl bych ...? [biH] could I ...? (said by man)

mohla [mo-hla] I was able to; you were able to; she was able to; it was able to

mohla bych [biH] could I ...? (said by woman)

mohu [mohoo] I can

mohu ...? [mohoo] may I ...?, can I ...?

moje* [mo-yeh] my; mine

moji* [mo-yi] my

mokrý [mokree] wet

molo pier; dock

moment, prosím! wait a moment, please!

Morava [moruva] Moravia

Moravan m [moruvun], Moravanka f Moravian

moravský [morufskee] Moravian (adj)

morový sloup [morovee slohp] plague column

moře n [morJeh] sea

motocykl [moto-tsikul] motorbike

motor engine

motorový olej [motorovee olay] engine oil

mou* [moh] (by) my; (by) mine

moudrý [mohdree] wise

moucha [moh-Ha] fly

mozek brain

možná [moJnah] maybe, perhaps

možný [moJnee] possible

mrak [mruk] cloud

mráz [mrahs] frost

mrazivý [mruzivee] frosty

mraznička [mruznitchka] freezer

mražené potraviny fpl [mruJeneh potruvini] frozen food

mrtvice f [murtvitseh] stroke (attack)

mrtvý [murtvee] dead

mše f [musheh] mass

mu* [moo] him

můj* [moo-i] my; mine

muset [mooset] must; to have to

muzeum [moozeh-oom] museum

muž [moosh] man

můžete ...? [mooJeteh] can you ...?

muži mpl [mooJi] men; gents' toilet, men's room

mužský [moosh-skee] men's; male

my* [mi] we

mýdlo [meedlo] soap

mých* [meeH] my; mine

mým* [meem] my; mine; to my/mine;

mými* [meemi] (by) my; (by) mine

myslet [mislet] to think

myš [mish] mouse

myšlenka [mishlenka] idea

mýt/umýt [meet] to wash

N

na* on; onto; for; to

nabídka [nubeetka] offer

nabízet/nabídnout [nubeezet/ nubeednoht] to offer

náboženský [nahboJenskee] religious

náboženství [nahboJenstvee] religion

nabroušený f [nubrohshenee] sharp

nábřeží [nahbrJeJee] quay

nábytek [nahbitek] furniture

nad [nut] above; over

nadaný [nudunee] gifted

nádherný [nahdhernee] wonderful

nádobí [nahdobee] crockery

nádraží [nahdruJee] station; railway station

nádrž f [nahdursh] tank

nadšený [nudshenee] enthusiastic

nadváha [nudvah-ha] excess baggage

nafta [nufta] diesel

náhoda chance

nahoru [nuhoroo] up

nahoře [nuhorJeh] upstairs

náhradní díly mpl [nah-hrud-nyee dyeeli] spare parts

náhradní součástka [sohtchahstka] spare part

náhrdelník [nah-hurdel-nyeek] necklace

náhrobek [nah-hrobek] tombstone

nahý [nuhee] naked

nacházet/najít [nuHahzet/nī-eet] to find

nachlazení [nuHluzenyee] cold (illness)

naivní naive

najednou [nuyednoh] suddenly

nájemné n [nah-yemneh] rent

najezený [nī-ezenee] full (up) (not hungry)

najímat/najmout [nī-eemut/ nīmoht] to rent; to hire

najíst se [nī-eest] to eat one's fill

najít [nī-yeet] to find

najmout [nīmoht] to rent; to hire

náklad [nahklut] load

nákladní auto [nahklud-nyee] lorry

nákladní vlak [vluk] goods train

nákladní výtah goods lift/ elevator

nakoupit [nukohpit] to go shopping

nákup [nahkoop] shopping

nákupní kurs [nahkoop-nyee koors] buying rate

nákupní středisko [strJeh-dyisko] shopping centre

nákupní taška [tushka] shopping bag

nakupovat/nakoupit [nukoopovut/ nukohpit] to go shopping

nakyslý [nukislee] slightly sour

nálada [nahluda] mood

nalačno [nulutchno] on an empty stomach

náledí icy surface

naléhavý [nuleh-huvee] urgent

naléhavý případ [prJeeput] emergency

nálepka label

nalevo [nulevo] on/to the left

naleziště n [nulezish-tyeh] archaeological site

náležet [nahleJet] to belong

nám* [nahm] (to) us

namáčet/namočit [numahtchet/ numotchit] to soak

namalovat [numulovut] to paint

namasírovat [numuseerovut] to massage

náměstek [nah-mnyestek] deputy; vice-president

náměstí [nah-mnyes-tyee] square (in town)

námi [nahmi] (by) us

namočit [numotchit] to soak

naneštěstí [nunesh-tyestyee] unfortunately

nanuk [nunook] ice lolly

napětí voltage

napínavý film [nupeenuvee] thriller

napít se [nupeet seh] to have a drink

náplast f [nahplust] (sticking) plaster

naplnit [nupulnyit] to fill

náprava [nahpruva] axle

napravo [nupruvo] on/to the right

na prodej [proday] for sale

náprsní taška [nahpursnyee tushka] wallet

například [nuprJeeklut] for example

napsat [nupsut] to write

náramek [narumek] bracelet

nárazník [naruz-nyeek] bumper, (US) fender

narkoman drug addict

národnost nationality

narozen [nurozen] born

narozeniny fpl [nurozenyini] birthday

nařizovat/nařídit [nurJizovut/ nurJee-dyit] to order

nás* [nahs] (of) us

nashle [nus-Hleh] bye

nashledanou [nus-Hledunoh] goodbye

nashledanou zítra [zeetra] see you tomorrow

naslouchátko [nusloh-Hahtko] hearing aid

nasraný: jsem nasraný/nasraná (said by man/woman) [sem nusrunee/nusrunah] I'm pissed off

nástroj [nahstroy] tool

nástup [nahstoop] entrance, entry

nástupiště [nahstoopish-tyeh] platform, (US) track

nastupovat/nastoupit [nustoopovut/nustohpit] to get in, to get on

náš* [nash] our(s)

naše [nusheh], našeho [nusheho], našem* [nushem] our(s)

našemu* [nushemoo] (to) our(s)

naši [nushi], naší* [nushee] our(s)

našich* [nushiH] (of) our(s)

našim* [nushim] (to) our(s)

našÍm [nusheem], našimi*
[nushimi] (by) our(s)
naštěstí [nush-tyes-tyee]
fortunately
natáčet/natočit [nutahtchet/
nutotchit] to set (hair)
natáčky fpl [nutahtchki] curlers
natahovat/natáhnout [nutuhovut/
nutaнnoht] to stretch
natočit [nutotchit] to set (hair)
Natural [nutoorul] unleaded
petrol/gas
na účet volaného [00chet
voluneho] collect call
naučit se [nowchit seh] to learn
naušnice f [nowsh-nyitseh]
earrings
náves f [nahves] village centre
návod k použití instructions for
use
návštěva [nahfshtyeva] visit
návštěvní hodiny fpl
[nahfshtyevnyee ho-dyini]
visiting hours
navštívenka [nuf-shtyeevenka]
business card
navštěvovat/navštívit [nuf-
shtyevovut/nuf-shtyeevit] to visit
nazdar [nuzdur] hello; goodbye
na zdraví! [zdruvee] cheers!
názor [nahzor] opinion
ne [neh] no; not
ně [nyeh] it; them
nebezpečí [nebespetchee]
danger
nebezpečí lavin danger of
avalanches
nebezpečí smyku danger of
skidding

nebezpečná zatáčka dangerous
bend
nebezpečný [nebespetch-nee]
dangerous
nebo or
nebyl [nebil] he/it wasn't
nebyla she/it wasn't
nebyli they weren't
nebyl jsem [sem] I wasn't
nebyl jsi [si] you weren't
nebyli jsme [smeh] we weren't
nebyli jste [steh] you weren't
necelý [netselee] almost whole
něco [nyetso] something
nedaleko f [neduleko] not far
neděle f [nedyeleh] Sunday
nedorozumění [nedorozoo-
mnyenyee] misunderstanding
nedotýkat se do not touch
nehet fingernail
něho* [nyeho] (of) him/it
nehoda accident
nechutný [neнootnee] disgusting
nějací [nyayutsee] some; any
nějaká [nyayukah], nějaké
[nyayukeh], nějaký [nyayukee] a;
some; any
nejasný [nayusnee] unclear
nejbližší [nay-bliJshee] the
nearest
nejede v ... does not run on ...
nejhorší [nay-horshee] the worst
nejistý [nay-istee] uncertain
nejlepší [nay-lepshee] the best
nejmenší [nay-menshee] the
smallest
nejsem [naysem] I am not
někde [nyegdeh] somewhere
někdo [nyegdo] somebody

někdy [nyegdi] sometimes

několik [nyekolik] a few

nekonečný [nekonetchnee] neverending

některá [nyekuterah], **některé** [nyekutereh] some (of them); others

některý some (of them); one (of them)

někteří [nyekuterJee] some (of them); others

nekuřáci mpl [nekoorJahtsi] non-smokers

nekuřte, prosím please do not smoke

nelíbit se [neleebit seh] to dislike

něm* [nyem] him; it

nemám ... [nemahm] I don't have ...

nemáte: nemáte ...? [nemahteh] have you got ...?

němčina [nyemtchina] German (language)

Němec m [nyemets] German (man)

Německo [nyemetsko] Germany

německý [nyemetskee] German (adj)

Němka f [nyemka] German (woman)

nemluvte za jízdy s řidičem do not speak to the driver when the vehicle is in motion

nemoc [nemots] disease

nemocnice f [nemots-nyitseh] hospital

nemocný [nemotsnee] ill

nemorální [nemorahl-nyee] immoral

nemožný [nemoJnee] impossible

nemrznoucí směs f [nehmurz-nohtsee smnyes] antifreeze

němu* [nyemoo] (to) him/it

nenahýbejte se z oken do not lean out of the windows

nenávidět [nenahvidyet] to hate

není [nenyee] he/she/it is not; there is not

není tady [nenyee tudi] he's not in

není zač [zutch] you're welcome; don't mention it

neobsazovat dětmi do 12 let not for children under 12

neobvyklý [neh-obviklee] unusual

neočekávaný [neh-otchekahvunee] unexpected

neochotný [neh-oHotnee] unwilling

neomezený [neh-omezenee] unlimited

neotravuj! [nehotruvoo-i] stop bothering me!

neparkovat no parking

nepohodlný [nepo-hodulnee] uncomfortable

nepochopitelný [nepoHopitelnee] incomprehensible

nepopulární [nepopoolar-nyee] unpopular

nepořádný [neporJahdnee] disorderly

nepřesný [neprJesnee] imprecise

nepřetržitý provoz [neprJeturJitee provos] 24-hour service

nepříjemný [neprJee-yemnee] annoying; unpleasant

nepřístojný [neprJees-toynee] obnoxious

nepřístupný [neprJeestoopnee] inaccessible

nerost mineral

nerovný [nerovnee] unequal

nerozumím [nerozoomeem] I don't understand

nervózní [nervawznyee] nervous

neslaný nemastný [neslunee nemustnee] unexciting

nesmělý [nesmnyelee] shy

nést [nest] to carry

nestaví v ... does not stop in ...

neškodný [neshkodnee] harmless

neteř f [neterJ] niece

neúspěšný [neh-OOspyeshnee] unsuccessful

neustálý [neh-oostahlee] constant

neuvěřitelný [neh-oovyerJitelnee] incredible

nevhodný [nevhodnee] unsuitable

nevím [neveem] I don't know

nevinný [nevinee] innocent

nevkusný [nefkoosnee] tasteless

nevstupovat do not enter

nevyklánějte se z okna do not lean out of the window

nevystupovat! do not get off

nezajímavý [nezī-eemuvee] uninteresting

nezákonný [nezahkonee] illegal

nezaměstnaný [nezum-nyestnunee] unemployed

nezávislý [nezahvislee] independent

nezbytný [nezbitnee] necessary

nezpevněná krajnice soft verges

nezvěstný f [nezvyestnee] missing

nezvyklý [nezviklee] unusual

než [nesh] than

nežádoucí [neJahdohtsee] undesirable

ni* [nyi] her

ní* [nyee] her; of her; to her; by her

nic [nyits] nothing

nich* [nyiH] (to) them

nikde [nyigdeh] nowhere

nikdo [nyigdo] nobody

nikdy [nyigdi] never

nim* [nyim] of them

ním* [nyeem] (by) him/it

nimi* [nyimi] (by) them

nit f [nyit] thread

nízký [nyeeskee] low

Nizozemí n [nyizozemee] the Netherlands

noc [nots] night

nocleh se snídaní [notsleH seh snyeedunyee] bed and breakfast

noční klub [notchnyee] nightclub

noční košile [koshileh] nightgown

noční krém night cream

noční teplota night temperature

noční vinárna wine bar open at night

noha [noha] leg

Nor m Norwegian (man)

Norka f Norwegian (woman)

normální [normahlnyee] normal

Norsko Norway

norský [norskee] Norwegian (adj)

norština [norsh-tyina] Norwegian (language)

nos nose

nosič [nositch] porter

nosit/nést to carry

nosnost capacity

nouzový východ [nohzovee veeHot] emergency exit

novinář m [novinarJ], **novinářka** f journalist

noviny fpl [novini] newspaper

noviny-časopisy newspapers and magazines

Novozéland'an m [novozelun-dyun], **Novozéland'anka** f New Zealander

nový [novee] new

Nový rok New Year

Nový Zéland [novee zelund] New Zealand

nudný [noodnee] boring

nula [noola] zero

nůž m [nOOsh] knife

nůžky fpl [nOOshki] scissors

nyní [ninyee] now

O

oba both

obálka [obahlkah] envelope

obarvit vlasy [oburvit vlusi] to dye one's hair

občan m [optchun], **občanka** f citizen

občanský [optchunskee] civic

občanský průkaz [optchunskee prOOkus] ID card

občerstvení [optcherstvenyee] refreshments, snacks

období [obdobee] period

oběd [obyet] lunch

obědvat [obyedvut] to have lunch

obědy mpl [obyedi] lunches

oběť f [obyet^yeh] victim

obchod [opHot] business; shop

obchodní [opHodnyee] business

obchodní cesta [tsesta] business trip

obchodní dům [dOOm] department store

obchodní zástupce m [opHodnyee zahstooptseh] agent

objasňovat/objasnit [obyusnyovut/obyusnyit] to make clear; to explain

objektiv [obyektif] lens

objížd'ka [obyeeshd^yehka] diversion

oblečený [obletchenee] dressed

oblek suit

oblékat/obléknout [oblekut/oblekhoht] to dress (someone)

oblékat se/obléknout se [seh] to get dressed

obleva thaw

oblíbený [obleebenee] favourite

obloha sky

oblý [oblee] round

obnošený [obnoshenee] worn out

obočí [obotchee] eyebrow

obraz [obrus] painting, picture

obrázkový [obrahskohvee] pictorial

obrovský [obrofskee] tremendous

obsah [opsuн] contents

obsahovat [opsuhovut] to include

obsahuje [opsuhoo-yeh] it contains

obsazeno [opsuzeno] no vacancies; engaged; occupied; full up

obsloužit [opslohJit] to serve

obsluha [opslooнa] service

obsluhovat/obsloužit [opsloohovut/opslohJit] to serve

obtížný [op-tyeeJnee] difficult

obuv f [oboof] footwear

obvaz [obvus] bandage

obviněný [obvi-nyenee] accused

obvod [obvot] district

obvykle [obvikleh] usually

obvyklý [obviklee] usual

obyčejné poštovné inland postage

obyčejný [obitchaynee] ordinary, usual

obytný automobil [obitnee owtomobil] camper van

obytný přívěs [prJee-vyes] caravan, (US) trailer

obývací pokoj [obeevutsee pokoy] living room

ocas [otsus] tail

ocel [otsel] steel

očkování [otchkovah-nyee] vaccination

oční lékař [otchnyee lekurJ] eye specialist

oční stín [styeen] eye shadow

oční víčko [veetchko] eyelid

od [ot] since

odbarvovač [odburvovutch] bleach (for cleaning)

odbavení [odbuvenyee] check-in

odděleně [od-dyelenyeh] separately

oddělení [od-dyelenyee] compartment; department

oddělený [od-dyelenee] separate

oddíl [od-dyeel] club (sport)

odejít [odeh-yeet] to leave (on foot)

odešel [odeshel] he left (on foot)

odesílatel [odeseelutel] sender

oděvy mpl [odyevi] garments

odjet [odyet] to leave

odjezd [odyezt] departure

odjíždět/odjet [odyeeJdyet/odyet] to leave

odlakovač [odlukovutch] nail polish remover

odlety departures

odlišný [odlishnee] different

odměřený [od-mnyerenee] measured

odnášet/odnést [odnahshet] to take away, to remove

odpadky mpl [otputki] rubbish, garbage

odpočatý [otpotchutee] rested

odpočinek [otpotchinek] rest (sleep)

odpočívat si/odpočinout si [otpotcheevut si/otpotchinoht] to take a rest

odpoledne [otpoledneh] afternoon

odporný [otpornee] disgusting

odpověď f [otpovyet^{yeh}] answer

odpovědět/odpovídat
[otpovyedyet/otpoveedut] to
answer

odpovědný [otpovyednee]
responsible

odpovídat [otpoveedut] to
answer

odstartovat [otsturtovut] to take
off

odstín [otstyeen] shade

odstraňte z dosahu dětí keep
out of reach of children

odtáhnout [ot-tah-hnoht] to pull
away (remove)

odtahová služba [ot-tuhovah
slooJba] towing service

odvážit se [odvahJit seh] to dare

ofina fringe

oheň [ohen^yeh] fire
(ne)máte oheň? [(ne)mahteh]
have you got a light?

ohlašovna poruch faults service

ohnutý [oHnootee] bent

ohňostroj [oHnyostroy] fireworks

oholení [oholenyee] shave

ohrožovat/ohrozit [oHroJovut] to
threaten

ochutnávat/ochutnat
[oHootnahvut/oHootnut] to
taste, to try

okamžitě [okumJityeh]
immediately

okenice f [okenitseh] shutter

okno window

oko eye

okresní [okresnyee] regional;
district

okresní silnice f [okresnyee
silnitseh] country lane

olej [olay] oil

olej na opalování [opulovah-nyee]
suntan oil

omlívat/omdlít [omdleevut/
omdleet] to faint

omezení rychlosti speed limit

omluvit/omlouvat [omloovit/
omlohvut] to apologize
omluvte mě [omloofteh mnyeh]
excuse me

omyl [omil] wrong number
to je omyl [omil] you've got
the wrong number

on he; it

ona she; it; they

oni [onyi] they

ono it

ony they

opakovat/zopakovat [opukovut]
to repeat

opálený [opahlenee] suntanned

opalovat se/opálit se [opahlovut
seh/opahlit seh] to sunbathe; to
get a tan

opatrný [oputurnee] careful

opékač topinek [opekutch]
toaster

operace f [operutseh] operation

opěrka hlavy [opyerka] headrest

opilec [opilets] drunkard

opilý [opilee] drunk

opouštět/opustit [opohshtyet/
opoostyit] to leave

opozdit se [opozdyit seh] to be
late

opravdový [opruvdovee] true

opravdu? [opruvdoo] really?, is
that so?

opravený [opruvenee] repaired

opravit [opruvit] to mend; to repair

opravna [opruvna] repair shop

opravna automobilů [owtomobiloo] garage, service station

opravovat/opravit [opruvovut/opruvit] to mend; to repair

opravy [opruvi] repairs

optik optician

opuchlý [opooHlee] swollen

opustit [opoostyit] to leave

opuštěný [opoosh-tyenee] left behind

oranžový [orunJovee] orange (colour)

organizace f [orgunizutseh] organisation

organizovat [orgunizovut] to organize

orloj [orloy] clock; town clock

osamělý [osumnyelee] lonely

oslava [osluva] party (celebration)

osm [osum] eight

osmdesát [osumdesaht] eighty

osmnáct [osumnahtst] eighteen

osmnáctý [osumnahtstee] eighteenth

osmý [osmee] eighth

osoba person

osobní vlak [osobnyee] local train

osobní výtah customer lift/elevator; passenger lift/elevator

ospalý [ospulee] sleepy

ostrov island

ostrý [ostree] sharp

ostří [ostrJee] edge

ostříhání [ostrJeeahah-nyee] haircut

ostřikovač skla [ostrJikovutch] windscreen washer

ostýchavý [osteeHuvee] shy

osuška [osooshka] bath towel

osvobození liberation

ošklivý [oshklivee] ugly

otáčet/otočit [otahtchet/ototchit] to turn

otázka [otahska] question

otec [otets] father

oteklý [oteklee] swollen

otevírací doba [oteveerutsee] opening times

otevřeno [otevrJeno] open

otevřený [otevrJenee] open

otevřít [otevrJeet] to open

otočit [ototchit] to turn

otok swelling

otrava [otruva] poisoning

otrava jídlem [yeedlem] food poisoning

otvírák konzerv [otveerahk konzerf] tin-opener

otvírák lahví [luhvee] bottle-opener

otvírat/otevřít [otveerut/otevrJeet] to open

ovce f [oftseh] sheep

ovoce-zelenina [ovotseh-zelenyina] fruit and vegetables

ozářený [ozahrJenee] lit, lighted

oznamovací tón [oznumovutsee tawn] dialling tone

P

padák [pudahk] parachute

padat/upadnout [pudut/ oopudnoht] to fall

padělek [pudyelek] forgery

padesát [pudesaht] fifty

padesátikoruna [pudesah- tyikoroona] 50-crown coin or banknote/bill

pádlo [pahdlo] paddle

pahorek [puhorek] hill

páchnoucí [pahнnohtsee] smelly

páka [pahka] lever

palác [pulahts] palace

palec [pulets] toe

pálit [pahlit] to burn

pálivý [pahlivee] hot (spicy)

paluba [pulooba] deck

palubní vstupenka [paloob-nyee fstoopenka] boarding pass

památník [pumahtnyeek] monument

pamatovat si/zapamatovat si [zupumutovut si] to remember

pan [pun] Mr

pán [pahn] gentleman

pane [puneh] Mr; sir

panelák [punelahk] apartment block

panenka [punenka] doll

pánev f [pahnef] frying pan

paní [punyee] Mrs; married; madam

páni mpl [pahnyi] gents' toilet, men's room

pánské oděvy mpl [pahnskeh odyevi] menswear

pantofle mpl [puntofleh] slippers

papír [pupeer] paper

papírnictví [pupeer-nyitstvee] stationer's

papírový kapesník [pupeerovee kupesnyeek] tissue, Kleenex®

pár pair

paragon [purugon] receipt

parfém [purfem] perfume

parkovat/zaparkovat [zupurkovut] to park

parkoviště [purkovishtyeh] car park, parking lot

parný [purnee] hot, sultry

pas [pus] passport

pás [pahs] waist

pasáž [pusahsh] archway

pasažér m [pusuʌair]/**pasažérka** f passenger

pásek [pahsek] belt; cassette

pasová kontrola passport control

pasta na zuby [pusta na zoobi] toothpaste

pastelky fpl [pustelki] crayons

pastilky fpl [pustilki] throat pastilles

pata [puta] heel

pátek [pahtek] Friday

patnáct [putnahtst] fifteen

patnáctý [putnahtstee] fifteenth

patro [putro] floor

patrové postele fpl [putroveh posteleh] bunk beds

pátý [pahtee] fifth

pavouk [puvohk] spider

paže f [puʌeh] arm

péct* [petst] to bake; to roast; to grill

pečlivý [petchlivee] neat

pekař [pekarJ] baker

pekařství [pekurJ-stvee] baker's shop

pěkně oblečený [pyeknyeh obletchenee] well-dressed

pěkný [pyeknee] beautiful; pretty; fine (weather)

pěna do koupele [pyena do kohpeleh] bath foam

pěna na holení [holenyee] shaving foam

peněženka [penyeJenka] purse

peněžní poukázka [penyeJnyee pohkahska] money order

peníze mpl [penyeezeh] money

penzión [penzi-awn] boarding house

perfektní [perfektnyee] perfect

perla pearl

pero pen

peří [perJee] feather

peřina [perJina] duvet

pes dog

pěšina [pyeshina] path

pěšinka [pyeshinka] parting

pěší zóna pedestrian precinct

pěšky [pyeshki] on foot

pět [pyet] five

pětisetkoruna [pyetiset-koroona] 500-crown banknote/bill

píchat/píchnout [peeHut/ peeHnoht] to sting; to prick

píchnutí [peeHnootyee] puncture

pikantní [pikuntnyee] savoury

pila seesaw

pilník na nehty [pilnyeek na neHti] nailfile

pilný [pilnee] fast

pilulka [piloolka] pill

pinzeta tweezers

písek [peesek] sand

píseň [peesen^(yeh)] song

pistole [pistoleh] gun

pít/napít se [peet/nupeet seh] to drink

pitná voda [pitnah] drinking water

pitomec [pitomets] idiot
pitomče! f [pitomtcheh] you idiot!

pivnice f [pivnyitseh] pub

placené parkoviště paying car park/parking lot

plachetnice f [pluHet-nyitseh] sailing boat

plachta [pluHta] sail

plakat [plukut] to cry

plakát [plukaht] poster

plánovaný let [plahnovunee] scheduled flight

plášť [plahsht^(yeh)] overcoat

plášť do deště [deshtyeh] raincoat

pláštěnka [plahshtyenka] raincoat

platební karta [plutebnyee kurta] credit card

platit/zaplatit [zuplutyit] to pay
platit v hotovosti [vhotovostyi] to pay cash

platnost 35 minut od označení valid for 35 minutes after the ticket has been validated

platný [plutnee] valid

plavání [pluvahnyee] swimming

plavat [pluvut] to swim

plavčík [plufcheek] lifeguard

plavecký bazén [pluvetskee

buzen] swimming pool

plavky fpl [plufki] swimming costume; swimming trunks

plavky vcelku [ftselkoo] one-piece swimsuit

plenka nappy, diaper

ples ball, dance

plešatý [pleshutee] bald

plést/uplést [oopletst] to knit

pleť f [plet^yeh] complexion

pleťová voda toilet water

pleťové mléko [pletyoveh] skin lotion

pleťový čisticí krém [pletyovee chis-tyitsee] cleansing cream

pleťový krém cold cream

plíce fpl [pleetseh] lungs

plná penze [pulnah penzeh] full board

plnovous [pulnovohs] beard

plný [pulnee] full

plochý [ploHee] flat (level)

plomba filling (in tooth)

plot fence

plyn [plin] accelerator; gas

plynulý [plinoolee] fluent

pneumatika [puneh-oohmutika] tyre

PNS Mail and Newspaper Service

po after

pocit [potsit] feeling

počasí [potchusee] weather

počáteční [potchahtetch-nyee] initial

počítač [potcheetutch] computer

počkat [potchkut] to wait

počkejte! [potchkayteh] wait!

počkejte na mě! [mnyeh] wait

for me!

pod [pot] below; under

podací lístek [podutsee leestek] postal receipt

podávejte chlazené serve chilled

poděkovat [podyekovut] to thank

podělit se [podyelit seh] to share

podepsat [podepsut] to sign

podchod [potHot] pedestrian underpass

podívaná [podyeevunah] show

podívat se [podyeevut seh] to look

podivný [podyivnee] strange, peculiar, weird

podjezd [podyest] pedestrian underpass

podkladový krém [potkludovee] foundation cream

podkroví [potkrovee] attic

podlaha [podluha] floor (of room)

podloubí [podlohbee] arcade

podnebí [podnebee] climate

podnik [podnyik] enterprise

podnos tray

podobný [podobnee] similar

podpis signature

podprsenka [potpursenka] bra

podrážka [podrahshka] sole (of shoe)

podrobný [podrobnee] detailed

podzim autumn, (US) fall

pohádat se [pohahdut seh] to argue

pohlaví [po-Hluvee] sex; sexual

pohlavní choroby fpl [Horobi] VD

pohled [po-hlet] view

pohlednice f [po-hlednyitseh]

postcard

pohnout [po-hnoht] to move a
little

pohodlný [po-hodulnee]
comfortable

pohoří [po-horJee] mountain
range

pohostinnost f [po-hostyinost]
hospitality

pohostinství [po-hostyinstvee]
pub

pohotovostní služba
emergencies

pohraničí [po-hrunyitchee]
border region

pohřeb [po-hrJep] funeral

pochopitelný [po-Hopitelnee]
understandable

pojďte dál! [poyt^{yeh}teh dahl]
come in!

pojistka [po-yistka] fuse

pojištění [po-yishtyenyee]
insurance

pokaždé [pokuJdeh] every time

pokažený [pokuJenee] faulty;
broken

pokládat/položit [poklahdut/
poloJit] to put

pokladna [pokludna] till, cash
desk; cashier; ticket office

poklička [poklitchka] lid

pokoj [pokoy] room

pokoj pro dvě osoby [dvyeh
osobi] double room

pokojská [pokoyskah]
chambermaid

pokrývka [pokreefka] quilt;
blanket

Polák m [polahk] Pole (man)

pole n [poleh] field

poledne n [poledneh] midday

políbit [poleebit] to kiss

police f [politseh] shelf

policejní ředitelství [politsaynee
rJeh-dyitelstvee] police
headquarters

policejní stanice f [stunyitseh]
police station

policie f [politsi-eh] police

policista m [politsista]
policeman

policistka policewoman

politická strana [polititskah
struna] political party

politický [polititskee] political

politika politics

polytý [politee] wet

Polka f Pole (woman)

polknout [pol-knoht] to swallow

polní cesta [polnyee tsesta] dirt
road

polo- half-

polodrahokam [polodruhokam]
semi-precious stone

pololetí [pololetyee] half-year

polopenze f [polopenzeh]
halfboard

položit [poloJit] to put

Polsko Poland

polský [polskee] Polish (adj)

polštář [polshtarJ] pillow

polština [polsh-tyina] Polish
(language)

polykat/polknout [polikut/pol-
knoht] to swallow

pomáhat/pomoci [pomah-hut/
pomotsi] to help

pomalu [pomuloo] slowly

pomalý [pomulee] slow

pomník [pomnyeek] memorial

pomoc [pomots] help

  pomoc! help!

pomoci [pomotsi] to help

pondělí [pondyelee] Monday

ponožky fpl [ponoshki] socks

popelnice f [popelnyitseh]
  dustbin, trashcan

popelník [popelnyeek] ashtray

popisovat/popsat [popisovut/
  popsut] to describe

poplach [popluH] alarm

poplatek [poplutek] fee; charge

popsat [popsut] to describe

poptávka [poptahfka] demand

populární [popoolarnyee]
  popular

populární hudba [hoodba] pop
  music

poradit [porudyit] to advise

porazit [poruzit] to knock down

porce [portseh] portion

porcelán [portselahn] china

porucha [porooHa] breakdown
  (car); out of order

pořad [porJut] feature

pořádek [porJahdek] order
  v pořádku [fporJahtkoo] OK, all
  right

posadit se [posudyit seh] to sit
  down

posádka [posahtka] crew

poschodí [posHodyee] floor
  (storey)

posílat/poslat [poseelut/poslut] to
  send

poslanec [poslunets] deputy

poslanecký [poslunetskee]
  deputy (adj)

poslat [poslut] to send

poslat poštou [poshtoh] to post,
  to mail

poslat za adresátem
  [udresahtem] to forward (mail)

poslední [poslednyee] last

poslouchat [poslohHut] to listen
  to

poslušný [poslooshnee] obedient

postel f bed

poškozovat/poškodit
  [poshkozovut/poshkodyit] to
  damage

pošta [poshta] post office; mail

pošťák [poshtyahk] postman

poštovní schránka [poshtovnyee
  sHrahnka] letterbox, mailbox

poštovní směrovací číslo
  [smnyerovutsee cheeslo]
  postcode, zip code

potápět se/potopit se [potahpyet
  seh] to dive; to sink

potěšení [potyeshenyee] pleasure

potěšený [potyeshenee] pleased

potěšit [potyeshit] to please

potit se [potyit seh] to sweat

potkávat/potkat [potkahvut/
  potkut] to meet

potok brook

potom then

potopit se [seh] to dive; to sink

potraviny fpl [potruvini]
  groceries

potřebovat [potrJebovut] to need

potvrdit [potvurdyit] to confirm

pouť f [pohtᵞᵉʰ] funfair

pouze pro dopravní obsluhu for
  authorised vehicles only

pouze pro personál staff only

pouze v doprovodu rodičů must be accompanied by parents

použití a dávkování usage and dosage

povlečení [povletchenyee] bedding

pozdě [pozdyeh] late

pozdrav Pánbůh! [pozdruf ·pahnbooH] bless you!

pozítří [pozeetrJee] the day after tomorrow

poznávat/poznat [poznahvut/ poznut] to recognize

pozor! attention!, look out!; caution!

pozor, děti! caution, children (crossing)!

pozor! na cestě se pracuje caution! roadworks

pozorovat/zpozorovat [spozorovut] to watch; to notice

pozvání [pozvahnyee] invitation

pozvat/zvát [pozvut/zvaht] to invite

požádat/žádat [poJahdut] to ask for; to demand

požár [poJar] fire (emergency)

požární útvar [poJarnyee OOtvur] fire brigade

požehnání [poJehnahnyee] blessing

práce f [prahtseh] work

práce na silnici f roadworks

pracný [prutsnee] laborious

pracovat [prutsovut] to work

pracovitý [prutsovitee] hard-working, diligent

pracovní den [prutsovnyee] working day

pračka [prutchka] washing machine

prádelna [prahdelna] laundry (place)

prádlo [prahdlo] laundry, washing; underwear

Praha [pruha] Prague

prachovka [pruHofka] duster

praktický [pruktitskee] practical

pramen [prumen] spring (water)

prapor [prupor] flag

prase n [pruseh] pig

prášek [prahshek] pill; powder

prášek na praní [prunyee] washing powder

prášek na spaní [spunyee] sleeping pill

prát [praht] to do the washing

prát se [seh] to fight

pravdivý [pruvdyivee] true

pravidelný [pruvidelnee] regular

pravidla silničního provozu [pruvidla silnyitch-nyeeho provozoo] highway code

pravidlo [pruvidlo] rule

právnička f [prahv-nyitchka]/ právník m [prahvnyeek] lawyer

pravý [pruvee] genuine

prázdná pneumatika [prahzdnah puneh-oomutika] flat tyre

prázdninový [prahzdnyinovee] holiday (adj)

prázdniny fpl [prahz-dnyini] holidays, vacation

prázdný [prahzdnee] empty; vacant

pražský [prushskee] Prague (adj)

preferovat [−ovut] to prefer

prezervativ [prezervutif] condom

princ m [prints] prince

princezna f [printsezna] princess

pro for

  pro mě [mnyeh] for me

  pro tebe [tebeh] for you

procento [protsento] per cent

proč? [protch] why?

prodaný [produnee] sold

prodat [produt] to sell

prodavač m [produvutch],

  prodavačka f shop assistant

prodavač květin [kvyetyin] florist

prodávat/prodat [prohdahvut] to

  sell

prodej [proday] sale

prodejna [prodayna] shop

prodejní kurs [prodaynyee koors]

  selling rate

prodloužený [prodlohJenee]

  prolonged

prodlužovačka [prodlooJovutchka]

  extension lead

procházet se/projít se [proHahzet

  seh/pro-yeet] to walk around

procházka [proHahska] walk

projímadlo [pro-yeemudlo]

  laxative

projít se [pro-yeet] to walk

  around

proměnlivý [pro-rɪnyenlivee]

  changeable

promiňte [promin^yeh teh] sorry

pronájem [pronī-em] hire;

  letting

pronájem automobilů

  [owtomobiloo] car rental

pronájimat/pronajmout [pronī-

imut/pronīmoht] to hire, to

  rent; to let

pronajmutí: k pronajmutí

  [pronīmoo-tyee] for hire, to

  rent

prosím [proseem] please; here

  you are; you're welcome,

  don't mention it

  prosím? pardon (me)?

  prosím vás excuse me

prosinec [prosinets] December

prostěradlo [prostyerudlo] sheet

prostředek [prostrJedek] means

prostřední [prostrJed-nyee]

  middle

prošlý [proshlee] expired;

  overdue

proti [protyi] opposite; against

protože [protoJeh] as, since;

  because

proud [proht] stream

provaz [provus] rope

provázek [provahzek] string

provoz [provos] traffic

provozní doba [provoznyee]

  opening hours

pro zásobování for delivery

  only

prs [purs] breast

pršet [purshet] to rain

  prší [purshee] it's raining

prst [purst] finger

prsten [pursten] ring (on finger)

prudký [prootkee] steep

průhledny [proo-hlednee]

  transparent

průchod zakázán no

  thoroughfare

průjem [proo-yem] diarrhoea

průjezd zakázán no thoroughfare (on foot)

průkaz [prOOkus] card; certificate; licence

průměrný [prOO-mnyernee] average

průmyslový [prOOmislovee] industrial

průsmyk [prOOsmik] mountain pass

průvan [prOOvun] draught

průvodce m [prOOvotseh] guide (man); guidebook

průvodčí (m/f) [prOOvotchee] conductor (on train)

průvodkyně f [prOOvotki-nyeh] guide (woman)

pružina [prOOJina] spring (in seat etc)

pružný [prOOJnee] elastic

první [purvnee] first

první pomoc [pomots] first aid

první poschodí [pos-Hodyee] first floor, (US) ground floor

první třídou [purvnee trJeedoh] first class (travel etc)

první třídu! [trJeedoo] first class!

přání [prJahnyee] wish; congratulations

před [prJet] before; in front of

předčíslí [prJet-cheeslee] dialling code

předek [prJedek] ancestor; front (part)

předeprat prádlo [prJedeprut prahdlo] to prewash

předevčírem [prJedef-cheerem] the day before yesterday

předchozí [prJetHozee] preceding

předjíždět/předjet [prJedyeeJ-dyet/ prJedyet] to overtake

předloni [prJedlonyi] the year before last

předložit [prJedloJit] to show; to submit

předložte jízdenky! tickets please!

předměstí [prJed-mnyestyee] suburbs

přední [prJednee] front (adj)

přední světla [svyetla] headlights

přednost [prJednost] preference; priority

přednost v jízdě right of way

předpověď f [prJetpovyet^yeh] forecast

předpověď počasí [potchusee] weather forecast

předprodej [prJetproday] advance booking

předseda vlády [prJetseda vlahdi] prime minister

představovat/představit [prJedstuvovut/prJetstuvit] to introduce

přehánět/přehnat [prJehah-nyet/ prJehnut] to exaggerate

přeháňka [prJehahn^yehka] shower (rain)

přehnat [prJehnut] to exaggerate

přecházet/přejít [prJeHahzet/ prJeh-yeet] to cross

přechod [prJeHot] crossing

přechod pro chodce [Hotseh] pedestrian crossing

přejet [prJeh-yet] to run over; to miss

přejímka zboží closed for deliveries

přejít [prJeh-yeet] to cross

překládat/přeložit [prJeklahdut/ prJeloJit] to translate; to reload

překvapení [prJekvupenyee] surprise

překvapený [prJekvupenyee] surprised

překvapivý [prJekvupivee] surprising

přeliv [prJelif] tint (hair)

přeložit [prJeloJit] to translate; to reload

přenos [prJenos] transmission, broadcast

přenosná kamínka npl [prJehosnah kumeenka] heater; portable stove

přepadení f [prJepudenyee] hold-up

přepojím [prJepo-yeem] I will transfer you

přes [prJes] over; across; through

přesedat/přesednout [prJesedut/ prJesednoht] to change (trains)

přesnídávka [prJes-nyeedahfka] mid-morning snack

převléknout se [prJevleknoht seh] to change (clothes), to get changed

převodovka [prJevodofka] gearbox

přezdívka [prJezdeefka] nickname

při [prJi] during, close at

přibarveno contains artificial colouring

příběh [prJeebyeH] story

příbory mpl [prJeebori] cutlery

příbuzní mpl [prJeebooznyee] relatives

příčina [prJeetchina] cause

přihodit se [prJi-hodyit seh] to happen

přicházet/přijít [prJi-Hahzet/prJi-yeet] to come

přijdu hned [prJeedoo hnet] back in a moment

příjem [prJee-yem] receiving

příjemce m [prJee-yemtseh] addressee

příjemný [prJee-yemnee] pleasant

přijet [prJi-yet] to arrive

příjezd [prJee-yest] arrival

přijímat/přijmout [prJi-yeemut/ prJeemoht] to receive

přijít [prJi-yeet] to come

přijíždět/přijet [prJi-yeeJdyet/prJi-yet] to arrive

příjmení [prJee-menyee] surname

přijmout [prJeemoht] to receive

příklad [prJeeklut] example

přílety mpl arrivals

příliš [prJeelish] too

příliš časně [chusnyeh] too early

příliš mnoho too much

přímá volba [prJeemah] direct dialling

přímo [prJeemo] straight ahead, straight on; directly

přímý [prJeemee] direct

přímý let direct flight

přinášet/přinést [prJinahshet/
prJinest] to bring

přinejmenším [prJinaymensheem]
at least

přinést [prJinest] to bring

připravený [prJipruvenee] ready

připravovat/připravit
[prJipruvovut/prJipruvit] to
prepare

příroda [prJeeroda] nature

přirozený [prJirozenee] natural

příruční zavazadlo
[prJeerootchnyee zuvuzadlo]
hand luggage/baggage

přistávat/přistát [prJistahvut/
prJistaht] to land

přístroj [prJeestroy] device

přišel [prJishel] he came

příští [prJeeshtyee] next

přitažlivý [prJituJlivee] attractive

přítel [prJeetel] friend;
boyfriend

přítelkyně f [prJeetelkinyeh]
friend; girlfriend

přívěs [prJeevyes] trailer

přívoz [prJeevos] ferry

přízemí [prJeezemee] ground
floor, (US) first floor;
downstairs

přízvuk [prJeezvook] accent

psací papír [psutsee pupeer]
writing paper

psací stroj [stroy] typewriter

psát/napsat [psaht/nupsut] to
write

PSČ postcode, zipcode

pták [ptahk] bird

publikum n [pooblikoom]

audience

pudr [poodr] talcum powder

puchýř [pooHeerJ] blister

půjčit [poo-itchit] to lend

půjčká [poo-itchka] loan

půjčovat/půjčit [poo-itchovut/poo-
itchit] to lend

půjčovna aut [poo-itchovna owt]
car rental

půjčovna loděk [lodyek] rowing
boats for hire/to rent

půjčovna lyží [liJee] skis for
hire/to rent

půl [pool] half

půl hodiny [pool ho-dyini] half
an hour

půlka [poolka] half

půlnoc [poolnots] midnight

pulovr [poolovr] sweater

pult [poolt] counter

pumpa [poompa] pump

punčocháče fpl [poontcho-
Hahtcheh] tights, pantyhose

punčochy fpl [poontchoHi]
stockings

pupínek [poopeenek] spot
(pimple)

puška [pooshka] gun (rifle)

pyj [pi-i] penis

pyšný [pishnee] proud

pyžamo [piJumo] pyjamas

R

rád [raht] glad

radit/poradit [rudyit] to advise

radnice f [rudnyitseh] town hall

Rakousko [rukohsko] Austria

rakouský [rukohskee] Austrian

Rakušan m [rukooshun], **Rakušanka** f Austrian
rameno [rumeno] shoulder
ramínko na šaty [rumeenko na shuti] coathanger
ranní [runyee] morning (adj)
ráno [rahno] morning
recepce f [retseptseh] reception
recepční m/f [retseptchnyee] receptionist
recept [retsept] prescription; recipe
reflektor light (on car)
refundovat [–dovut] to refund
regál [regahl] shelf
rentgen X-ray
repelent insect repellent
restaurace f [restowrutseh] restaurant
ret lip
revizor ticket inspector
revmatismus [refmutizmoos] rheumatism
revoluce f [revolootseh] revolution
rezavý [rezuvee] rusty
rezervace f [rezervutseh] reservation
rezervní pneumatika [rezervnyee puneh-oomutika] spare tyre
rezervovat [rezervovut] to book; to reserve
riziko risk
roční doba [rotchnyee] season
rodiče mpl [ro-dyitcheh] parents
rodina [ro-dyina] family
rodinné balení family-size pack
rodné jméno [rodneh yumeno] maiden name

roh [roH] corner
rohy mpl [rohi] horns
rok year
roleta blind, shutter
Róm m [rawm] Romany (man)
román [romahn] novel
Rómka f [rawmka] Romany (woman)
rosa dew
rostlina plant
rovně [rovnyeh] straight on
rovný [rovnee] straight
rozcestí [rostses-tyee] fork (in road)
rozdělovač [roz-dyelovutch] distributor
rozhlas [roz-hlus] broadcasting, radio
rozhodovat se/rozhodnout se [roz-hodovut seh/roz-hodnoht] to decide
rozkošný [roskoshnee] lovely
rozkousejte je chew them
rozmazlený [rozmuzlenee] spoiled
rozsvěcovat/rozsvítit [rosvyetsovut/rosveetyit] to switch on (light)
rozsvícený [rosveetsenee] lit, lighted
rozsvítit [rosveetyit] to switch on (light)
roztrpčený [rosturptchenee] annoyed
rozumět [rozoomnyet] to understand
rozumný [rozoomnee] sensible
rozvážný [rozvahJnee] deliberate
rozvedený [rozvedenee] divorced

rozvinout/rozvíjet [rozvinoht/ rozvee-yet] to develop

rozlobený [rozlobenee] angry

rtěnka [rutyenka] lipstick

rty [ruti] lips

ruční brzda [rootchnyee burzda] handbrake

ručník [rootchnyeek] (hand) towel

rudovlasý [roodovlusee] red-headed

ruka [rooka] hand

rukavice fpl [rookavitseh] gloves

rukopis [rookopis] manuscript

ruksak [rooksuk] rucksack

Rumunsko [roomoonsko] Romania

rumunský [roomoonskee] Romanian (adj)

rumunština [roomoonsh-tyina] Romanian (language)

Rus m [roos], Ruska f Russian Rusko Russia

ruský [rooskee] Russian (adj)

rušit/zrušit [rooshit] to cancel

rušný [rooshnee] busy

ruština [roosh-tyina] Russian (language)

různý [rOOznee] various

růže f [rOOJeh] rose

růžový [rOOJovee] pink

rvačka [ruvutchka] fight

rybaření [riburJenyee] fishing

rybářský lístek [ribarJskee leestek] fishing permit

rybářský prut [proot] fishing rod

rybí speciality fpl [ribee] fishmonger's; fish dishes

rybník [ribnyeek] pond;

fishpond

rýč [reetch] spade

rychlík [riHleek] fast train

rychlost f [riHlost] gear; speed

rychlý [riHlee] quick

ryzí [rizee] genuine

Ř

řadicí páka [rJuh-dyitsee pahka] gear lever

řasenka [rJusenka] eyeliner

Řecko [rJetsko] Greece

řecký [rJetskee] Greek (adj)

řečtina [rJetch-tyina] Greek (language)

ředitel m [rJedyitel], ředitelka f manager; director

Řek [rJek] Greek (man)

řeka [rJeka] river

řekl [rJekul] he said

Řekyně f [rJekinyeh] Greek (woman)

řemen [rJemen] belt

řemen ventilátoru [–lahtoroo] fan belt

řemesla npl [rJemesla] crafts

řetěz [rJetyes] chain

řetízek [rJetyeezek] small chain

řeznictví [rJeznits-tvee] butcher's

řezník [rJeznyeek] butcher

říct* [rJeetst] to say; to tell můžete mi říct ...? [mooJeteh] can you tell me ...?

řidič m [rjidyitch], řidička f driver

řidičský průkaz [rJidyitchskee prOOkus] driving licence

řídit [rJeedyit] to drive

řídký [rJeetkee] sparse

říjen [rJee-yen] October
říkat/říct [rJeekut/rJeetst] to say;
to tell
řízení [rJeezenyee] steering
říznout se [rJeeznoht seh] to cut
oneself

S

s* with
sáček [sahtchek] paper bag
sádra [sahdra] plaster
sako [suko] jacket
sakra! [sukra] damn!
salónek [sulawnek] function
room
sám m [sahm] myself; yourself;
himself; alone; on my/your/
his own; on one's own
sama f [suma] myself; yourself;
herself; alone; on my/your/
her/their own; on one's own
samet [sumet] velvet
sami [sumi] on their own;
themselves
samo [sumo] itself; on its own
samoobsluha [sumo-opslooha]
self-service
samostatný [sumostutnee]
independent
samozřejmě [sumozrJay-mnyeh]
of course
samy [sumi] themselves; on
their own
sandály mpl [sundahli] sandals
saně fpl [sunyeh] sledge
sanitka [sunitka] ambulance
sáňkování [sahn^yehkovahnyee]
sledging

saponát [suponaht] detergent
sazba [suzba] charges
sbírat/sebrat [zbeerut/sebrut] to
collect
sbírka [zbeerka] collection
(stamps etc)
sbohem [zbo-hem] goodbye
scenérie [stseneri-eh] scenery
se oneself; myself; yourself;
himself; herself; itself;
ourselves; yourselves;
themselves; one another
sedačka [sedutchka] pushchair
sedačkový výtah [sedutchkohvee
veetuH] chairlift
sedadlo [sedudlo] seat
sedm [sedum] seven
sedmdesát [sedumdesaht]
seventy
sedmnáct [sedumnahtst]
seventeen
sedmnáctý [sedumnahtstee]
seventeenth
sedmý [sedmee] seventh
sedněte si! [sednyeteh si] sit
down!
sejít se [seh-yeet seh] to come
together
sekat [sekut] to cut
sekretářka f [sekretarJka]
secretary
sekunda [sekoonda] second (in
time)
sem pull
semafor [semufor] traffic lights
sen dream
senná rýma [senah reema]
hayfever
seno hay

seřídit [sehrJeedyit] to adjust; to tune

sestra sister

sestřenice f [sestrJeh-nyitseh] cousin (female)

sešit [seshit] notebook

set*: pět set [pyet] five hundred

setkávat se/setkat se [setkahvut/ setkut seh] to meet

sever north

severní [severnyee] northern

Severní Irsko [severnyee] Northern Ireland

seznam [seznam] list

sezónní [sezawnyee] seasonal

shnilý [sHunyilee] rotten

scházet/sejít [sHahzet/say-eet] to go down, to walk down

schody mpl [sHodi] stairs

schovávat/schovat [sHovahvut/ sHovut] to hide

schránka [sHrahnka] letterbox, mailbox

schránku vybírá [sHrahnkoo vibeerah] collection times

schůze f [sHOOzeh] meeting

schůzka [sHOOska] appointment

si (for) oneself; each other, one another

sídliště [seedlish-tyeh] housing estate

silnice se v zimě neudržuje road not cleared in winter

silný [silnee] thick; strong

Silvestr New Year's Eve

sirky fpl [sirki] matches

síť f [seet^{yeh}] net

sjezdovka [syezdofka] downhill course

sjízdné pouze se sněhovými řetězy passable with snow chains only

sjízdný [syeezdnee] passable (slope)

skákat/skočit [skahkut/skotchit] to jump

skála [skahla] rock

skalnatý f [skulnutee] rocky

skanzen [skunzen] open air museum

skladatel [skludutel] composer

skladujte v chladu a suchu store in cool and dry place

sklenice f [sklenyitseh] glass

sklep basement

sklo glass

skoky do vody [skoki do vodi] diving

skoky na lyžích [liJeeH] ski jump

skončit [skonchit] to finish

skoro [skoro] almost

Skot m, Skotka f Scot

Skotsko [skotsko] Scotland

skotský [skotskee] Scottish (adj)

skromný [skromnee] modest

skrz* [skurs] through

skříň f [skrJeen^{yeh}] cupboard

skupina [skoopina] group

skutečný [skootetchnee] real

skvělý [skvyelee] excellent

skvrna [skvurna] stain

slabý [slubee] weak

sladký [slutkee] sweet (to taste)

sláma [slahma] straw

slavnost [sluvnost] celebration

slavnostní [sluvnost-nyee] festive

slavný [sluvnee] famous

slečna [sletchna] Miss; single

woman
slečno! Miss!
sledovat [–ovut] to follow
slepá ulice f blind alley
slepý [slepee] blind
sleva discount
slibovat/slíbit [sleebovut/sleebit]
to promise
slipy [slipi] briefs
slonovina [slonovina] ivory
Slovák m [slovahk], **Slovenka** f
Slovak
Slovensko Slovakia
slovenský [slovenskee] Slovak
(adj)
slovenština [slovensh-tyina]
Slovak (language)
slovník [slovnyeek] dictionary
slovo word
složitý [sloJitee] complex
slunce [sloontseh] sun
sluneční brýle [sloonetch-nyee
breeleh] sunglasses
slunečný [sloonetchnee] sunny
slušný [slooshnee] fair; decent
slyšet [slishet] to hear
smát se [smaht seh] to laugh
smažit [smuJit] to fry
směnárenský kurs
[smnyenarenskee koors]
exchange rate
směnárna [smnyenarna] bureau
de change
směr [smnyer] direction, way
směrové číslo [smnyeroveh
cheeslo] dialling code
směr prodeje queue this way
směšný [smnyeshnee] ridiculous
smetanový [smetunovee]

creamy; cream-coloured
smíchat [smeeHut] to mix
together
smlouva [smlohva] agreement
smluvit [smloovit] to arrange
(something)
smokink dinner jacket
smrt f [smurt] death
smutný [smootnee] sad
smyk [smik] skid
snadný [snudnee] easy
snědý [snyedee] tanned
sněhové řetězy [snyehoveh
rJetyezi] snow chains
sněžit [snyeJit] to snow
sněží [snyeJee] it is snowing
snídaně f [snyeedunyeh]
breakfast
snídat [snyeedut] to have
breakfast
sníh [snyeeH] snow
sníh s blátem [zblahtem] slush
snoubenec [snohbenets] fiancé
snoubenka fiancée
sobecký [sobetskee] selfish
sobota Saturday
socha [soHa] statue
sochař m [soHurJ], **sochařka** f
sculptor
součástka [sohchahstka] part
soudce m [soht-tseh], **soudkyně** f
[sohtkinyeh] judge
souhlasit [soh-hlusit] to agree
soukromá společnost f
[sohkromah spoletchnost]
private company
soukromý [sohkromee] private
soukromý majetek private
property

soused m [sohset], **sousedka** f
 neighbour
spací pytel [sputsee pitel]
 sleeping bag
spadnout [spudnoht] to fall
spáchat f [spah-Hut] to commit
spálenina [spahlenyina] burn
spálení sluncem [spahlenyee
 sloontsem] sunburn
spalničky fpl [spulnyitchki]
 measles
spát [spaht] to sleep
speciál [spetsi-ahl] lower-grade
 petrol/gas; charter flight
spěchat f [spyeHut] to hurry
 spěchej! [spyeh-Hay] hurry up!
spěšnina [spyesh-nyina] express
 parcel (delivered and collected at
 the station)
spěšniny fpl express parcels
spisovatel m [spisovutel],
 spisovatelka f writer
spíše [speesheh] rather
spodky mpl [spotki] underpants
spoj [spoy] connection
Spojené státy americké mpl [spo-
 yeneh stahti umeritskeh] United
 States of America
spojka [spoyka] clutch
spojovatel m [spoyovutel],
 spojovatelka f operator
spokojený [spoko-yenee]
 content; satisfied
společně [spoletch-nyeh]
 together
společnost f [spoletchnost]
 company; society
spolknout [spol-knoht] to
 swallow

sporák [sporahk] cooker
sportovec [sportovets]
 sportsman
sportovkyně f [sportofki-nyeh]
 sportswoman
sportovní potřeby fpl [–nyee
 potrJebi] sporting facilities
spořitelna [sporJitelna] savings
 bank
spotřebovat do use before
spotřebujte do use before
spousta [spohsta] a lot (of)
spravedlivý [spruvedlivee] fair,
 just
spravit [spruvit] to repair
správně [sprahvnyeh] right,
 that's right; OK
správný [sprahvnee] correct
spravovat/spravit [spruvovut/
 spruvit] to repair
sprcha [spurHa] shower
sprchovat se [spur-Hovut seh] to
 take a shower
sprchy fpl [spurHi] showers
spropitné n [sropitneh] tip
SPZ [es peh zet] number plate
srážka [srahshka] crash
srdce n [surdtseh] heart
srdečný [surdetchnee] cordial
srpen [surpen] August
srub [sroop] log cabin
sta*: tři sta [trJi] three
 hundred
stačit: to bude stačit [stutchit]
 that'll do nicely
stadión [studi-awn] stadium
stan [stun] tent
stánek [stahnek] kiosk
stanice f [stunyitseh] station;

stop

stanice první pomoci f [puhrvnyee pomotsi] first aid post

stanoviště taxi n [stunovishtyeh tuksi] taxi rank

starat se [sturut seh] to take care of

starobní důchodce m [sturobnyee dOOHotseh], starobní důchodkyně f [dOOHotki-nyeh] old-age pensioner

starost f [sturost] worry

starověký [sturovyekee] ancient

starožitnictví [sturoJitnits-tvee] antique shop

starožitnost f [sturoJitnost] antique

start [sturt] take-off

starý [sturee] old

starý mládenec [sturee mlahdenets] bachelor

stáří [stahrJee] old age

stát [staht] to cost; to stand

statečný [stutetchnee] brave

státní [stahtnyee] state (adj)

státní poznávací značka [poznahvutsee znutchka] number plate

státní příslušnost f [prJeeslooshenost] citizenship

státní svátek [svahtek] public holiday

státní škola [shkola] state school

stav [stuf] marital status

stávat se/stát se [stahvut seh/staht] to become

stě*: dvě stě [dvyeh styeh] two hundred

stehno [stehno] thigh

stejně [stay-nyeh] anyway

stejný [staynee] same

stěrač [styerutch] windscreen wiper

stevard [stevurd] steward

stevardka [stevurtka] stewardess

stezka [steska] path

stezka pro cyklisty cycle path

stěžovat si [styeJovut si] to complain

stín [styeen] shadow; shade

sto* hundred

stojí to ... korun [sto-yee to ... koroon] it costs ... crowns

stokoruna [stokoroona] 100-crown banknote/bill

století [stoletyee] century

stostupňový [stostoopnyovee] centigrade/Celsius

strach [struH] fear

strašný [strushnee] horrible; terrible

strava [struva] diet

strom tree

strop ceiling

stručný [strootchnee] brief

struna [stroona] wire

strýc [streets] uncle

střed [strJet] centre; middle
střed města [mnyesta] city centre

středa [strJeda] Wednesday

střední [strJednyee] middle

střední škola [shkola] secondary school

střecha [strJeHa] roof

střelba [strJelba] shooting

stříbro [strJeebro] silver

střídavý [strJeeduvee] alternate

střízlivý [strJeezlivee] sober

studentka f [stoodentka] student (female)

studený [stoodenee] cold

stůj! [stOO-i] stop!

stůl f [stOOl] table

stupeň [stoopen^{yeh}] degree

stýkat se [steekut seh] to be in touch

stýská: stýská se mi ... [steeska seh] I miss ...

sudý [soodee] even (number)

suchý [sooHee] dry

sukně f [sooknyeh] skirt

sůl do koupele [sOOl do kohpeleh] bath salts

super [sooper] four-star petrol, premium gas

surf [soorf] sailboard

sušák na prádlo [sooshahk na prahdlo] clothes horse

sušička [sooshitchka] dryer

suvenýry mpl [soovehneeree] souvenirs

svá* [svah] my; your; his/her/ its; our; their; one's

svačina [svutchina] midmorning snack

svačit [svutchit] to eat snacks

svah [svuH] slope

sval [svul] muscle

svatba [svudba] wedding

svátek [svahtek] public holiday

své* [sveh] my; your; his/her/ its; our; their; one's

svědit [svyedyit] to itch

svět [svyet] world

světlo [svyetlo] light

světlý [svyetlee] light (adj: colour)
 světle modrý [svyetleh modree] light blue

svetr [svetur] jumper

svíčka [sveetchka] candle

svislý [svislee] vertical

svobodný [svobodnee] free; unmarried

svůj* [svOO-i] my; your; his/her/ its; our; their; one's

syn [sin] son

synovec [sinovets] nephew

sytič [sityitch] choke (in car)

sytý [sitee] rich (food)

Š

šachy mpl [shuHi] chess

šála [shahla] scarf

šálek [shahlek] cup
 šálek čaje [chĬ-eh] a cup of tea

šampón [shumpawn] shampoo

šátek [shahtek] wrapper

šatna [shutna] cloakroom, (US) checkroom

šaty mpl [shuti] clothes; dress

šedesát [shedesaht] sixty

šedý [shedee] grey

šéf m [shef], šéfová [shefovah] boss

šek [shek] cheque

šeková knížka [shekovah kunyeeshka] cheque book

šel [shel] he went

šest [shest] six

šestnáct [shestnahtst] sixteen

šestnáctý [shestnahtstee] sixteenth

šestý [shestee] sixth

šílený [sheelenee] crazy

široký [shirokee] wide

šít [sheet] to sew

škoda [shkoda] pity
  to je škoda [yeh] it's a pity

škodlivý [shkodlivee] harmful

škola [shkola] school

školačka [shkolutchka]
  schoolgirl

školák [shkolahk] schoolboy

školní hřiště [shkolnyee
  hurJishtyeh] school
  playground

šla [shla] she went

šlechta [shleHta] nobility

šlo [shlo] it went

šňůra na prádlo [shnyoOra na
  prahdlo] clothes line

šok [shok] shock

šokující [shokoo-yeetsee]
  shocking

šortky fpl [shortki] shorts

Španěl m [shpunyel], Španělka f
  Spaniard

Španělsko Spain

španělský [shpunyelskee]
  Spanish (adj)

španělština [shpunyel-shtyina]
  Spanish (language)

špatné číslo [shputneh cheeslo]
  wrong number

špatné trávení [trahvenyee]
  indigestion

špatný [shputnee] bad
  je mi špatně [shputnyeh] I feel
  sick

špendlík [shpendleek] pin

špinavý [shpinuvee] dirty

šroub [shrohp] screw

šroubovák [shrohbovahk]
  screwdriver

šťastnou cestu [shtyustnoh
  tsestoo] have a good journey!

šťastný [shtyustnee] happy

šťastný Nový rok! [novee] happy
  New Year!

štíhlý [shtyeeHlee] slim

štípnutí [shtyeepnootyee] insect
  bite

šváb [shvahp] cockroach

švadlena [shvudlena]
  dressmaker

Švýcar m [shveetsur], Švýcarka f
  Swiss

Švýcarsko [shveetsursko]
  Switzerland

švýcarský [shveetsurskee] Swiss
  (adj)

T

ta* this (one); that (one);
  these; those

tabák [tubahk] tobacco

tableta [tubleta] tablet

táboření [tahborJenyee] camping

tábořiště [tahborJishtyeh]
  campsite

tady [tudi] here
  tady je [yeh] here is
  tady jsou [soh] here are
  je tady ...? is there ...?
  jsou tady ...? are there ...?

tahat/táhnout [tah-Hnoht] to pull

tahle [tuhleh] this (one)

tachometr [tuHometr]
  speedometer

tajný [tīnee] secret

tak [tuk] so

také [tukeh] also, too, as well

taková [tukovah], takové
 [tukoveh], takoví [tukovee],
 takový [tukovee] such

talíř [tuleerJ] dish; plate

talířek [tuleerJek] saucer

tam [tum] there; push

 tam dole [doleh] down there

tamhle [tum-hleh] over there

tampóny mpl [tumpawni]
 tampons

tamta [tumta] those; that (one)

tamten [tumten] that (one)

tamti [tumtyi] those

tamto [tumto] that (one)

tamty [tumti] those

tancovat [tuntsovut] to dance

taška [tushka] bag

tát [taht] to thaw

tatínek [tutyeenek] dad

tato [tuto] this (one); these

taxametr [tuksumetur] taxi
 meter

taxikář [tuksikarJ] taxi-driver

té* [teh]·this, that; of this, of
 that; to

tě* [tyeh] (of) you

tebe* [tebeh] you; of you; to
 you

tebou* [teboh] (by) you

teď [tet^yeh] now

těhotná [tyeh-hotnah] pregnant

těch* [tyeH] (of) these; (of)
 those

tekutý [tekootee] liquid

telefonní budka [telefonyee
 bootka] phone box

telefonní číslo [cheeslo] phone
 number

telefonní informace fpl
 [informutseh] directory
 enquiries, information

telefonní kabina [kubina] phone
 box (at post office)

telefonní karta [kurta] phone
 card

telefonní seznam [seznum]
 phone directory

telefonovat [telefonovut] to
 phone

telegramy telegrams

televize f [televizeh] television

tělo [tyelo] body

tělocvična [tyelotsvitchna] gym

těm* [tyem] (to) these; (to)
 those

téměř [teh-mnyerJ] nearly

těmi* [tyem] (by) these; (by) those

ten* that (one)

tenhle* [ten-hleh] this (one)

tenisky fpl [teniski] trainers

tenisový kurt [–ovee koort] tennis
 court

tenký [tenkee] thin

tento this (one)

tepláková souprava [teplahkovah
 sohpruva] tracksuit

teplo warmth

 je teplo [yeh] it's warm

teploměr [teplo-mnyer]
 thermometer

teplota temperature

terénní vůz [terenyee vOOs] off-
 the-road vehicle

termální prameny mpl
 [termahlnyee prumeni] thermal
 springs

termofor hot-water bottle

termoska thermos flask

těší mě! [tyeshee mnyeh] pleased to meet you!

těsný [tyesnee] tight

teta aunt

těžkopádný [tyeshkopahdnee] cumbersome

těžký [tyeshkee] heavy

ti* [tyi] (to) you; these; those

ticho [tyiHo] silence
ticho! quiet!

tichý [tyiHee] quiet

tím* [tyeem] (by) this; (by) that

tisíc [tyiseets] thousand

tisíce: dva tisíce [tyiseetseh] two thousand

tisícikoruna [tyiseetsi-koroona] 1000-crown banknote/bill

tiskárna [tyiskarna] printer's

tiskoviny fpl [tyiskovini] printed matter

tísňové volání [tyeesnyoveh volahnyee] emergency call

tito* these

tkaničky (do bot) fpl [tkunyitchki] shoelaces

tlačit [tlutchit] to push

tlak v pneumatikách tyre pressure

tlak vzduchu air pressure

tlustý [tloostee] fat

tmavý [tmuvee] dark

to* it; that
to je ... [yeh] it is ...

toaleta [to-uleta] toilet, restroom

toaletní papír [to-uletnyee pupeer] toilet paper

tobě* [tobyeh] (to) you

tohle* [to-hleh] this (one)

toho*, tom* this; that

tomu* [tomoo] (to) him; (to) it

topení [topenyee] heating

toto* this (one)

tou* [toh] (by) this; (by) that

továrna factory

tradice f [truditseh] tradition

tradiční [truditchnyee] traditional

trafika [trufika] tobacconist's

trajekt [truh-yekt] ferry

tramvaj f [trumvî] tram

trápit se [trahpit seh] to worry

trapný [trupnee] embarrassing

trasa [trusa] route

tráva [trahva] grass

trávení [trahvenyee] digestion

trenýrky fpl [treneerki] running shorts; boxer shorts

trestný [trestnee] criminal (adj)

tričko [tritchko] T-shirt

trochu [troHOO] a little bit (of); some

trosky fpl [troski] ruins

trpělivý [turpyelivee] patient (adj)

trpět [turpyet] to suffer

trpký [turpkee] bitter

trvalá [turvulah] perm

trvalé bydliště permanent residence

třetí [trJetyee] third

tři [trJi] three

třicátý [trJitsahtee] thirtieth

třicet [trJitset] thirty

třída [trJeeda] class; avenue; main street

třikrát denně three times a day

třikrát denně před jídlem three times a day before meals

třináct [trJinahtst] thirteen

třináctý [trJinahtstee] thirteenth

tu* [too] this; that

turista m [toorista] tourist (man)

turistická stezka tourist path

turistickou třídou [tooristitskoh trJeedoh] tourist class

turistka f tourist (woman)

turnaj [toornI] tournament

tužidlo na vlasy [tooJidlo na vlusi] styling mousse

tužka [tooshka] pencil

tužka na rty [ruti] lipliner

tvá* [tvah] your(s)

tvář [tvarJ] face

tvé* [tveh] your

tvého* [tveho] (of) your(s)

tvém* [tvem] your(s)

tvému* [tvemoo] (to) your(s)

tví* [tvee] your(s)

tvoje [tvo-yeh], tvoji* [tvo-yi] your

tvou* [tvoh] (by) your(s)

tvrdý [tvurdee] hard

tvůj* [tvOO-i] your(s)

tvých* [tveeH] (of) your(s)

tvým* [tveem] (by) your(s); (to) your(s)

tvými* (by) your(s)

ty* [ti] you; these; those

týden [teeden] week

týdeník [teedenyeek] weekly

tyto* [tito] these

U

u* [oo] by; at

ubohý [oobo-hee] poor

ubrousek [oo-brohsek] napkin

ubrus [oobroos] tablecloth

ubytovací řád [oobytovutsee rJaht] hotel rules

ubytování [oobitovah-nyee] accommodation

ubytování v soukromí [fsohkromee] accommodation in a private house or apartment

ubytovna [oobitovna] hostel

ubytovna mládeže [mlah-deJeh] youth hostel

ucpaný [ootspunee] blocked

učebnice f [ootcheb-nyitseh] textbook

učební osnovy fpl [ootcheb-nyee osnovi] curriculum

učesat [ootchesut] to comb

učesat se [oochesut seh] to comb one's hair

účet [OOchet] bill, (US) check; account

učit [oochit] to teach

učitel m [ootchitel], učitelka f teacher

učit se/naučit se [ootchit seh/nowchit] to learn

ucítit/cítit [ootsee-tyit] to smell

udělat [oo-dyelut] to make; to do

udeřit [ooderJit] to hit, to strike a blow

udivující [oo-dyivoo-yeetsee] astonishing

údolí [oodolee] valley

uhasit/hasit [oo-husit] to extinguish

uhlí [ooh-lee] coal

ucho [ooHo] ear

uchovejte v chladu keep in a cool place

uchovejte v suchu keep in a dry place

ukázat [ookahzut] to show můžete mi ukázat ...? [mooJeteh] can you show me ...?

uklidnit se [ooklidnyit seh] to calm down

uklizený [ooklizenee] tidied up, tidy

ukončete výstup a nástup, dveře se zavírají! stand back please, the doors are closing!

Ukrajina [ookrĭ-eena] Ukraine

Ukrajinec m [ookrĭ-inets], Ukrajinka f Ukrainian

ukrajinský [ookrĭ-inskee] Ukrainian (adj)

ulice f [oolitseh] street

uložit [ooloJit] to deposit

umělá hmota [oo-mnyelah humota] plastic

umělec m [oo-mynelets], umělkyně f [oo-mnyelki-nyeh] artist

umělecká škola [oo-mnyeletskah shkola] art school

umělý [oo-mnyelee] artificial

umění [oo-mnyenyee] art

umýt [oomeet] to wash (up)

umýt a natočit [nutotchit] wash and set

umyvadlo [oomivudlo] washbasin

umývárna automobilu [oomeevarna owtomobiloo] car wash

unavený [oonuvenee] tired

únik [OOnyik] escape; leak

univerzita [ooniverzita] university

únor [OOnor] February

upadnout [oopudnoht] to fall

úpal [OOpul] sunstroke

upevněte si bezpečnostní pás fasten seat belt

úplně [OOpulnyeh] quite

upřímný [ooprJeemnee] sincere

úraz [OOrus] injury

urazit [ooruzit] to offend

úrok [OOrok] interest

urostlý [oohrostlee] well-built

úroveň [OOroven^yeh] level

úrovňová křižovatka level crossing, (US) grade crossing

úřad [OOrJut] office

úřednice f [OOrJed-nyitseh] clerk (woman)

úřední hodiny office hours; opening times

úředník m [OOrJed-nyeek] clerk (man)

úschovna zavazadel [OOsHovna] left luggage, (US) baggage check

úsek častých nehod accident blackspot

úsměv [OOs-mnyef] smile

usmívat se [oosmeevut seh] to smile

usnout/usínat [oosnoht] to fall asleep

úspěch [OOspyeH] success

úspěšný [OOspyeshnee] successful

ústa npl [OOsta] mouth

ústní voda [OOstnyee] mouthwash

ústředna [OOstryedna] operator

ústřední [OOstryednyee] central

ústřední topení [topenyee] central heating

uší, nosní a krční [ooshnyee nosnyee a krutchnyee] ear, nose and throat

úterý n [OOteree] Tuesday

útes [OOtes] cliff

utěrka [ootyerka] tea towel

útok [OOtok] attack

utrácet/utratit [ootrahtset/ ootrutyit] to spend

úvěr [OOvyer] credit

uvidět [oovidyet] to catch sight of

území [OOzemee] area

úzký [OOskee] narrow

už [oosh] already

užitečný [ooJitetchnee] useful

užít/užívat [ooJeet/ooJeevut] to use

užívejte při hlavním jídle take with the main meal

V

v* in; at

vadit [vudyit] to mind

vadilo by vám, kdybych ...? [vudylo bi vahm gudibiH] do you you mind if I ...?

vagón [vugawn] carriage

váha [vah-ha] weight

válka [vahlka] war

valuty fpl [valooti] foreign currency

vám* [vahm] (to) you

vámi* (by) you

vana [vuna] bathtub

vánice f [vahnyitseh] blizzard, snowstorm

Vánoce mpl [vahnotseh] Christmas

Varšava [vurshuva] Warsaw

vařič [vurJitch] cooker

vařit [vurJit] to cook; to boil

vás* [vahs] (of) you

váš* [vahsh] your; yours

vaše [vusheh], vašeho [vusheho], vašem* [vushem] your(s)

vašemu* [vushemoo] (to) your(s)

vaši* [vushi] your(s)

vašich* [vushiH] (of) your(s)

vašim* [vushim] (to) your(s)

vaším [vusheem], vašimi* [vushimi] (by) your(s)

vata [vuta] cotton wool, absorbent cotton

váza [vahza] vase

vážný [vahJnee] serious

včas [ftchus] on time

včela [ftchela] bee

včera [ftchera] yesterday

včetně [fchetnyeh] inclusive of

včetně všeho [fsheho] all-inclusive

vdaná [vdunah] married (of woman)

vděčný [vdyetchnee] grateful

vdova widow

vdovec [vdovets] widower

ve* [veh] in; at

věc f [vyets] thing; matter

večer [vetcher] evening

večeře [vetcherJeh] supper; dinner (evening meal)

večeřet [vetcherJet] to have supper

večerka [vetcherka] grocer's open in the afternoons and late evenings

večírek [vetcheerek] party

věda [vyeda] science

vědec [vyedets] scientist (man)

vědět* [vyedyet] to know

vědí [vyedyee] they know

vědkyně f [vyetki-nyeh] scientist

vedl [vedul] he lead

vedle* [vedleh] next to, beside

vedoucí m/f [vedohtsee] manager; manageress

vědro [vyedro] bucket

věk [vyek] age

velehory fpl [velehori] high mountains

Velikonoce mpl [velikonotseh] Easter

velikost f [velikost] size

Velká Británie [velkah britahni-eh] Great Britain

velký [velkee] big; large

velmi mnoho very much

Velšan [velshun] Welshman

Velšanka Welshwoman

velšský [velshskee] Welsh

velvyslanectví [velvislunetstvee] embassy

ven out

venkovský [venkofskee] rural

venku [venkoo] outside

ventil valve

ventilátor [ventilahtor] fan

veřejný [verJaynee] public

věřit [vyerJit] to believe

veselé Vánoce! [veseleh vahnotseh] Merry Christmas!

veselý [veselee] merry

veslice f [veslitseh] rowing boat

veslo oar

vesnice f [vesnyitseh] village

vést to lead

věšák [vyeshahk] hanger

veterinář m [veterinarJ], **veterinářka** f vet

větev f [vyetef] branch

větší [vyetshee] bigger

většina [vyetshina] (the) most (of); the majority (of)

vevnitř [vev-nyiturJ] inside

vězení [vyezenyee] prison

věž f [vyesh] tower

vhodný [vuhodnee] suitable

vhoďte minci insert money

vcházet/vejít [fHahzet/vay-yeet] to enter

vchod [fHot] way in, entrance

vchod vedle entry next door

ví [vee] he/she/it knows

více [veetseh] more

Vídeň f [veeden^yeh] Vienna

vidět [vidyet] to see

vidlička [vidlitchka] fork

víkend [veekend] weekend

víko [veeko] lid

vila villa

vilová čtvrť f [vilovah chutvurt^yeh]

suburb

vím [veem] I know

víme [veemeh] we know

vinárna wine bar

vinice [vinyitseh] vineyard

vinná réva grapevine

vinný sklep [vinee sklep] wine cellar

víš [veesh] you know

vítáme vás! [veetahmeh vahs] welcome!

vítat [veetut] to welcome

víte [veeteh] you know

vítr [veetur] wind

vízum [veezoom] visa

vjezd zakázán no entry

vklad [fklut] deposit, money paid into account

vláda [vlahda] government

vlajka [vlīka] flag

vlak [vluk] train

k vlakům to the trains

vlasy mpl [vlusi] hair

vlažný [vluJnee] lukewarm

vlhký [vul-Hkee] damp

vlna [vulna] wool; wave (in sea)

vloni [vulonyi] last year

vloupání [vlohpahnyee] break-in

vložky fpl [vloshki] sanitary towels/napkins

vnitrostátní linky fpl domestic flights

vnitrozemí [vnyitrozemi] inland

vnitřní [vnyiturJ-nyee] inner

voda water

voda po holení [holenyee] aftershave

vodní lyže fpl [vodnyee liJeh] waterski

vodní lyžování [liJovahnyee] waterskiing

vodopád [vodopaht] waterfall

vojenský [vo-yenskee] military

volant [volunt] steering wheel

volat [volut] to call

kdo volá? [gudo volah] who's calling?

volá meziměsto [mezi-mnyesto] there is a long-distance call for you

volby fpl [volbi] elections

volič [volitch] voter

volno vacancy; free time

volný [volnee] free; vacant

vonět/zavonět [vonyet] to smell (nice)

vosa wasp

vosk na vlasy [vlusi] wax (for hair)

vozidlo vehicle

vpravo [fpruvo] right

vracet se/vrátit se [vrutset seh/vrahtyit] to come back

vracet/vrátit to give back

vrátnice f [vrahtnyitseh] reception

vrchol [vurHol] top; peak

vstávat/vstát [fstahvut/fstaht] to get up

vstupenka [fstoopenka] ticket

vstup jen ve společenském oděvu jacket and tie required

vstupné [fstoopneh] entrance fee

vstup pouze s košíkem customers must use a basket

vstupte! [fstoopteh] come in!

vstup volný admission free

vstup zakázán no admittance, no entry

všední den [fshednyee] weekday

všechno [fsheHno] everything; all

všechno nejlepší! [naylepshee] best wishes!

všechno nejlepší k narozeninám! [nahrozenyinahm] happy birthday!

všichni [fshiHnyi] all

všude [fshoodeh] everywhere

vteřina [fterJina] second (in time)

vůl [vOOl] stupid man

vůně f [vOOnyeh] nice smell

vy* [vi] you

vybalit [vibulit] to unpack

výběr [veebyer] withdrawal

vybírat/vybrat [vibeerut/vibrut] to choose

výborně! [veebornyeh] well done!

vyčistit/čistit [vichis-tyit] to clean up

výdej [veeday] issue

výdejna jízdenek [veedayna yeezdenek] ticket office

výdej zavazadel [veeday zuvuzadel] baggage claim

vydělávat/vydělat [vidyelahvut] to earn

vydržet [vidurJet] to endure; to hold out

vyfotografovat [vifotogrufovut] to photograph

vyfoukat [vifohkut] to blow-dry

výfuk [veefook] exhaust

vyhledat [vihledut] to look up

vyhodit [vihodyit] to throw away

vyhrávat/vyhrát [vihrahvut] to win

vyhublý [vihooblee] thin

východ [veeHot] exit; gate; east

východní [veeHodnyee] eastern

východ slunce [sloontseh] sunrise

výklad [veeklut] shop window

vykoupat se [vikohput seh] to take a bath

výkup purchase

výlet [veelet] trip

vyluxovat [vilooksovut] to vacuum-clean

vyměnit/vyměňovat [vi-mnyenyit/vi-mnyen^yeh^ovut] to exchange; to change

vypadat [vipudut] to look, to seem

vypadat jako [yuko] to look like

výpadek elektřiny [veepudek elektrJini] power cut

vypadněte! [vipud-nyeteh] get out!

vypínač [vipeenutch] switch

vypít [vipeet] to drink up

vyplnit/vyplňovat [vipulnyit/vipuln^yeh^ovut] to fill; to fill in

vypnout [vipnoht] to switch off (engine)

vypracovat [viprutsovut] to work out

vyprat [viprut] to do the washing

vyprodáno [viprodahno] sold out

výprodej [veeproday] sale

výroba klíčů [veeroba kleetchoO] locksmith's

výročí [veerotchee] anniversary

výron [veeron] sprain
  mám výron v kotníku [mahm – fkotnyeekoo] I've sprained my ankle

vyrušovat/vyrušit [virooshovut/ virooshit] to disturb

vysavač [visuvutch] vacuum cleaner

vysilující [visiloo-yeetsee] exhausting

vyslovit [vislovit] to pronounce

vysoké napětí high voltage

vysoký [visokee] high

vysoušeč vlasů [visohshetch] hair dryer

vysoušet/vysušit [visohshet/ visooshit] to dry

výstava [veestuva] exhibition

výstup [veestoop] exit

vystupovat/vystoupit [vistoopovut/ vistohpit] to get off

vysvětlit/vysvětlovat [vi-svyetlit] to explain

vyšetření [vishet-rJenyee] check-up

vyšetřovat [vishet-rJovut] to investigate

vyšívaný [visheevunee] embroidered

výšivka [veeshifka] embroidery

výtah [veetuH] lift, elevator

vytahovat/vytáhnout [vituhovut/ vitahHnoht] to pull up; to lift

výtah pro … osob lift/elevator for … persons

vytočte číslo dial number

vyučovací hodina [vi-ootchovutsee ho-dyina] lesson

vyučovat [vi-ootchovat] to teach

vyvolat film [vivolut] to develop a film

vývrtka [veevurtka] corkscrew

vyzkoušet [viskohshet] to try on

významný [veeznumnee] important

vzal [vuzul] I took; you took; he took

vzbudit [vuzboodyit] to wake up

vzdálenost f [vuzdahlenost] distance

vzdělání [vuzdyelahnyee] education

vzdělaný [vuzdyelunee] educated

vzduch [vuzdooH] air

vzhůru [vuzhOOroo] awake

vzít* [vuzeet] to take

vzkaz [fskus] message
  nechat vzkaz [neHut] to leave a message

vzlétnout [vuzletnoht] to take off

vzrušující [vuzrooshoo-yeetsee] exciting

vždy [vuJdi] always

W

WC muži gents' toilet, men's room

WC ženy ladies' toilet, ladies' room

Z

z of; from

za behind; in; after, past the; per

zabalit [zubulit] to wrap; to pack

zábava [zahbuva] fun; dance, party

zábavný [zahbuvnee] amusing

zabít [zubeet] to kill

zabočte ... [zubotchteh] turn ...

záclona [zahtslona] curtain

zácpa [zahtspa] constipation

začal [zutchul] I began; you began; he began

začátečnice f [zutchahtetchnitseh], začátečník [zutchahtetch-nyeek] beginner

začátek [zutchahtek] beginning

začínat/začít* [zutcheenut/zutcheet] to begin, to start

záda npl [zahda] back (of body)

zadáno [zudahno] reservation

zadek [zudek] bottom (of body)

zadní [zudnyee] back (adj)

zadní kolo back wheel

zadní sedadlo [sedudlo] back seat

zadní sklo rear window

zadní světla [svyetla] rear lights

zahanbený [zuhunbenee] ashamed

zahněte ... [zaHnyeteh] turn ...

zahodit [zuhodyit] to throw away

zahrada [zuhruda] garden

zahrádka na automobil [zuhruhtka na owtomobil] roof rack

zahraniční [zuhrunyitchnyee] foreign; international; overseas

zahraniční linky fpl international flights

záchod [zahHot] toilet, restroom

záchody mpl [zahHodi] toilets, restroom

zachránit [zuHrahnyit] to save

záchranná brzda [zahHrunah burzda] emergency cord

záchranná služba [slooJba] ambulance

záchranná vesta life jacket

záchranný pás [zahHrunee pahs] lifebelt

zajímavý [zī-eemuvee] interesting

zakašlat [zukushlut] to cough

zákaz [zahkus] prohibition, bar

zakázaný [zukahzunee] forbidden; prohibited

zákaz koupání no swimming

zakazovat/zakázat [zukuzovut/zukahzut] to forbid

zákaz parkování no parking

zákaz prodeje sale forbidden

zákaz předjíždění no overtaking

zákaz rybaření no fishing

zákaz vstupu no trespassing

základní škola [zahkludnyee shkola] primary school

zákon [zahkon] law

záležet [zahleJet] to depend

záliv [zahlif] bay

záloha [zahloha] deposit; advance payment

zámek [zahmek] castle; lock

zamést [zumest] to sweep

zaměstnání [zuh-mnyestnahnyee] job; employment

zaměstnat [zuh-mnyestnut] to

employ
zamíchat [zumeeHut] to mix
zamračeno [zumrutcheno] cloudy
zaneprázdněný [zuneprahz-dnyenee] busy
zánět [zahnyet] inflammation
zánět mandlí [mundlee] tonsillitis
zánět slepého střeva [strJeva] appendicitis
západ [zahput] west
západně od [zahpud-nyeh ot] west of
západní [zahpud-nyee] western
západ slunce [sloontseh] sunset
zápach [zahpuH] bad smell
zapálit [zupahlit] light
zápalky fpl [zahpulki] matches
zapalovací svíčka [sveetchka] spark plug
zapalovač [zupulovutch] lighter
zapalování [zupulovahnyee] ignition
zápal plic [zahpul plits] pneumonia
zapamatovat si [zupumutovut] to remember
zaparkovat [zupurkovut] to park
zápas [zahpus] match (sport)
zápasení [zahpusenyee] wrestling
zápěstí [zahpyestyee] wrist
zapínat/zapnout [zupeenut/zupnoht] to switch on
zápisník [zahpis-nyeek] notebook
zaplatit [zuplutyit] to pay
záplavy fpl [zahpluvi] floods

zapomínat/zapomenout [zupomeenut/zupomenoht] to forget; to leave behind
zapomnětlivý [zupo-mnyetlivee] forgetful
za prvé [purveh] firstly
zardénky fpl [zardyenki] German measles
záruční lhůta best before
záruka [zahrooka] guarantee
září [zahrJee] September
zařízený [zarJeezenee] furnished
zařízený byt [bit] furnished flat/apartment
zasmát se [zusmaht seh] to have a laugh
zastavárna [zustuvarna] pawnshop
zastávka [zustahfka] bus stop
zastávka na znamení request stop
zastavovat/zastavit [zustuvit] to stop
zástrčka [zahsturtchka] plug (electrical)
zástrčka zámku [zahmkoo] bolt
zástupce m [zahstooptseh], **zástupkyně** f [zahstoopki-nyeh] agent
zásuvka [zahsoofka] socket
zatáčka [zutahtchka] bend
zatancovat si [zutuntsovut] to have a dance
zatčení [zutchenyee] arrest
zatímco [zutyeemtso] while
zátka [zahtka] plug (in sink)
zatknout [zutknoht] to arrest
zátoka [zahtoka] inlet
za týden [teeden] per week; this

time next week

zavazadla npl [zuvuzudla] luggage, baggage

závěj f [zahvyay] snowdrift

závěrka [zahvyerka] shutter (in camera)

závěsné létání [zahvyesneh lehtahnyee] hang-gliding

závěsy mpl [zahvyesi] curtains, drapes

zavírací špendlík [zuveerutsee shpendleek] safety pin

zavírat/zavřít [zuveerut/zuvurJeet] to close

zavolat [zuvolut] to call

zavolejte později [zuvolayteh pozdyayi] call later

zavřeno [zuvrJeno] closed

zavřený [zuvrJenee] closed

zazpívat si [zuspeevut] to sing

zbraně f [zbranyeh] arms, weapons

zbytek [zbitek] rest, remainder

zde [zdeh] here

zde je [yeh] here is

zde jsou [soh] here are

zde otevřít open here

zdraví [zdruvee] health

zdravotní sestra [zdruvotnyee sestra] nurse

zdravý [zdruvee] healthy

z druhé ruky [zdrooheh rooki] secondhand

zdvořilý [zdvorJilee] polite

zeď f [zet^yeh] wall

zejména [zaymena] especially

zelený [zelenee] green

země [zeh-mnyeh] earth

zemědělec [zeh-mnyedyelets]

farmer

zemřít [zem-rJeet] to die

zeť [zet^yeh] son-in-law

zhasínat/zhasnout [zuhuseenut/zuhusnoht] to switch off

zhasni! [zuhusnyi] switch it off!

zima winter

je zima [yeh] it's cold

zítra [zeetra] tomorrow

zjevný [zyevnee] obvious

zklamaný [sklumunee] disappointed

zkontrolovat [–lovut] to check

zkouřit [zukohrJit] to smoke

zkoušet/zkusit [skohshet/skoosit] to try

zkratka [skrutka] shortcut

zkusit/zkoušet na sebe [skoosit/skohshet na sebeh] to try on

zkušený [skooshenee] experienced

zlaté stránky [zluteh strahnki] yellow pages

zlato [zluto] gold

zlepšovat/zlepšit [zlepshovut/zlepshit] to improve

zlobit se [seh] to be angry

zloděj m [zlodyay], **zlodějka** f thief

zlomenina [zlomenyina] fracture

zlomený [zlomenee] broken

zlomit si ... to break one's ...

zlý [zlee] bad

zmatek [zmutek] mix-up

zmatený [zmutenee] confused

zmeškat [zmeshkut] to miss (bus, train etc)

změna přednosti v jízdě traffic priority changes

změnit [zmnyenyit] to change

zmizet [zmizet] to disappear

známka [znahmka] stamp

známky fpl stamps

znát [znaht] to know (person)

znečištěný [znetchish-tyenee] polluted

zneužití se trestá penalty for misuse

znovu [znovoo] again

zoologická zahrada [zo-ologitskah zuhruda] zoo

zopakovat [zopukovut] to repeat

zoufalý [zohfulee] desperate

zpátečka [spahtetchka] reverse (gear)

zpáteční jízdenka [spahtetchnyee yeezdenka] return ticket, round-trip ticket

zpětné zrcátko [spyetneh zurtsahtko] rearview mirror

zpěvačka [spyevutchka], zpěvák [spyevahk] singer

zpívat [speevut] to sing

zpozdit se [spozdyit seh] to be late

zpozorovat [spozorovut] to notice; to watch

zpoždění [spoJdyenyee] delay

zpráva [sprahva] message

zprávy fpl [sprahvi] news

zralý [zrulee] ripe

zranění [zrunyenyee] wound

zraněný [zrunyenee] injured; wounded

zrcadlo [zurtsudlo] mirror

zrušit [zrooshit] to cancel

ztrácet/ztratit [strahtset/strutyit] to lose

ztráta [strahta] loss

ztráty a nálezy [strahti a nahlezi] lost property office

zub [zoop] tooth

zubař [zooburJ] dentist

zubní lékař m [zoobnyee lekurJ], zubní lékařka f dentist

zubní protéza dentures

zuřivý [zoorJivee] furious

zůstávat/zůstat [zOOstahvut/ zOOstut] to stay, to remain

zvát [zvaht] to invite

zvedák [zvedahk] jack

zvědavý [zvyeduvee] curious

zvedněte sluchátko lift receiver

zvětšení [zvyetshenyee] enlargement

zvíře n [zveerJeh] animal

zvon bell (in church)

zvonek bell (on door)

zvonit [zvonyit] to ring

zvracet [zvrutset] to vomit

Ž

žába [Jahba] frog

žádat [Jahdut] to ask; to demand

žádná [Jahdnah], žádné [Jahdneh], žádní [Jahdnyee], žádný [Jahdnee] no ...; none

žádné další [dulshee] no more

žádost f [Jahdost] application form

žák [Jahk] schoolboy

žákyně f [Jahki-nyeh] schoolgirl

žaludek [Juloodek] stomach

žaluzie [Juloozi-eh] Venetian blind

žárlivý [Jarlivee] jealous

žárovka [Jarofka] light bulb

žebro [Jebro] rib

žebřík [JebrJeek] ladder

žehlicí prkno [Jehlitsee purkno] ironing board

žehlička [Jehlitchka] iron (for ironing)

žehnat [Jehnut] to bless

železářství [JelezarJstvee] hardware store

železnice f [Jeleznyitseh] railway

železniční přejezd railway crossing

železo [Jelezo] iron (metal)

žena [Jena] woman

ženatý [Jenutee] married (of man)

ženský [Jenskee] female; women's; ladies' (toilet), ladies' room

žert [Jert] joke

židle [Jidleh] chair

židovský [Jidofskee] Jewish

žiletky fpl [Jiletki] razor blades

žít [Jeet] to live

život [Jivot] life

živý [Jivee] alive

žízeň [Jeezen^yeh] thirst

žíznivý [Jeeznyivee] thirsty

Žlutí andělé [Jlootyee undyeleh] Yellow Angels (breakdown recovery organization)

žlutý [Jlootee] yellow

župan [Joopun] dressing gown

žvýkačka [Jveekutchka] chewing gum

Menu Reader:

Food

ananas [ununus] pineapple

anglická slanina [unglitskah slunyina] bacon

anglická telecí játra [unglitskah teletsee yahtra] fried calves' liver with streaky bacon

anglický rostbíf [unglitskee rostbeef] English-style roast beef

angrešt [ungresht] gooseberry

arašídy [urusheedi] peanuts

bábovka [bahbofka] light sponge cake

baklažán [bukluJahn] aubergine/ eggplant

baklažány s česnekovou omáčkou [bukluJahni s chesnekovoh omahtchkoh] aubergines/eggplants with garlic sauce

banán [bunahn] banana

banán v čokoládě [chokolahdyeh] banana in chocolate sauce

bavorské vdolečky [buvorskeh vudoletchki] doughnuts with jam, cottage cheese or cream

bažant [buJunt] pheasant

bažant dušený na žampionech [dooshenee na Jumpi-awneH] pheasant casserole with mushrooms

bažant na slanině [slunyinyeh] roast pheasant with bacon

bezmasá jídla [bezmusah yeedla] meatless dishes

biftek s vejcem [vaytsem] steak with an egg

bílý rybíz [beelee ribees] white currants

bochník [boH-nyeek] loaf

bomba Malakov [mulukof] sponge cake soaked in milk and rum and filled with butter cream

boršč [borshtch] Russian-style beetroot and cabbage soup

borůvky [boroOfki] bilberries, blueberries

bramborák [brumborahk] potato pancake, usually containing small pieces of salami

bramborová kaše [brumborovah kasheh] mashed potatoes

bramborová polévka [polefka] potato soup

bramborové hranolky [brumboroveh hrunolki] chips, French fries

bramborové knedlíky [kunedleeki] potato dumplings

bramborové knedlíky plněné uzeným [pulnyeneh oozeneem] potato dumplings filled with smoked meat

bramborové knedlíky s cibulkou [tsiboolkoh] potato dumplings with onions

bramborové lupínky [loopeenki] crisps, potato chips

bramborové placky [plutski] potato pancake

bramborové šišky [shishki] small flour and potato dumplings

bramborový guláš [brumborovee goolahsh] potato goulash

bramborový salát [sulaht] potato salad

brambory [brumbori] potatoes

brokolice [brokolitseh] broccoli

brokolice s vejci [vaytsi] broccoli with eggs

broskev [broskef] peach

broskev plněná kuřecím salátem [pulnyenah koorJetseem sulahtem] peach stuffed with chicken salad

brukev na paprice [brookeʄ na pupritseh] kohlrabi with red peppers

brynza [brinza] sheeps' cheese

brynzové halušky [brinzoveh hulooshki] small flour and potato dumplings with sheeps' cheese

buchty [booHti] baked yeast dumpling filled with cottage cheese, jam, apples or plums

burské oříšky [burskeh orJeeshki] peanuts

byliny [bilini] herbs

celer [tseler] celery

celerová polévka [tselerovah polefka] celery soup

celerový salát [tselerovee sulaht] celery salad

celozrnný chléb [tselozurnee Hlep] wholemeal bread

cibule [tsibooleh] onion

cibulová omáčka [tsiboolovah omahtchka] onion sauce

cikánská hovězí pečeně [tsikahnskah hovyezee petchenyeh] gypsy-style beef stew, with onions, mushrooms, peppers, smoked sausage and tomatoes

citrón [tsitrawn] lemon

citrónový [tsitrawnovee] lemon (adj)

cukína [tsookina] courgettes, zucchini

cukr [tsukur] sugar

cukroví [tsookrovee] biscuits, cookies

čajové pečivo [chī-oveh petchivo] tea biscuits/cookies

černý rybíz [chernee ribees] blackcurrants

čerstvý [cherstvee] fresh

červená řepa [chervenah rJepa] beetroot

červený rybíz [chervenee ribees] redcurrants

český chléb bread with rye, wheat and whey

česnek [chesnek] garlic

česneková omáčka [chesnekovah omahtchka] garlic sauce

česneková polévka [polefka] garlic soup

čevapčiči [chevuptchitchi] spicy meatballs

čínské zelí [cheenskeh zelee] Chinese cabbage, Chinese leaf

čočka [chotchka] lentils

čočka s vejcem [vaytsem] boiled lentils with a fried egg

čočka vařená [vurJenah] boiled

lentils

čočková polévka [polefka] lentil soup

čočková polévka s párkem lentil soup with sausage

čočkový salát [chotchkovee sulaht] lentil salad

čokoládový krém se šlehačkou [chokolahdovee krem seh shlehutchkoh] chocolate custard dessert with whipped cream

daněk [dunyek] venison

daňčí hřbet na smetaně [dun^(yeh)tchee hurJbJet na smetunyeh] saddle of venison with cream sauce

daňčí roštěná [roshtyenah] sirloin of venison

datle [dutleh] dates

dezert dessert

divoký kanec [dyivokee kunets] wild boar

divoký králík na česneku [krahleek na chesnekoo] wild rabbit with garlic

divoký králík na smetaně [smetunyeh] wild rabbit with cream sauce

do krvava [kurvuva] rare

domácí [domahtsee] homemade

domácí pečená klobása [petchenah klobahsa] homemade grilled smoked sausage

dort cake; gâteau

dortík [dortyeek] tart

dršťková polévka [dursht^(yeh)kovah

polefka] tripe soup with paprika

dršťky [dursht^(yeh)ki] tripe

dršťky na paprice [pupritseh] tripe in paprika sauce

drůbež [dr00besh] poultry

drůbeží salát [dr00beJee sulaht] chicken salad

drůbková polévka [dr00pkovah polefka] giblet soup

drůbky [dr00pki] giblets

dukátové buchtičky s vanilkovým krémem [dookahtoveh booHtyitchki svunilkoveem] small doughnuts in hot vanilla custard

dušená brokolice [dooshenah brokolitseh] stewed broccoli

dušená brukev [brookef] stewed kohlrabi

dušená kapusta [kupoosta] stewed curly kale

dušené hovězí maso [doosheneh hovyezee] beef stew

dušené telecí [teletsee] veal stew

dušené vepřové [veprJoveh] pork stew

dušené zelí [zelee] stewed sauerkraut

dušený [dooshenee] stewed

dušený špenát [shpenaht] stewed spinach

dýňová semena [deenyovah] pumpkin seeds

džem [jem] jam

fazole [fuzoleh] beans

fazole na kyselo [kiselo] sour

bean stew
fazolkový salát [fuzolkovee sulaht]
   French bean salad
fazolky [fuzolki] green beans
fazolová polévka [fuzolovah
   polefka] bean soup
fazolový salát [fuzolovee sulaht]
   bean salad
feferonkový salát [feferonkovee
   sulaht] hot pepper and pea
   salad
fíky [feeki] figs
filé [fileh] fillet
francouzské brambory
   [fruntsohskeh brumbori] boiled
   potatoes baked with eggs,
   peas and onions
francouzský salát [fruntsohskee
   sulaht] salad of potatoes,
   vegetables and mayonnaise
fritovaný [fritovunee] deep-fried

gaskoňský kotlet [guskon^yeh skee]
   pork chop with cream and
   mushrooms
graham [gruhum] wholemeal
   bread
grilované kuře [grilovuneh
   koorJeh] grilled chicken
grilovaný [grilovunee] grilled
guláš [goolahsh] goulash, meat
   stew with paprika
gulášová omáčka [goolahshovah
   omahtchka] goulash sauce
gulášová polévka [polefka]
   goulash soup
guláš z daňčího masa
   [dun^yeh tcheeho muso] venison
   goulash

guláš z husích žaludků [hooseeH
   Julootkoo] goulash made with
   goose's stomach

hašé [husheh] minced meat
hašé z telecího masa [teletseeho
   musa] minced veal
hermelín [hermeleen]
   Camembert-type cheese
hlávkové zelí [hlahfkoveh zelee]
   cabbage
hlávkový salát [hlahfkovee sulaht]
   lettuce
hlávkový salát se slaninou [seh
   slunyinoh] lettuce with
   vinegar dressing and small
   pieces of fried bacon
hlávkový salát s kyselou
   smetanou [smetunoh] lettuce
   with sour cream
hlávkový salát s kyselým mlékem
   [kiseleem] lettuce with sour
   milk dressing
hodně vypečený [hodnyeh
   vipetchenee] well-done
holub [holoop] pigeon
horký [horkee] hot
hořčice [horJtchitseh] mustard
hotová jídla [hotovah yeedla]
   ready-made meals
houbová omáčka [hohbovah
   omahtchka] mushroom sauce
houbová polévka [polefka]
   mushroom soup
houbový guláš [goolahsh]
   mushroom goulash
houby [hohbi] mushrooms
houska [hohska] roll
houskové knedlíky [hohskoveh

kunedleeki] bread dumplings

hovězí [hovyezee] beef

hovězí dušené na hřbkách
[doosheneh na hrJeebkaн] beef
stew with mushrooms

hovězí dušené v mrkvi [murkvi]
beef stew with carrots

hovězí guláš [goolahsh] beef
goulash

hovězí játra na slanině [yahtra na
slunyinyeh] calves' liver
stewed with onions and
bacon

hovězí maso [muso] beef

**hovězí maso s houbovou
omáčkou** [hohbovoh
omahtchkoh] boiled beef with
mushroom sauce

**hovězí maso s koprovou
omáčkou** [koprovoh] boiled
beef with dill sauce

hovězí maso s rajskou omáčkou
[rīskoh] boiled beef with
tomato sauce

hovězí pečeně na houbách
[petchenyeh na hohbahн]
stewed beef with
mushrooms

hovězí pečeně na paprice
[pupritseh] stewed beef with
paprika

hovězí pečeně na víně [veenyeh]
stewed beef in wine sauce

hovězí polévka [polefka] beef
broth

**hovězí polévka se žemlovým
svítkem** [Jemloveem sveetkem]
beef broth with bread
omelette

hovězí polévka s knedlíčky
[kunedleetchki] beef broth
with dumplings

**hovězí polévka s masem a
nudlemi** [musem a noodlemi]
beef broth with meat and
vermicelli

**hovězí polévka s masovými
knedlíčky** [musoveemi
kunedleetchki] beef broth with
meatballs

hovězí polévka s noky [noki]
beef broth with small flour
and potato dumplings

hovězí polévka s rýží [sreeJee]
beef broth with rice

hovězí tokáň [tokahn^yeh] beef
stewed in wine and tomato
purée

hovězí vývar s nudlemi [veevahr
snoodlemi] beef broth with
vermicelli

hrách [hrahн] (dried) peas

hrachová kaše [hruнovah kusheh]
boiled peas with pieces of
bacon

hrachová kaše s cibulkou
[tsiboolkoh] peas with fried
onions

**hrachová polévka s uzeným
masem** [polefka soozeneem
musem] pea soup with
smoked meat

hrách s kyselým zelím [hrahн
skiseleem zeleem] peas and
sauerkraut

hranolky [hrunolki] chips,
French fries

hrášek [hrahshek] peas

hrášek s mrkví [murkvee] peas
and carrots

hráškový krém [hrahshkovee]
cream of pea soup

hroznové víno [hroznovee veeno]
grapes

hrozny [hrozni] grapes

hruška [hrooshka] pear

hříbky s vejci [hrJeepki svaytsi]
baked mushrooms with eggs

humr [humur] lobster

husa [hoosa] goose

husí játra pečená na cibuli
[hoosee yahtra petchenah na
tsibooli] fried goose liver
with onions

husí játra s jablky [syubulki]
fried goose liver with apples

husí játra smažená [smuJenah]
goose liver fried in
breadcrumbs

husí prsa nebo stehýnka na
česneku [hoosee pursa
steheenka na chesnekoo] breast
or leg of goose with garlic

husí žaludky zadělávané
[Julootki zudyelahvuneh] goose
stomach in white sauce

chléb [Hlep] bread

chlebíčky [Hlebeetchkee] open
sandwiches

chlupaté knedlíky se zelím
[Hlooputeh kunedleeki seh
zeleem] Bohemian potato
dumplings with cabbage

chřest [HrJest] asparagus

chuťovky [Hootyofki]
savouries

jablka v županu [yubulka
vJoopunoo] apples baked in
puff pastry with nuts and
jam

jablko [yubulko] apple

jablková žemlovka [yubulkovah
Jemlofka] apple charlotte
made from baked apples,
white bread soaked in milk,
cottage cheese and raisins

jablkový závin [yubulkovee
zahvin] apple strudel

jahodový [yuhodovee]
strawberry (adj)

jahody [yuhodi] strawberries

jarní míchaný salát [yurnyee
meeHunee sulaht] mixed
vegetable salad

jaternicová polévka
[yuternyitsovah polefka] soup
with black pudding and
jitrnice sausage

játra [yahtra] liver

játrová omáčka [yahtrovah
omahtchka] liver sauce

jazýček [yuzeetchek] tongue

jazyk [yuzik] tongue

ječmen [yetchmen] barley

jedlý kaštan [yedlee kushtun]
chestnut

jednotlivá jídla [yednotlivah
yeedla] à la carte

jehně [yehnyeh] lamb

jehněčí maso [yehnyehtchee
muso] lamb

jehněčí maso dušené na kmíně
[doosheneh na kumeenyeh]
lamb stewed with caraway
seeds

jelení hřbet přírodní [yelenyee hurJbet prJeerodnyee] saddle of venison

jelení maso [yelenyee muso] venison

jelito [yelito] black pudding

jídelní lístek [yeedelnyee leestek] menu

jídla na objednávku meals made to order

jitrnice [yiturnyitseh] sausage made from minced meat and breadcrumbs

jogurt [yogoort] yoghurt

kadeřávek [kuderJahvek] savoy cabbage

kachna [kuHna] duck

kachna pečená [petchenah] roast duck

kachna s pomerančem dušená v papilotě [seh pomeruntchem dooshenah v pupilotyeh] duck in orange sauce en papillote

kachna v šouletu [fshohletoo] duck in a pea and pearl barley purée

kančí [kuntchee] wild boar

kančí filé [fileh] roast fillet of wild boar

kančí kýta s brusinkovou omáčkou [keetah s broosinkovoh omahtchkoh] boiled leg of wild boar with cranberry sauce

kapr [kupur] carp

kapr dušený na paprice [dooshenee na pupritseh] stewed carp with paprika

kapr na kmíně [kumeenyeh] carp baked with caraway seeds

kapr na modro carp cooked in fish stock with wine and spices

kapr na rožni [roJnyi] carp on a skewer

kapr pečený [petchenee] baked carp

kapr smažený [smuJenee] fried carp

kapusta [kupoosta] curly kale

kapustové karbanátky [kupoostoveh kurbunahtki] fried curly kale rissoles

karbanátky minced meat rissoles

karotka [kurotka] carrots

kaše [kusheh] buckwheat cereal; purée

kaviár [kuvi-ar] caviar

kaviárové vejce [kuvi-aroveh vaytseh] hard-boiled egg with caviar

kedluben [kedlooben] kohlrabi

klobása [klobahsa] smoked sausage

klopsy na smetaně [klopsi na smetunyeh] stewed meatballs with cream sauce

kmín [kumeen] caraway seed

kmínová polévka s vejcem [kumeenovah polefka svaytsem] caraway seed soup with egg

kmínový chléb bread with caraway seeds

knedlíky [kunedleeki] dumplings

knedlíky s vejci [vaytsi] dumplings and egg

kobliha doughnut

kokos coconut

koláč [kolahtch] small cake with marmalade or cottage cheese

koláček [kolahtchek] small sweet pie or tart

kompot stewed fruit

kopr [kopur] dill

koprová omáčka [koprovah omahtchka] dill sauce

koroptev pečená na slanině [koroptef petchenah na slunyinyeh] roast partridge with bacon

koření [korJenyee] spice

kotleta chop

krabí maso na másle [krubee muso na mahsleh] crab meat with butter

krajíc [krī-yeets] slice of bread

králík [krahleek] rabbit

krevety [kreveti] shrimps

krocan [krotsun] turkey

krocan pečený na slanině [petchenee na slunyinyeh] roast turkey with bacon

krocan s kaštanovou nádivkou [kushtunovoh nahdyifkoh] roast turkey stuffed with chestnuts

krokety [kroketi] croquettes

krupice [kroopitseh] semolina

krupicová kaše [kroopitsovah kusheh] semolina purée

krupicové noky [kroopitsoveh noki] semolina dumplings

krupicový nákyp [kroopitsovee nahkip] semolina pudding

krvavý [kurvuvee] rare

křehký koláč s jablky [krJeнkee kolahtch s yubulki] apple pie

křen [krJen] horseradish

křenová šlehačka [krJenovah shlehutchka] horseradish sauce

křepelčí hnízdo [krJepeltchee hunyeezdo] quail's egg with ham

křepelčí vajíčka [krJepeltchee vī-eetchka] quail's eggs

křídlo [krJeedlo] wing

kukuřice [kookoorJitseh] maize; sweet corn; corn on the cob

kuře [koorJeh] chicken

kuřecí polévka [koorJetsee polefka] thin chicken soup

kuřecí prsa s broskví a sýrem [koorJetsee prusa sbroskvee a seerem] fried chicken breast with peaches and cheese

kuřecí prsíčka s masitou náplní [pruseetchka smusitoh nahpulnyee] roast chicken breast stuffed with veal and ham

kuřecí vývar s masem a nudlemi [kurJetsee veevur smusem a noodlemi] chicken broth with meat and vermicelli

kuře na paprice [kurJeh na pupritseh] chicken in paprika, onion and cream sauce

kuře na rožni [roJnyi] chicken on a skewer

kuře na způsob bažanta [spoosop buJunta] roast chicken with bacon and spices

kůzle pečené [kOOzleh petcheneh] roast kid

květák [kvyetahk] cauliflower

květáková polévka [kvyetahkovah polefka] cauliflower soup

květák s vejci [kvyetahk svaytsi] cauliflower with eggs

kynuté knedlíky [kinooteh kunedleeki] dumplings filled with jam or fruit

kyselé zelí [kiseleh zelee] sauerkraut

kyselý [kiselee] sour

kýta [keeta] thigh; joint; haunch

langoše [lungosheh] deep-fried dough, covered in garlic

lečo s klobásou [letcho sklobahsoh] green or red peppers stewed with onions, tomatoes and smoked sausage

lečo s vejci [svaytsi] green or red peppers stewed with onions, tomatoes and eggs

ledvinky [ledvinki] kidneys

lískové ořechy [leeskoveh orJeHi] hazelnuts

lívance [leevuntseh] pancakes with jam

losos salmon

losos na másle [mahsleh] salmon with butter

loupáky [lohpahki] similar to croissants

luštěninová jídla [looshtyenyinovah yeedla]

dishes containing beans or pulses

majonéza [mī-oneza] mayonnaise

majoránka [mī-orahnka] marjoram

mák [mahk] poppy seeds

makrela [mukrela] mackerel

makrela na žampionech [na Jumpi-awneH] stewed mackerel with mushrooms

maliny [mulini] raspberries

mandarinka [mundurinka] tangerine

mandle [mundleh] almond

máslo [mahslo] butter

maso [muso] meat

masová směs na roštu [musovah smnyes na roshtoo] mixed grill of beef, veal, pork, calves' or pigs' kidney, smoked sausage and ham

máta peprná [mahta pepurnah] peppermint

med [met] honey

meloun [melohn] melon

menu [meni] table d'hôte, set menu

meruňka [meroon^{yeh}ka] apricot

míchaná vejce [meeHanah vaytseh] scrambled eggs

míchaná vejce na cibulce [tsibooltseh] scrambled eggs with onions

míchaná zelenina [zelenyina] boiled mixed vegetables

minutky fast meals to order

moravský vrabec [morufskee

vrubets] 'Moravian Sparrows'
– pieces of pork sprinkled
with caraway seeds and
roasted
mořské ryby [morJskeh ribi]
saltwater fish
moučník [mohtchnyeek] dessert
moučníky [mohtchnyeeki]
desserts
mouka [mohka] flour
mražený [mruJenee] frozen
mrkev [murkef] carrot
mrkvový salát [murkuvovee
sulaht] carrot salad
mušle [mooshleh] mussels

nadívané holoubě [nudyeevuneh
holohbyeh] stuffed young
pigeon
nadívaný [nudyeevunee] stuffed
na jehle [yehleh] on a skewer
nakládaný [nuklahdunee]
pickled
na kmíně [kumeenyeh] with
caraway seeds
nanukový dort [nunookovee] ice
cream gâteau
na roštu [roshtoo] grilled
ne moc vypečený [neh mots
vipetchenee] medium-rare
niva soft, crumbly blue cheese
noky [noki] small flour and
potato dumplings
nudle [noodleh] noodles
nudle s mákem [mahkem]
noodles with poppy seeds
nudle s tvarohem a cukrem
[tvuro-hem a tsookrem] noodles
with cottage cheese and

sugar
nudlový nákyp s tvarohem
[noodlovee nahkip] noodle
pudding with cottage cheese

obilí [obilee] corn
obložené vejce [obloJeneh
vaytseh] hard-boiled egg,
mayonnaise, ham and
pickles
**obložený biftek se smaženým
vejcem** [obloJenee – seh
smuJeneem vaytsem] beef
steak with an egg and
garnish
obložený chléb [Hlep] sandwich
obložený chlebíček [Hlebeetchek]
open sandwich, canapé
ocet [otset] vinegar
okurka [okoorka] cucumber
okurková omáčka [okoorkovah
omahtchka] cucumber sauce
okurkový salát [okoorkovee
sulaht] cucumber salad
okurkový salát se smetanou [seh
smetunoh] cucumber salad
with cream
olej [olay] oil
olejovky s cibulí [olay-ofki
sutsiboolee] sardines with
onions
olivový olej [olivovee olay] olive
oil
omáčka [omahtchka] sauce
omeleta s drůbežími játry
[drOobeJeemi yahtri] omelette
with poultry liver
omeleta se šunkou [shoonkoh]
ham omelette

omeleta se zavařeninou [seh
zuvurɟenyinoh] jam omelette

omeleta s hráškem [hrahshkem]
pea omelette

opékané brambory [opekuneh
brumbori] fried potatoes

oplatky [oplutki] waffles

ořech [orɟeʜ] nut

ostružiny [ostrooɟini]
blackberries

ovarové vepřové koleno
[ovuroveh veprɟoveh] boiled
pigs' knuckle

oves oats

ovoce [ovotseh] fruit

ovocné knedlíky [ovotsneh
kunedleeky] fruit dumplings

ovocný [ovotsnee] fruit (adj)

ovocný talíř [tuleerɟ] fruit bowl

palačinka [pulutchinka] pancake

palačinky se šlehčkou
[pulutchinki seh shlehutchkoh]
pancakes with jam and
whipped cream

palačinky se zavařeninou
[zuvurɟenyinoh] pancakes with
jam

pálivá paprika [pahlivah puprika]
hot red pepper

paprika green or red pepper

paprikový lusk pepper,
capsicum

paprikový salát [puprikovee
sulaht] green or red pepper
salad

párek sausage, frankfurter

párek s hořčicí [horɟtchitsee]
sausage with mustard

párek smažený v těstíčku
[smuɟenee ftyestyeetchkoo] fried
sausage in batter

párek v rohlíku [rohleekoo] hot
dog

pařížský krém [purɟeeshskee]
whipped cream and
chocolate custard dessert

paštika [pahshtyika] pâté

paštika z bažantů [buɟuntoo]
pheasant pâté

paštika z husích jater [hooseeʜ
yuter] goose liver pâté

pažitka [puɟitka] chives

pečená husa [petchenah hoosa]
roast goose

pečená šunka s vejci [petchenah
shoonka svaytsi] ham and eggs

pečené hovězí maso [petcheneh
hovyezee muso] roast beef

pečené kuře s nádivkou [koorɟeh
s nahdyifkoh] stuffed roast
chicken

pečený [petchenee] roast;
baked; grilled

pečivo [petchivo] bread;
pastries

pepř [pepurɟ] pepper (spice)

perlička pečená na slanině
[perlitchka petchenah na
slunyinyeh] roast guinea fowl
with bacon

perník [pernyeek] gingerbread;
crackers

petržel [petruɟel] parsley

pivní sýr [pivnyee seer] cheese
flavoured with beer

plátek [plahtek] slice

platýs na roštu [plutees na

roshtoo] grilled flounder

plněná kapusta [pulnyenah kupoosta] curly kale leaves stuffed with minced meat and stewed

plněná paprika [puprika] stewed stuffed green or red peppers

plněné rajče zapečené [pulnyeneh rĭtcheh zupetcheneh] stuffed tomato au gratin

plněné žampiony [Jumpi-awni] stuffed mushrooms au gratin

plněný telecí řízek [teletsee rJeezek] stuffed veal steak

plzeňská pivní polévka [pulzen^yeh skah pivnyee polefka] Pilsen-style beer soup

poháry [pohari] sundae

pochoutky k vínu [poHohtki k veenoo] snacks eaten with wine

polévka [polefka] soup

pomazánka [pomuzahnka] spread

pomeranč [pomeruntch] orange

pomerančový [pomeruntchovee] orange (adj)

porcovaný chléb [portsovunee Hlep] sliced bread

pórek leek

pórková polévka s vejcem [porkovah polefka svaytsem] leek soup with egg

poulard dušený v rýži [pohlurd dooshenee vreeJi] stewed poulard with rice

povidla homemade thick

plum jam

povidlové taštičky [povidloveh tushtyitchki] small potato and cottage cheese dough parcels filled with plum jam

pražské telecí hrudí [prushskeh teletsee hroodyee] Prague-style breast of veal stuffed with a mixture of scrambled eggs and ham, green peas, whipped cream and roasted with butter

předkrmy [prJedkurmi] starters, appetizers

přesnídávka [prJes-nyeedahfka] mid-morning snack

přesnídávková polévka [prJes-nyeedahfkovah polefka] thick soup, eaten as a meal in itself

příliš propečený [prJeelish propetchenee] overdone

přílohy [prJeelohi] side dishes

přírodní hovězí pečeně [prJeerodnyee hovyezee petchenyeh] beef spread with bacon fat and stewed with onions

přírodní roštěná [roshtyenah] sirloin stewed with onions

přírodní vepřové žebírko [veprJoveh Jebeerko] grilled pork chop

pstruh [pustrooH] trout

pstruh na roštu [roshtoo] grilled trout

pstruh na rozmarýnu [rozmureenoo] trout with rosemary

pstruh na smetaně [smetunyeh] poached trout with cream

pstruh s máslem [smahslem] grilled trout with herb butter

pšenice [pshenyitseh] wheat

pšeničný chléb [pushenyitchnyee ʜlep] white bread

ragú [rugoo] stew

rajčatový salát [rĭtchutovee sulaht] tomato salad

rajče [rĭtcheh] tomato

rajská omáčka [rĭskah omahtchka] tomato sauce

rajská polévka [polefka] tomato soup

rajské jablko [rĭskeh yubulko] tomato

rak [ruk] crayfish

ražniči z kuřecího masa [ruJnyitchi skoorJetseeho musa] pieces of chicken with onion and bacon grilled on a skewer or fried

restovaná telecí játra [restovunah teletsee yahtra] roast calves' liver with onion and spices

rizoto ze žampinů [zeh Jumpi-awnoo] stewed rice with mushrooms

rohlík [rohleek] roll

roláda [rolahda] Swiss roll

rostlinný tuk [rostlinee took] vegetable fat

roštěná na česneku [roshtyenah na chesnekoo] sirloin with garlic

roštěná na paprice [pupritseh] stewed sirloin with paprika

roštěná přírodní na roštu [prJeerodnyee na roshtoo] grilled sirloin steak

roštěná se šunkou a vejcem [seh shoonkoh a vaytsem] stewed sirloin with ham and egg

rozinky [rozinki] raisins

rožeň [roJenʸᵉʰ] spit; skewer

ruská polévka [rooskah polefka] Russian-style beetroot and cabbage soup

růžičková kapusta [rooJitchkovah kupoosta] Brussels sprouts

ryba [riba] fish

rybí filé na másle [ribee fileh na mahsleh] fillet of fish in butter

rybí filé na roštu [roshtoo] grilled fillet of fish

rybí kost fishbone

rybí polévka z kapra [polefka skupra] carp soup

rybí salát [sulaht] fish salad

rybí speciality [ribee] fish dishes

rybíz [ribees] currants

ryby [ribi] fish

rychlé občerstvení [riʜleh optcher-stvenyee] snack

rýže [reeJeh] rice

rýže dušená [dooshenah] stewed rice

rýžová kaše [reeJovah kusheh] sweet or savoury rice purée

rýžový nákyp s jablky [reeJovee nahkip syubulki] rice pudding with apples

ředkev [rJetkef] type of radish
ředkvička [rJetkvitchka] radish
řez [rJes] lighter, square cakes,
usually containing fruit
řízek [rJeezek] fillet

salám [sulahm] salami
salát [sulaht] lettuce; salad
saláty [sulahti] salads
salát z červeného zelí
[cherveneho zelee] red
cabbage salad
salát z červené řepy [cherveneh
rJepi] beetroot salad
salát z čínského zelí [cheenskeho
zelee] Chinese cabbage salad
salát z fazolových lusků
[fuzoloveeн looskoo] French
bean salad
salát z kyselého zelí [kiseleho
zelee] sauerkraut salad
salát z těstovin [tyestovin] pasta
salad
sardinka [surdinka] sardine
segedínský guláš [segedeenskee
goolahsh] pork goulash with
sauerkraut
sekaná [sekunah] minced meat
sekaná pečeně [petchenyeh]
meatloaf
sekaná svíčková [sveetchkovah]
meatloaf with cream sauce
sekaný [sekunee] chopped
selská pečeně [selskah
petchenyeh] peasant-style
saddle of pork roasted with
garlic, salt and onions
selská polévka [polefka]
peasant-style soup with

noodles and mushrooms
selské jaternice [yuternyitseh]
peasant-style white pudding
skopová kýta na česneku
[skopovah keeta na chesnekoo]
leg of mutton with garlic
skopová kýta na divoko [dyivoko]
leg of mutton spread with
bacon fat and stewed with
onions and root vegetables
in red wine
skopová kýta na smetaně
[smetunyeh] leg of mutton in
cream sauce
skopové maso [skopoveh muso]
mutton
skopové maso na rožni [roJnyi]
grilled mutton
skopové na majoránce [mī-
orahntseh] mutton with
marjoram
skopové ragú [rugoo] mutton
stew
sladká paprika [slutkah puprika]
sweet red pepper
sladkovodní ryby [slutkovodnyee
ribi] freshwater fish
sladký [slutkee] sweet
slanina [slunyina] bacon
slaný [slunee] salty
sleď [sletʸᵉʰ] herring
sleď vařený s křenovou
omáčkou [vurJenee skrJenovoh
omahtchkoh] herring in
horseradish sauce
slepice [slepitseh] chicken
slepice na paprice [pupritseh]
chicken with paprika and
cream sauce

slepice na slanině [slunyinyeh]
chicken with bacon
slepice v nudlové polévce
[noodloveh poleftseh] chicken
noodle soup
slepičí vývar s nudlemi
[slepitchee veevur snoodlemi]
chicken broth with
vermicelli
sluka [slooka] snipe
slunečnicová semena
[sloonetchnyitsovah] sunflower
seeds
slunečnicový olej
[sloonetchnyitsovee olay]
sunflower oil
smažená roštěnka s vejcem
[smuJenah roshtyenka svaytsem]
fried sirloin with an egg
smažená telecí játra [teletsee
yahtra] fried calves' liver in
breadcrumbs
smažená vejce [vaytseh] fried
eggs
smažené baklažány [smuJeneh
bukluJahni] fried aubergines/
eggplants
smažené bramborové hranolky
[brumboroveh hrunolki] chips,
French fries
smažené bramborové lupínky
[loopeenki] crisps, potato
chips
smažené jehně [yehnyeh] fried
lamb in breadcrumbs
smažené kuře [koorJeh] fried
chicken
smažené kůzle [koozleh] fried
kid in breadcrumbs

smažené rybí filé [ribee fileh]
fried fillet of fish
smažené telecí [teletsee] fried
veal
smažené telecí hrudí [hroodyee]
fried breast of veal
smažené telecí žebírko [Jebeerko]
veal chop fried in
breadcrumbs
smažené vepřové [veprJoveh]
fried pork
smažené žampiony [Jumpi-awni]
mushrooms fried in
breadcrumbs
smažený [smuJenee] fried (in
breadcrumbs)
smažený celer [tseler] fried
celery
smažený hermelín [hermeleen]
fried Camembert-type
cheese
smažený hermelín se šunkou
[seh shoonkoh] fried
Camembert-type cheese
with ham
smažený karbanátek
[kurbunahtek] fried meatballs
smažený květák [kvyetahk] fried
cauliflower
smažený sýr [seer] fried cheese
in breadcrumbs
smažený telecí brzlík [teletsee
burzleek] fried calves'
sweetbread
smažený uzený sýr [oozenee
seer] fried smoked cheese
smažený vepřový jazýček
[veprJovee yuzeetchek] fried
pig's tongue

smažený vepřový řízek [rJeezek] pork steak fried in breadcrumbs

smetana [smetuna] cream

sója [saw-ya] soya

sójové oříšky [saw-yoveh orJeeski] soya beans

sójový salát [saw-yovee sulaht] soya bean salad

srnčí [suruntchee] venison

srnčí hřbet přírodní [hurJbet prJeerodnyee] saddle of venison

srnčí kýta na smetaně [keeta na smetunyeh] leg of venison in cream sauce

srnčí ragú na víně [rugoo na veenyeh] venison stew with wine

steak z tuňáka po provensálsku [toonyahka po provensahlskoo] tuna, tomatoes, white wine and garlic

studené předkrmy [stoodeneh prJetkurmi] hors d'œuvres, starters, appetizers

sůl [sool] salt

sušenka [sooshenka] biscuit, cookie

svačina [svutchina] snack between main meals

svíčková [sveetchkovah] sirloin

svíčková omáčka [omahtchka] sour cream sauce, usually served with fillet of beef

svíčková pečeně na smetaně [petchenyeh na smetunyeh] fillet of beef with cream sauce

svíčkové řezy se šunkou a vejcem [sveetchkoveh rJezi seh shoonkoh a vaytsem] fillet steaks with ham and eggs

svíčkové řezy s husími játry [hooseemi yahtri] fillet steaks with goose liver

sýr [seer] cheese

syrečky [siretchki] small cakes of spicy, strong-smelling cheese

syrový [sirovee] raw

sýrový salát [seerovee sulaht] cheese salad

škubánky s mákem [shkoobahnki smahkem] potato dumplings with poppy seeds and sugar

šlehačka [shlehutchka] whipped cream

šlehaný tvaroh [shlehunee tvuroH] whipped cottage cheese

špagety [shpugeti] spaghetti

španělský ptáček [shpunyelskee putahtchek] stewed beef roll with sausage, cucumber, onions and eggs

špekové knedlíky [shpekoveh kunedleeki] bread and bacon dumplings

špenát [shpenaht] spinach

špikovaná telecí kýta [shpikovunah teletsee keeta] fried larded leg of veal

štika na pivě [shtyika na pivyeh] pike in beer

šunka [shoonka] ham

šunka po cikánsku [po tsigahnskoo] gypsy-style ham with bacon, potatoes,

onions, mushrooms and
paprika

šunka s křenem [skrɹenem] ham
with horse radish

šunková rolka [shoonkovah] ham
roll

šunkový [shoonkovee] ham (adj)

švestkové knedlíky [shvestkoveh
kunedleeki] plum dumplings

švestky [shvestki] plums

tatarská omáčka [tuturskah
omahtchka] tartar sauce

telecí [teletsee] veal

telecí droby [drobi] calves' liver,
kidneys and tongue

telecí dušené s hráškem
[doosheneh shrahshkem] veal
stew with peas

telecí filé se šunkou a chřestem
[fileh seh shoonkoh a HrɹestEm]
veal fillet with ham and
asparagus

telecí filé s husími játry [s
hooseemi yahtri] veal fillet
with goose liver

telecí hrudí nadívané [hroodyee
nudyeevuneh] stuffed breast
of veal

telecí kolínko na způsob bažanta
[koleenko na spoosob buJunta]
calves' knuckle stewed with
spices

telecí kýta na smetaně [keeta na
smetunyeh] leg of veal with
cream sauce

telecí ledvinka pečená
[petchenah] roast calves'
kidneys

telecí medailonky [meda-ilonki]
veal medallions

telecí mozeček s vejci [mozetchek
svaytsi] fried calves' brains
with eggs

telecí na houbách [hohbahH]
veal stew with mushrooms

telecí na kmíně [kumeenyeh] veal
stew with caraway seeds

telecí na paprice [pupritseh] veal
in paprika sauce

telecí pečeně [petchenyeh] roast
veal

telecí perkelt stewed veal in
paprika sauce

telecí plíčky na smetaně
[pleetchki na smetunyeh]
calves' lung with cream
sauce

telecí řízek přírodní [rɹeezek
prɹeerodnyee] veal steak

telecí řízek smažený [smuɹenee]
veal steak fried in
breadcrumbs

telecí srdce na smetaně [surdtseh
na smetunyeh] calves' heart in
cream sauce

telecí žebírko na žampionech
[Jebeerko na Jumpi-awneH] veal
chop with mushrooms

teplá šunka [teplah shoonka]
boiled ham, served hot

teplé předkrmy [tepleh
prɹetkurmi] entrées

teplý [teplee] hot; warm

těstoviny [tyestovini] noodles;
pasta

topinka s česnekem [chesnekem]
toasted rye bread rubbed

with garlic

topinka s drůbežími játry
[sdroobeJeemi yahtri] toast
with chicken liver

topinka se šunkou [seh
shoonkoh] ham on toast

tresčí játra [trestchee yahtra]
cod's liver

treska na roštu [roshtoo] grilled
cod

treska s hořčicovou omáčkou
[horJtchitsovoh omahtchkoh]
stewed cod in mustard
sauce

trhanec s malinovou šťávou
[truhunets smulinovoh
shtyahvoh] pancakes with
raspberry syrup

třešně [trJeshnyeh] cherries

třešňová bublanina [trJeshnyovah
booblanyina] sponge biscuit
with cherries

tuňák [toonyahk] tuna fish

tvaroh [tvuroH] cottage cheese

tvarohová žemlovka [tvurohovah
Jemlofka] sweet pudding
made from white bread and
cottage cheese

tvarohové knedlíky [tvurohoveh
kunedleeki] cottage cheese
dumplings

tvarohové palačinky
[palutchinki] cottage cheese
pancakes

tvarůžky [tvurooshki] small
cakes of spicy, smelly
cheese

tykev [tikef] marrow

uherský salám [ooherskee
sulahm] Hungarian spicy
salami with cucumber

uzené vařené [oozeneh vurJeneh]
boiled smoked meat

uzené vepřové [veprJoveh]
smoked pork

uzeniny [oozenyini] smoked
meats

uzený [oozenee] smoked

uzený hovězí jazyk [hovyezee
yuzik] smoked ox tongue

uzený losos smoked salmon

uzený sýr [seer] smoked cheese

uzený úhoř [oohorJ] smoked eel

vaječná jídla [vī-etchnah yeedla]
egg dishes

vajíčkový salát [vī-eetchkovee
sulaht] egg salad

vanilková zmrzlina [vunilkovah
zmurzlina] vanilla ice cream

vanilkový [vunilkovee] vanilla
(adj)

vánočka [vahnotchka] oblong
Christmas cake

vařená kukuřice [vurJenah
kookoorJitseh] boiled
sweetcorn

vařená vejce [vaytseh] boiled
eggs

vařené brambory [brumbori]
boiled potatoes

vařené fazolky [fuzolki] boiled
green beans

vařené hovězí maso [hovyezee
muso] boiled beef

vařené telecí [teletsee] boiled
veal

vařené vepřové [veprJovee]
boiled pork

vařený [vurJenee] boiled

vařený kukuřičný klas
[kookoorJitchnee klus] boiled
corn on the cob

vejce [vaytseh] egg

vejce naměkko [vaytseh
numnyeko] soft-boiled egg

vejce natvrdo [nutvurdo] hard-
boiled egg

vejce plněné humří majonézou
[pulnyeneh hoomrJee mī-onezoh]
hard-boiled egg filled with
lobster mayonnaise

vejce plněné šunkovou pěnou
[shoonkovoh pyenoh] hard-
boiled egg filled with ham

veka white French-style bread

věneček [vyenetchek] chocolate
éclair

vepřenky [veprJenki] grilled
minced pork with onion and
mustard

vepřová játra na cibulce
[veprJovah yahtra na tsibooltseh]
pigs' liver stewed with
onions

vepřová játra pečená na cibulce
[petchenah] fried pigs' liver
and onions

vepřová krkovička po selsku
[kurkovitchka po selskoo] roast
neck of pork with onions

vepřová kýta na paprice [keeta
na pupritseh] stewed leg of
pork with paprika

vepřová kýta na smetaně
[smetunyeh] stewed leg of

pork in cream sauce

vepřová pečeně [petchenyeh]
roast pork

vepřové dušené v kedlubnách
[veprJoveh doosheneh v
kedloobnahH] pork stewed
with kohlrabi

vepřové maso [muso] pork

vepřové na kmíně [kumeenyeh]
pork stew with caraway
seeds

vepřové plíčky na smetaně
[pleetchki na smetunyeh] pigs'
lungs in cream sauce

vepřové ražniči [ruJnitchi] pork
on skewer with bacon and
onions

vepřové žebírko na kmíně
[Jebeerko na kumeenyeh]
stewed rib of pork with
caraway seeds

vepřové žebírko přírodní
[prJeerodnyee] stewed rib of
pork

vepřový bůček nadívaný
[veprJovee bOOtchek
nudyeevunee] stuffed side of
pork

vepřový guláš [goolahsh] pork
goulash

vepřový jazyk na bylinkách [yuzik
na bilinkahH] pigs' tongue
stewed with herbs

vepřový mozeček s vejci
[mozetchek svaytsi] fried pigs'
brains with eggs

vepřový ovar [ovur] boiled pig's
head and liver

vepřový řízek [rJeezek] breaded

pork cutlet

větrník [vyeturnyeek] chocolate
éclair

vídeňský telecí řízek
[veeden^yehskee teletsee rJeezek]
fried veal fillet in
breadcrumbs

višně [vishnyeh] sour cherries;
morello

vlašské ořechy [vlushskeh orJeHi]
walnut

vlašský salát [vlushkee sulaht]
salad of potatoes, ham,
salami, vegetables, hard-
boiled eggs and mayonnaise

zadělávaná karotka
[zudyelahvunah kurotka] carrot
in white sauce

zadělávaná slepice [slepitseh]
chicken with white sauce

zadělávané dršťky [dursht^yehki]
tripe in white sauce

zadělávané kedlubny [kedloobni]
kohlrabi with white sauce

zajíc [zī-eets] hare

zajíc na černo [cherno] stewed
hare in thick, dark, sweet
and sour sauce

zajíc na divoko [dyivoko] saddle
and leg of hare spread with
bacon fat and cooked with
onions and root vegetables
in red wine

zajíc na smetaně [smetunyeh]
hare in cream sauce

zákusek [zahkoosek] sweet
pastry

zákusky [zahkooski] desserts

zapečená šunka s vejci
[zupetchenah shoonka] ham
and eggs

zapečený [zupetchenee] roast;
baked; grilled

zapékané brambory se sýrem
[zupekuneh brumbori seh
seerem] potatoes baked with
cheese

zapékané nudle [noodleh] baked
noodles with cheese and egg

zavařenina [zuvurJenyina]
preserves; jam

zavařený [zuvurJenee]
preserved; bottled

závin [zahvin] apple strudel

zavináč [zuvinahtch] rollmop
herring in vinegar

zelené fazole [zeleneh fuzoleh]
green beans

zelenina [zelenyina] vegetables

zeleninová jídla [zelenyinovah
yeedla] vegetable dishes

zeleninová polévka [polefka]
vegetable soup

zeleninové rizoto [zelenyinoveh]
stewed rice with vegetables

zeleninový řízek [zelenyinovee
rJeezek] fried vegetable
rissole

zelí [zelee] cabbage

zelná polévka [zelnah polefka]
cabbage soup

zelná polévka s klobásou
[klobahsoh] cabbage soup
with smoked sausage

zelný salát [zelnee sulaht]
cabbage salad

zmrzlina [zmurzlina] ice

cream

zmrzlinový pohár [zmurzlinovee] sundae

znojemská roštěná [znoyemskah roshtyenah] Znojmo-style sirloin

ztracená vejce [ztrutsenah vaytseh] poached egg

zvěřina [zuvyerJina] game

žampionová omáčka [Jumpi-awnovah omahtchka] mushroom sauce

žampióny [Jumpi-awni] mushrooms

žebírko [Jebeerko] ribs

želví polévka [Jelvee polefka] turtle soup

žemle [Jemleh] white bread roll

žemlovka [Jemlofka] bread pudding with apples and cinnamon

židovská česnečka [Jidofskah chesnetchka] Jewish garlic soup

žitný chléb [Jitnee Hlep] rye bread

žito [Jito] rye

žraločí řízek [zHrulotchee rJeezek] shark fillet

Menu Reader:

Drink

alkoholické nápoje alcoholic
drinks

Becherovka® [beHerofka] sweet
herbal digestive liqueur

bez kofeinu [bes kofaynoo]
decaffeinated

bez ledu [ledoo] without ice

bílá káva [beelah kahva] white
coffee

bílé víno [beeleh veeno] white
wine

Budvar [boodvur] Budweis beer

burčák [boortchahk] very young,
slightly alcoholic wine

cappuccino espresso with hot
milk

čaj [tchī] tea

čaj s citrónem [tsitrawnem]
lemon tea

čaj s mlékem tea with milk

černá káva [chernah kahva] black
coffee

černé pivo [cherneh] dark
beer

červené víno [cherveneh veeno]
red wine

čokoláda se šlehačkou
[chokolahda seh shlehutchkoh]
hot chocolate with whipped
cream

destiláty [destilahti] spirits

Dobrá voda® [dobrah] brand of
mineral water

dvě deci [dvyeh detsi] two gills
(two decilitres)

džus [joos] juice

espresso strong black coffee

Fernet® bitter digestive
liqueur

Frankovka® [frunkofka]
medium-dry, strong red
wine

horké kakao [horkeh kukuh-o]
hot chocolate

instantní káva [instuntnyee kahva]
instant coffee

kakao [kukuh-o] cocoa; hot
chocolate

kapucín [kupootseen] espresso
with hot milk

káva [kahva] coffee

káva se smetanou [seh
smetunoh] coffee with cream

Kláštorné červené® [klahshtorneh
cherveneh] medium-dry red
wine

koňak [konyuk] brandy, cognac

kostka ledu [ledoo] ice cube

láhev vína [lah-hef veena] bottle
of wine

led [let]

ledová káva [ledovah kahva]
cold, black coffee, often
served with ice cream and
whipped cream

ledový čaj [ledovee chī] iced tea

ležák [leJahk] lager

likér liqueur

limonáda [limonahda] soft
drink; lemonade

Ludmila® [loodmila] red wine
from Bohemia

malé pivo [muleh] small beer

Mattoniho kyselka® [kiselka] brand of mineral water

minerálka [minerahlka] mineral water

minerální voda [minerahlnyee] mineral water

mléko milk

mražená káva [mruᴊenah kahva] iced coffee

Müller Thurgau® [miler thoorgow] medium-dry white wine

nápoj [nahpoy] drink

nápojový lístek [nahpo-yovee leestek] drinks list

nealkoholický [neh-ulkoholitskee] non-alcoholic

nealkoholické nápoje soft drinks

nešumivá minerálka [neshoomivah minerahlka] still mineral water

ovocná šťáva [ovotsnah shtyahva] fruit juice

ovocný čaj [ovotsnee chī] herbal tea

pivo beer

Plzeňské pivo® [pulzen^yeh^skeh] Pilsner beer

pomerančová šťáva [pomeruntchovah shtyahva] orange juice

presso strong, black coffee

Rulandské bílé® [rooluntskeh beeleh] light, slightly sweet white wine

řezané pivo [rᴊezuneh] mix of light and dark beers

sladké [slutkeh] sweet

s ledem [sledem] with ice

slivovice [slivovitseh] plum brandy

smetana do kávy [smetuna do kahvi] cream for coffee

sodová voda [sodovah] soda water

Stock® type of brandy

suché víno [sooʜeh veeno] dry wine

svařené víno [svahrᴊeneh] mulled wine with lemon and spices

světlé pivo [svyetleh] light, pale beer

s vodou [zvodoh] with water

šampaňské [shumpun^yeh^skeh] champagne

šťáva [shtyahva] juice

šumivá minerálka [shoomivah minerahlka] fizzy mineral water

šumivý [shoomivee] fizzy

turecká káva [tooretskah kahva] Turkish coffee – small, dark, strong coffee with grounds at the bottom

vídeňská káva [veeden^yeh^skah kahva] Viennese coffee with whipped cream

vinný střik [vinee strᴊik] wine and soda water

víno [veeno] wine

víno rozlévané [rozlevuneh] wine

  by the glass
voda water
voda s ledem [sledem] water
  with ice